Effective Psychotherapy

THE CONTRIBUTION OF HELLMUTH KAISER

EFFECTIVE PSYCHOTHERAPY

The Contribution of HELLMUTH KAISER

Edited by Louis B. Fierman, M.D.

Foreword by Allen J. Enelow, M.D.,
and Leta McKinney Adler, Ph.D.

1026—FREE PRESS—(Fierman)—Sept. 10—sid

THE FREE PRESS
A Division of Macmillan Publishing Co., Inc.
New York

Collier Macmillan Publishers
London

The Free Press
A Division of Macmillan Publishing Co., Inc.
866 Third Avenue, New York, N.Y. 10022

Collier-Macmillan Canada Ltd.

Library of Congress Catalog Card Number: 65–23114

printing number
4   5   6   7   8   9   10

Acknowledgments

Many obstacles, delays and difficulties had to be overcome for this book to reach publication. At low times when continued effort appeared completely futile, some new and unexpected assistance invariably would appear, and the faltering effort would go on. For their unflagging encouragement and indispensable help I am gratefully indebted to:

Leta McK. Adler, Ph.D.
Daniel I. Alevy, Ph.D.
Henry E. Altenberg, M.D.
Mrs. Martha Crossen
Mr. Robert J. Engleman
Allen J. Enelow, M.D.
Ella Y. Fierman, M.A.
Irving H. Frank, Ph.D.
Mrs. Ruth Kaiser
Miss Inge Kaiser
Mrs. Eva Kessler
Mr. Martin Kessler
Robert R. Holt, Ph.D.
John A. Larson, M.D.
T. Keery Merwin, M.D.
Thomas A. Munson, M.D.
Philip Olson, Ph.D.
John M. Rakusin, Ph.D.
Mrs. Marge Schuster
Donald L. Shapiro, M.D.
Albert Sokanoff, M.D.
Ross Thomas, Ph.D.
Alan P. Towbin, Ph.D.
Harvey R. Wasserman, M.D.
Miss Estelle Whelan

L. B. F.

Foreword

ALLEN J. ENELOW, M.D.

AND LETA MCKINNEY ADLER, PH.D.

In 1934, an article appeared in the *Internationale Zeitschrift fuer Psychoanalyse*, entitled "Problems of Technique."[1] It was written by Hellmuth Kaiser, then a young psychoanalyst. In that article, Kaiser made his first proposal for the modification of the classical psychoanalytic procedure. His ideas were an extension of Wilhelm Reich's suggestion that the analyst pay special attention to the attitude, posture, mannerism, tone of voice and diction of the patient and that he make his observations known to the patient. Reich held that these aspects of behavior (which he called "character armor") were the starting point for therapy. To call these to the attention of the patient would throw light on repressed unconscious contents which would eventually be interpreted. Kaiser's paper proposed that the analyst's activities should be *confined* to confronting the patient with his defenses (resistances) as manifested in his behavior. He further suggested that interpretations of repressed or unconscious mental content were of little or no therapeutic value.

After this, Kaiser dropped out of the psychoanalytic world. Twenty-one years were to elapse before his next paper would appear. In fact, when this paper was published, Kaiser was already in Mallorca earning his living as a wood-turner and toymaker. The political climate of Hitler's Germany was clearly not going to be favorable for Jews, and Kaiser felt he should leave while he could. It was 1950 before Kaiser had the opportunity again to devote full time to treating patients and writing, and 1955 before his second paper on psychotherapy was to appear.

It is not possible to imagine what Kaiser's impact would have been had he been in a position to publish repeatedly, to teach, and to exchange ideas with his colleagues during that twenty-one-year period. His ideas were developed in isolation because of the over-riding importance of physical survival, his chief concern for many years. Yet, even in the six years between his paper on "The Problem of Responsibility in Psychotherapy"[2] and his death in 1961, he attracted a number of students, and influenced the thinking of many people. More indicative of the quality of his thinking was the fact that his ideas invariably provoked hot controversy. Though many disagreed with Kaiser's position, no thoughtful therapist could ignore it. Those who exchanged ideas with him were invariably favorably impressed with his soft-spoken manner, his tightly-reasoned ideas. He thought logically, expressed himself clearly and had the courage to speak out. He also was an innovator. Even when he was earning his living at wood-turning, he designed and invented toys and such things as boxes which more or less automatically produced cigarettes.

Kaiser was born November 3, 1893, in Heidelberg, Germany. His father had practiced medicine at Hamburg but decided that he preferred teaching and research. At the time of Hellmuth Kaiser's birth, his father was a professor of physiology at the University of Heidelberg. Kaiser's mother was considered gifted both intellectually and artistically. Max Weber and George Jellinek were close friends of the Kaiser family.

Hellmuth, at the age of four or five, astonished his father by solving advanced mathematical problems and by his grasp of number theory. He was looked upon as a *wunderkind* by his doting mother. He wrote poems, painted and made silhouettes with scissors and paper. Later he wrote dramas and novels. At twelve, he had committed all of Goethe's *Faust* to memory. His mother's adoration, however, grew increasingly burdensome since he felt it to be demanding. Throughout his life, Kaiser hated to have demands made upon him.

The years in the university atmosphere at Heidelberg came to an end when Kaiser was eight. His father, an outspoken man, was quite critical of the head of the department. The situation between them deteriorated until the elder Kaiser resigned in 1901 and moved to Berlin. While in Heidelberg, he had patented several useful inventions, so he now found a position as director of research in a large electrical firm. In 1912, Hellmuth Kaiser completed his gymnasium studies in Berlin.

Young Kaiser entered the University of Goettingen in 1912 to study law. However, the University possessed strong departments of mathematics and philosophy, and he soon became interested in both. He gave up law and studied in both departments for a time. He came under the influence of Leonard Nelson, a noted philosopher of that time. Nelson was a "neo-Kantian" and especially interested in ethics. A very strong person with considerable personal charisma, Nelson gathered devoted disciples who were willing to live and work for their ideas. He had made some changes in Kant's categorical imperative and was convinced that, by induction and deduction, he had found *the* true answer to the question of how people should act. Using the Socratic method, Nelson would bring his students to find these "truths" themselves—under his guidance, of course. Kaiser, later to develop a philosophy of psychotherapy that was the polar opposite of the Nelson position, became enthralled with Nelson and his prescription for living. He studied with him until 1915, when he was drafted into the German army to serve in the field artillery.

Kaiser fought in Flanders and at Verdun, was released because of illness, but was recalled for noncombat duty, serving until 1919. At twenty-six, he returned to Goettingen and rejoined Nelson, becoming the leader of a study group devoted to Nelson's ideas.

Soon Nelson decided to found a "leader school" in which he, with the help of his closest disciples, would educate teachers and children according to his ethical principles. These, of course, applied to every aspect of life. Kaiser enthusiastically agreed to devote his entire life to this project. To his great disappointment, Nelson, an arbitrary and authoritarian man, dropped him and a number of other disciples. Though a man of considerable stature, Nelson was a very controversial figure. He was intolerant and impatient with those who disagreed with him. He was deeply convinced that he had discovered the "truth" in regard to ethical questions, and was thoroughly dedicated to the mission of establishing, together with his followers, a "dictatorship of reason." Kaiser shared his convictions and attitudes in every way, feeling superior to the misguided adversaries of Nelson. Thus it was a terrible blow to him when Nelson dropped him, and one from which he did not recover easily.

However, Kaiser finally returned to his studies of mathematics and philosophy and took his Ph.D. at Munich in 1922. His thesis was "The Theory of Probability Judgement." He now planned to teach at a university.

The post-war inflation in Germany soon left Kaiser with too little capital to support a wife and two daughters on an academic salary. Accordingly, he found a position as Director of the Bureau of Statistics of Osram, a large electric manufacturing corporation. This proved to be a job without duties— the job having been created primarily for tax purposes. He became bored and depressed and decided to get psychoanalytic treatment. When asked if he thought his treatment had been successful, his answer was characteristic: "Psycholanalysis may not cure patients, but it sure does make psychoanalysts out of them. I decided to become an analyst myself."

But, it was not easy for a statistician with a doctorate in mathematics and philosophy to get admitted to the Psychoanalytic Institute in Berlin. In fact, they had begun to limit the training to physicians. Kaiser's application was rejected because he did not have an M.D. degree. Not discouraged by this, he wrote a psychoanalytic study of Kleist's play "The Prince of Homburg," which was published in *Imago*.[3] Freud liked it very much and intervened for Kaiser, thus opening the gates of the Institute for him. In 1929, Kaiser graduated as a psychoanalyst, having entered private practice toward the end of his training. He had had his training analysis with Gustav Bally and supervision with Sandor Rado, Karen Horney, Hanns Sachs and Wilhelm Reich.

Kaiser was soon dissatisfied with the therapeutic effects of psychoanalysis. Though he felt he learned from all of his teachers and supervisors, he was not convinced that the content interpretations (i.e., telling the patient what is presumed to be unconscious or repressed) were of therapeutic value. In his second year of private practice, he consulted several different training analysts abóut one specific case. To his discouragement, he found that no two of them gave advice even approximating each other. He began to search for some improvement on the classical psychoanalytic technique.

Kaiser sought further training and experience by taking a position at Schloss Tegel under Ernst Simmel. Here a dedicated, hard-working group of analysts was attempting to treat hospitalized psychiatric patients using psychoanalytic principles and techniques. However, Schloss Tegel was a financial failure and went out of existence in 1931.

From 1931 until 1933, when he left Germany, Kaiser treated patients and puzzled over problems of psychoanalytic technique. He had been impressed with several of the things he heard in Wilhelm Reich's seminars and during supervisory sessions with him. At that time Reich was still a respected member of the faculty of the Berlin Institute for Psychoanalysis. Though he found Reich's approach inflexible and pseudo-systematic, he was much influenced by Reich's emphasis on observation of the patient's behavior and making the observations known to the patient. Reich first suggested to Kaiser an element that remained central in all Kaiser's thinking: that how the patient speaks and behaves is more important than what he says.

In the following excerpt from his 1934 paper, "Problems of Technique," Kaiser described the experiences which led him to the proposals he set forth in that paper:

During my analytical practice, my attention was drawn to a group of patients unusually resistant to the technique I employed. At the beginning of treatment, the difficulties which each patient exhibited appeared distinctly different from those of the others. The more their analyses progressed, however, or at least as the number of hours increased, the apparent differences between the patterns of these difficulties lessened, and at last I gained the impression that the core of the resistance which had frustrated my analytical exertions was actually the same in all these cases. The patients behaved quite differently in life and were impaired by their neuroses in varying degrees (at least to more casual observation). In spite of the apparent differences between them, I observed that the resistance which made itself felt during their analyses always set up the same kind of feeling-reaction in me. The first movement I could induce in one of these patients followed my arriving at an understanding of the essence of his resistance as a kind of stubbornness. Soon afterwards I noticed that this same point of view helped me to clear away the resistance in the other members of the group.

This experience led me to a series of studies into two different problems. First, I tried to clarify the concept of the "stubborn character," to give an exact description of the common denominator of this character structure, to understand its genesis as far as possible, and to differentiate it from other character types. The second problem was to determine why these patients were so little influenced by the kind of analytical technique which to varying degrees helped others. In the course of this latter investigation I arrived at a formulation of several principles for the analytic treatment of the "*trotzhafte* character" and studied the application of these principles in practice. . . . The aim of the present paper is to discuss some thoughts about the theory of technique which arose in the course of studying the "*trotzhafte* character" and its typical resistance. These, I believe, are relevant to the development of analytical technique even outside the context of this special character formation.[4]

In brief, the paper proposed that the task of therapy is to overcome the resistances of the patient. Kaiser believed at that time that certain kinds of illogical thinking maintain the defenses of the patient against awareness of unconscious impulses or trends. When these are exposed by confronting the patient with his illogical thinking or commenting on certain aspects of his behavior which appear to be incongruous or ungenuine, Kaiser felt in 1933 that the patient develops insight whether verbalized or not. He further proposed that interpretation of the repressed impulse was not helpful and could even increase resistance. At that time he called this technique resistance analysis; later he called it defense analysis. Over the next twenty-one years his ideas and his terminology changed, but one can see their beginnings in this paper.

Kaiser's first paper was not well received. Otto Fenichel, in fact, brought his heavy artillery to bear on the paper and blasted it severely. However, Fenichel was misled by a particularly vivid description of what Kaiser then called a "true affective breakthrough." He felt that Kaiser was interested only in promoting abreaction, thereby missing the point of the paper.

However, Kaiser was not around for the ensuing controversy. Hitler became Chancellor of Germany, and Jews were *personae non grata*. Kaiser and his first wife left Germany. They were accompanied by two patients who wanted to continue treatment and had some savings. His daughters went to the United States, and the others traveled south. They went to Italy and other Mediterranean areas searching for a place where the living was pleasant and inexpensive. They finally chose Mallorca.

The four of them settled in an inland village to which tourists never came. Kaiser and his wife occupied a two-story stucco house with a large garden. At the other end of the garden was a small house into which one of the patients moved. The other patient lived nearby. In a little over a year, both patients finished treatment and left. For the following two years Kaiser did not practice at all.

Nonetheless, Mallorca seemed to have been a good choice. Though the house had neither plumbing nor running water, life was pleasant. Almonds and pomegranates could be picked from the window of the house. They cooked over wood or coal. Kaiser made most of their furniture, an olive grove at one end of their garden supplying wood. Kaiser made toys, intricate boxes and puzzles from the beautifully grained olive wood. Later he acquired a lathe and became a competent wood turner. In 1958, Kaiser once remarked that he might never have left Mallorca had history not taken a turn that uprooted him once again.

In July, 1936, the Spanish Civil War began. Some government planes flew over Mallorca to bomb military garrisons, and Kaiser watched them with binoculars. The Mallorcans were pro-Franco and thought Kaiser was signalling the government planes. He was arrested and imprisoned, but released on his promise to leave Mallorca at once.

Kaiser and his wife went to Switzerland. However, he could not obtain a work permit, and they came close to literal starvation. At one point, a chance encounter with a former patient was the only reason they were able to eat and had a place to stay. They soon had to leave Switzerland and, for two years, during 1936 and 1937, Kaiser lived the life of a stateless person. He could not legally stay in either France or Switzerland.

He contacted Ernest Jones, who suggested that he come to England to practice as an analyst. Kaiser got to Folkestone but there met with great suspicion from the immigration authorities. The word *Spanienfluechting* (Spanish refugee) on his passport made them very wary because this raised the possibility that Kaiser was a Communist. He tried to reach Jones, without success. Finally, an immigration officer asked Kaiser, "Where will you go if we don't admit you into England?" Kaiser shrugged. "I don't know," was all he said. His casualness apparently confirmed the officer's suspicions, and Kaiser was immediately rejected.

On the train crossing France back to Switzerland, where once again he would be unable to work and could stay only fourteen days, Kaiser decided to stay in France illegally. He and his wife simply stepped off the train at an intermediate station stop and made their way to Paris.

For one and a half years he lived in Paris without a visa, always aware of the danger of being deported to Germany and the Nazi concentration camps. He gave ice-skating lessons, worked as a guide at the Paris World Fair and took any odd job that was available. It was a hand-to-mouth existence.

During his stay in Paris, he had an interesting encounter with Otto Fenichel, who, after conversations and subsequent correspondence about Kaiser's ideas (which were continuing to change), finally conceded the logic of Kaiser's position. Fenichel, however, concluded warningly: "But remember, this is *not* psychoanalysis."

In 1938, through the help of a Zionist agency, he was able to obtain a visa and transportation to Israel (then Palestine).

He was never able to master Hebrew and had very few patients. His marriage ended soon after his arrival there. He remarried, living in one room with his second wife and their son. His wife used the room as a weaving workshop. Kaiser earned his living as a wood turner, chiefly making recorders.

In 1949, under the sponsorship of Karl Menninger, Kaiser came to the United States to work at the Menninger Clinic and serve as a training analyst in the Topeka Institute for Psychoanalysis. For the first time in seventeen years, he was able to devote full time to treating patients, teaching and writing.

During those seventeen years, his ideas had evolved considerably from the point at which they were when "Problems of Technique" was published. Once he had given up the interpretation of content, he began to have doubts about the so-called "basic rule" of free association. In the first place, it seemed to be impossible to follow. Most patients tried to be intelligible and did not take the rule literally. When he abandoned that rule, he now found the concept of resistance no longer had applicability. The patient's resistance to treatment, once he was not required to talk, could be manifested only by not coming to treatment. If he appeared at the therapy session, he was not resisting. At this point Kaiser changed the name of his proposed technique from resistance analysis to defense analysis.

The essence of defense analysis was that no requirements as to what he talked about (or even that he talk) be made of the patient. The therapist's activity was to point out how the patient defended himself from awareness of his true feelings, impulses and motives. At that time he frequently would say to the patient: "You arrange yourself thus-and-so" to describe to the patient how he felt the patient was dealing with unconscious conflict.

Sometime between 1950 and 1955, Kaiser made one more step away from the classical psychoanalytic technique. This one was crucial, as it made a truly qualitative change in his therapy. Until then he had been practicing psychoanalysis minus the basic rule and minus content interpretation. Now he decided that he could best understand the patient's behavior as an attempt to get very close to the therapist and to have an "illusion of fusion" with the therapist. His interest now changed from how the patient dealt with his inferred intrapsychic conflict to how the patient behaved with the therapist in his attempt to experience an illusion of fusion.

It was not long after arriving at this point that Kaiser ceased to describe what he did as a technique. He now called it a philosophy or approach to therapy. He had arrived at a position exactly 180 degrees from his youthful theoretical stance as a loyal disciple of Leonard Nelson. Where he once wanted to prescribe a complete way of life for people, he now felt that the best therapy was the least manipulative. Even the word "technique" connotes doing something to another person. It implies a prescription for the therapist's behavior. Kaiser came to believe that therapy should involve no such prescription. Rather, in his view, therapy involves an attitude on the part of the therapist which emanates naturally from his interest in making possible a relationship where the equality and autonomy of the patient are respected.

He had a great effect on the thinking of many people in Topeka. His forthrightness and his unequivocal statements of his theoretical differences from established ideas were stimulating, even to those who disagreed. Nevertheless, he became increasingly removed from contact with students. In 1954, feeling that the atmosphere was too unfriendly for comfort, he moved with his wife and son to Hartford, Connecticut. Here he established a private practice and had a small private study group.

At this time he wrote the paper which represented his crystallized concept of psychotherapy. It was entitled, "The Problem of Responsibility in Psychotherapy," and appeared in 1955. The thesis of this paper was that the neurotic individual communicates in such a way as to give himself the feeling that he is not really responsible for his own words and actions. The task of the therapist, Kaiser wrote, is to behave in such a way as to promote in the patient a feeling of responsibility for his words and deeds. However, Kaiser emphasized that the responsibility for the outcome of therapy belonged solely to the therapist. The therapist must have the same feeling of responsibility that he wishes to promote in his patient.

In this paper, Kaiser not only presented his views about therapy, but also the rudiments of a theory of neurosis in order better to conceptualize his therapy. Up until this time, he had been describing his observations of his patients and his attempts to modify his therapy in order to be of more benefit to them. Now he began to speculate on why his therapy seemed to work. The three concepts which he introduced in this paper were the *delusion of fusion,* the *universal symptom* and the *universal conflict* though the last two were not specifically named.

In reading Kaiser's monograph, one might not recognize that these concepts derive from psychoanalytic theory. Kaiser abandoned the terminology and never described in detail the evolution of his conceptual formulations, though some indication of their origin is given in "The Problem of Responsibility in Psychotherapy."

In this paper, Kaiser defined *fusion* as follows: The neurotic "wants either to incorporate himself into the other person and lose his own personality, or to incorporate the other person and destroy the other person's personality."[5] This was described as regressive by Kaiser in this paper. The concept of regression is psychoanalytic, but one can also recognize the phenomena usually labelled "oral incorporative" by the psychoanalytic theorist. The characteristic relationship of the neurotic has been identified as "oral" also by Fairbairn, who remains closer to classical psychoanalytic formulations.

The *universal symptom* derives from the attempts of the patient to achieve the delusion of fusion. In the paper "The Problem of Responsibility in Psychotherapy" he describes it by saying, "What the patient says is not quite representative of *him, his own self,* but something which the hearer experiences as distant, indirect, an artifact, not a straight-forward self-expression."[6] This is viewed by Kaiser as reflecting an "archaic relationship," a psychoanalytic concept. Both the fusion propensity and the universal symptom were described as "transference attitude." He referred to the universal symptom at one time as ungenuineness; later as duplicity. Sullivan also dealt with this phenomenon which he labelled parataxic distortion. Like Kaiser, Sullivan defined the behavioral manifestations as a discrepancy or incongruity between verbal and nonverbal communication. Sullivan, however, was concerned about uncovering the origin of the distortion in the patient's life history.

Kaiser is thus a forerunner of recent research attempts to link double communication and mental disorder. The "double-bind" is a specific type of duplicity in which two messages in a communication express two mutually exclusive directions, often one being verbal and the other nonverbal.[7] Those employing this concept see this form of communication as both etiologically related to, and symptomatic of, schizophrenia. The concept of *pseudo-mutuality* has many features in common with Kaiser's concept of the delusion of fusion, or the fusion relationship. Pseudo-mutuality is characterized by "a predominant absorption in fitting together, at the expense of the differentiation of the identities of the persons in the relationship."[8] Pseudo-mutuality is seen by those who developed the concept as leading to ambiguous communication and as both a cause and a symptom of mental disorder. They do not, however, as Kaiser does, relate it to loneliness as the general condition of man.

Kaiser's original idea was his conception of the *universal conflict*. In his view, man is essentially separate and alone. No matter how close he may get to someone else, he cannot fuse with him. There is a point where one person stops and another begins. Man is, however, usually not confronted with this basic aloneness except when he must make a decision and take action. At such times, faced with the necessity to make decisions, the neurotic patient attempts to surrender his autonomy; i.e., attempts to create an illusion of fusion through duplicitous communication. Having arrived at this conclusion, Kaiser attempted to reinterpret the data he observed in his patients using psychoanalytic concepts of regression, oral incorporation and transference. When he found that this required either changing his new basic assumptions or the concepts themselves, he abandoned psychoanalytic terminology.

Kaiser's theory provides a conceptual framework for his ideas about therapy rather than a comprehensive theory of personality and neurosis. Since his therapy was developed independently and empirically, it does not stand or fall on the adequacy of the theory.

In a letter written from Hartford, Kaiser described how his theoretical formulation is applicable to the therapy situation:

Patients are lonely persons. Many of them are literally isolated and have few contacts with people, but even those who move in a circle of friends, have wives and children, parents and other relatives around them, are at least alone with their neurotic problems, because these problems cannot be shared with other people. However painstakingly the patient may describe his symptoms to his wife or his friend, he will never feel completely understood; for good reason: He cannot tell what makes it all so hopelessly complicated because he does not know himself. What drives him into the office of the psychiatrist is not so much the realistic hope of getting cured as the wish to step out of his isolation, though he does not know this and might use the expectancy of cure as a good rationalization. The therapist (however poor a therapist he might be) is not taken aback or disturbed by the patient's complaints and the sad story of his symptoms. He does not interfere with remarks like "This is what you should do or what you should avoid." Even these things make it possible for the patient to tell him a bit more (not necessarily in quantity but in quality) about himself. Even if the patient is completely silent, and the therapist shows no irritation with the silence, that in itself makes the patient feel a bit relieved. Starved as he is for human contact, his interest in the therapist grows rapidly. But there is a limit. As long as the patient's interest in the therapist is not too intense, the patient can behave in an approximately adult fashion. When his interest increases beyond a certain limit the adult relationship becomes intolerable for the patient. Closeness as it is accessible for an adult illuminates more than anything else could the unbridgeable gap between two individuals and underlines the fact that nobody can get rid of the full responsibility for his own words and actions. Then is the time when the patient tends to form with the therapist what one could call a "fusion relationship." As his adult intellect does not allow him to maintain an illusion of unity he does something which is a compromise between fusion and mature relationship: Namely, he behaves either submissively or domineeringly. This behavior is what in the usual terminology is called transference behavior. It is characteristic for transference behavior (or, in my terminology, for an attempt at fusion relationship) that the patient is not really interested in communication (sharing of thought, feelings, experiences) but has to do things which create in him the illusion that there is some subterranean connection between him and the therapist.

The possibility of therapy is due to the fact that the patient's adult ego does not agree with the feeling that a mature relationship is intolerable, nor with the desirability or feasibility of fusion nor with the glory of dependency and domination. Therefore he needs a lot of thought constructs, more or less loosely formulated, to make dependency look like "reasonably taking advice from the expert," a domineering attitude look like virile independence, in short, illusion look like good reality testing. I could just as well say the patient has to interpret his transference actions (which have the purpose of establishing something like fusion) as mature communications with the purpose of sharing thoughts and experiences. Therefore, the therapist has a chance to point to the places where the patient's "rationalizations" are falling short of sound thinking, or where he expresses emotions not in keeping with the mature emotional attitude he claims to have.[9]

In Hartford, Kaiser had developed angina pectoris, and, in 1959, he moved to Pacific Palisades, California, where he found the mild climate much more comfortable. Here he wrote, carried on a limited private practice, and did some teaching.

His third and last paper on psychotherapy, "Emergency," was finished in 1961.[10] This was a complex allegory in which Kaiser expressed his views about the present state of psychotherapy. It consisted of a series of dialogues (actually, a play) in which one therapist (Dr. Terwin) goes to treat a depressed therapist (Dr. Porfirio) at the behest of Porfirio's wife. Terwin, who speaks for Kaiser and his views, pretends to be a patient because Porfirio (who represents the more conventional psychoanalytic therapist) refuses to have treatment. Since Terwin, like Kaiser, maintains that all that is needed for therapy is that patient and therapist be together in the same room, it should be possible for the "patient" to treat the "therapist" in this situation. At the allegorical level, Terwin (therapist) represents Kaiser's views on how the health of psychoanalysis (Porfirio) might be improved. Read this way, Kaiser proposed an antidote for the ills, as he saw them, of the psychoanalytic movement. At the end of the paper, Kaiser hints at still another idea; that the genuine communication afforded both therapist and patient in psychotherapy should have a beneficial effect on both. The paper appeared in *Psychiatry* about three months after Kaiser's death.

There are reasons to hypothesize that a therapy which sets no requirements, such as Kaiser's, might be more effective than one which sets such requirements as the rule of free association, lying on a couch and other rules laid down by traditional psychoanalysis. If we set the goal of therapy as behavioral change in the patient (rather than merely a new view of himself), then it is important to create a situation which fosters a wide range of adaptive social behavior. This is more likely when the therapy situation is ambiguous. To some extent all therapists create an ambiguous situation by failing to meet the expectations of the patient. They fail to provide the kind of control and "help" that the patient wants and expects. They do not fully reciprocate the affective aspects of the relationship. Specifically, the therapist attempts to limit his own self-gratification in the relationship to that derived from having benefitted the patient. He also sets limits to the kinds of emotional gratification he provides the patient.

The failure of the therapist to meet the patient's expectations produces problems for the patient to solve which are general to all social relationships. These include dealing with authority and the emotional responses that arise in social relationships. The patient tries his repertory of responses and develops new ones to solve these problems. The more specific the expectations of the therapist for the patient's behavior, the easier it is for the patient to find a simple solution to meeting the expectations.[11] (For example, one lies on the couch, free associates, stops asking for advice, and accepts the interpretations of the therapist.) Hence, when requirements other than the patient's presence are made, he has less opportunity to develop new ways of dealing with such problems as domination, submission, decision-making, liking, and disliking, which he must resolve in all his relationships.

In Pacific Palisades, Kaiser turned more of his attention toward writing the monograph which constitutes the body of this book. In this work he expanded the embryonic theory presented in "The Problem of Responsibility in Psychotherapy." The central thesis of this work is man's "aloneness." The neurotic is one who is unable to tolerate this, as evidenced by his failure to feel responsible for his own words and actions. The universal symptom, duplicitous communication, produces a "vicious circle" by driving others away, thus increasing the neurotic person's isolation. The goal of therapy is to improve the patient's ability to communicate in a genuine manner, which is to be done by helping him to face his essential "aloneness" and to make him feel more responsible for his own behavior. Such improvement in his communication breaks the "vicious circle," thus making his life less lonely and his communication with others more satisfying.

Kaiser's Freudian beginnings can be detected in his central thesis. Underlying Freud's theory was an assumption that man is distinct from society and has drives and needs the fulfillment of which places him at odds with his social environment. However, for Freud the essential problem of man was not his isolation, but this conflict between his instincts and the demands of culture. Kaiser's concept of the *universal conflict* thus goes beyond Freud's theories in recognizing man's social nature: The individual is not so much in conflict with society as unhappily aware that he is irrevocably separated from it.

Kaiser's views concerning man's essential conflict are strikingly similar to Erich Fromm's. "The experience of separateness arouses anxiety; it is, indeed, the source of all anxiety. . . . The deepest need of man, then, is the need to overcome his separateness, to leave the prison of his aloneness."[12] Fromm recognizes a number of ways in which man attempts to meet this need. Among these is *symbiotic union,* which may be accomplished either by passivity or domination. Fromm equates these latter with masochism and sadism and describes them in the way Kaiser described the neurotic's attempts at fusion in the "Problem of Responsibility in Psychotherapy."

Fromm's thesis that man must view freedom, not as "freedom from" but "freedom to" bears some similarity to Kaiser's views that acceptance of a feeling of responsibility for one's self is characteristic of mental maturity.[13]

However, Fromm's formulation in *The Art of Loving* parts company with Kaiser's. Fusion is possible through love; "union under the condition of preserving one's integrity."[14] Thus, "love" for Fromm has the same characteristic that Kaiser attributes to a healthy relationship, one formed "on the basis of equality or symmetry, keeping [one's] own personality intact and respecting the other personality's boundaries."[15] Thus, one might conclude that the only difference between Fromm and Kaiser is a semantic one: whether such a relationship should or should not be called *fusion*. However, there are other attributes which Fromm assigns to love, particularly feeling responsibility for others as well as one's self, on which Kaiser is silent.

The extent to which Kaiser and Fromm, who was also trained at the Berlin Institute for Psychoanalysis, may have influenced each other is not clear. It is known that Kaiser had the opportunity to become acquainted with the views of Karen Horney, to whose ideas his own have some resemblance. For Horney, the basic anxiety "may be roughly described as a feeling of being small, insignificant, helpless, deserted, endangered, in a world that is out to abuse, cheat, attack, humiliate, betray, envy."[16] Horney describes the means by which anxiety is overcome as securing affection, submissiveness, power, and withdrawal. Again there is a parallel to Kaiser's description of the ways in which the neurotic attempts to achieve fusion.

Kaiser's theory of the *universal conflict* stemming from man's fundamental aloneness is essentially a philosophic position. It is true that man's psychological processes, including "willing," seem to be related to a bounded physiological organism which may be reached only through his sensory organs. However, it is just as true that man could not survive as an organism, let alone develop human attributes, if he were truly, literally "alone." In a very real observable sense, others partake in his decisions since he behaves differently and makes different decisions in the presence of different associates or under the influence of different "reference" groups. In other words, interpersonal behavior is as "real" as individual behavior, and boundaries are relative to the criteria of the observer.

The extent to which man is "alone" is, from another point of view, an empirical matter. Kaiser's insights are in keeping with the observation of many behavioral scientists that modern western man, at least, is troubled by what is variously termed isolation, alienation, marginality, anomia, or other expressions denoting aloneness or some quality related to it. Sociologists since Durkheim have held that the special qualities of modern, industrialized, urbanized, secular societies produce these feelings in man. Durkheim, writing at the time of Kaiser's birth, was perhaps the first to point out clearly what he called the "anomic" nature of rapidly changing, industrialized society. He referred to the fact that such a society no longer sets limits to the goals and strivings of its members, or in other words, is in a state of "normlessness." He felt that unlimited goals produced disillusionment, depression and what he termed "anomic" suicide.[17] Later sociologists have spoken more of the failure of secular, urban industrial society to set unambiguous goals. It sets conflicting goals for individuals and offers a bewildering choice of means to achieve them. Both goals and means tend to be subject to "rational" choice rather than "traditional" acceptance. In traditional, sacred, or preindustrial, societies, the individual perceives fewer alternatives, and alternatives other than those culturally approved are made to appear extremely unattractive through the sanctions applied.

Much current sociological theory and research is directed toward greater understanding of the relationship between the state of anomia in a society and the corresponding psychological state of anomia or alienation in the members of such a society. Kaiser's insights illuminate this relationship. His monograph points out that man feels most alone when (1) he makes a decision which is not universally approved, (2) his thoughts lead to a conviction not supported by authority, (3) or he wants something not universally valued. Thus the anomic society provides many experiences of aloneness, since it prescribes few goals or means of achieving them.[18] He also formulated a hypothesis concerning the etiological relationship between anomia and neurosis, another problem which is currently among the more pressing concerns of behavioral science.

Kaiser's underlying philosophy that man is essentially alone and that his sense of participation in his culture is often a manifestation of the delusion of fusion bears much similarity to the psychological qualities of anomia described by behavioral scientists.[19] From the point of view of the sociology of knowledge, it might be maintained that they derive from Kaiser's experiences. He, more than most men, was exposed to the vicissitudes of life in the anomic society.

On October 12, 1961, while having lunch with his wife, Ruth, in a small restaurant near his office, Kaiser suffered a coronary thrombosis and died instantly. His work was not finished. His monograph had not yet been completed. His ideas had been communicated to relatively few people. Had he been born at another time or in another place, he might have had much more impact on the field of psychotherapy in his lifetime. It is too early to evaluate his influence, but psychotherapy today is increasingly moving in the direction Kaiser pioneered. History is with Kaiser though the political events of his lifetime prevented him from knowing this.

Notes

1. Kaiser, Hellmuth, "Probleme der Technic," *Internationale Zeitschrift fuer Psychoanalyse*, 1934, 20:490–522.

2. Kaiser, Hellmuth, "The Problem of Responsibility in Psychotherapy," *Psychiatry*, 1955, 18:205–211.

3. Kaiser, Hellmuth, "Kleist's Prinz von Homburg," *Imago*, 1930, 16:119–137.

4. Translated and privately circulated by Dr. Kaiser.

5. Kaiser, Hellmuth, "The Problem of Responsibility in Psychotherapy," *Psychiatry*, 1955, 18:206.

6. *Ibid.*, p. 206.

7. Bateson, G., D. D. Jackson, J. Haley, and J. Weakland, "Toward a Theory of Schizophrenia," *Behavioral Science*, 1956, 1:251–264.

8. Wynne, L. D., I. M. Ryckoff, J. Day, and S. I. Hirsch, "Pseudo-Mutuality in the Family Relations of Schizophrenics," *Psychiatry*, 1958, 21:207.

9. Personal communication to Allen J. Enelow, June 14, 1956. A few minor stylistic changes were made to make Kaiser's English more idiomatic.

10. Kaiser, Hellmuth, "Emergency," *Psychiatry*, 1962, 25:97–118.

11. In Bateson's terms, reduces the opportunity for deutero-learning. See also Henry L. Lennard and Arnold Bernstein, *The Anatomy of Psychotherapy*, New York: Columbia University Press, 1960, pp. 154–158, 196.

12. Fromm, Erich, *The Art of Loving*, New York: Harper and Row, 1956, pp. 8–9.

13. Fromm, Erich, *Escape From Freedom*, New York: Farrar and Rinehart, 1941.

14. Fromm, Erich, *The Art of Loving*, New York: Harper and Row, 1956, p. 20.

15. Kaiser, Hellmuth, "The Problem of Responsibility."

16. Horney, Karen, *The Neurotic Personality of Our Time*, New York: W. W. Norton & Co., 1937.

17. Durkheim, Emile, *Division of Labor in Society*, tr. George Simpson, Glencoe, Ill.: The Free Press, 1947; *Suicide*, tr. John A. Spaulding and George Simpson, Glencoe, Ill.: The Free Press, 1951.

18. Howard Becker, who places special emphasis on unfavorable response to the new in the sacred society and favorable response to the new in the secular society, provides an especially clear link between sociological theory and Kaiser's views. See Howard Becker, "Current Sacred-Secular Theory and Its Development," in Howard Becker and Alvin Boskoff, eds., *Modern Sociological Theory*, New York: Dryden Press, 1957, pp. 133–176.

19. See especially Robert K. Merton, *Social Theory and Social Structure*, Glencoe, Ill.: The Free Press, 1957, pp. 131–194, and Leo Srole, "Social Integration and Certain Corollaries: An Exploratory Study," *American Sociological Review*, 1956, 21: 709–716.

Contents

Effective Psychotherapy

THE CONTRIBUTION OF HELLMUTH KAISER

The Problem of Responsibility

in Psychotherapy*

When a psychoanalytic treatment—unhampered by insurmountable obstacles from the outside—war, revolution, earthquake, or the interference of relatives—fails to cure the patient, either the treatment is at fault or the prognostic evaluation which led to the treatment was inadequate. Since the theory and technique of psychotherapy are still in their childhood, and since the same is true for the prognostic abilities of psychotherapists, the unsuccessful outcome of a therapeutic attempt does not mean that by necessity the therapist is guilty of negligence either in his prognostic evaluation or in the management of therapy. But still the responsibility for what happened in treatment, or failed to happen, is his; to blame any failure in treatment on the patient is as illogical and silly as to abuse a chair because one has bumped into it. Yet as psychotherapists we sometimes feel inclined to do just this. We say that it was the patient's fault; that he was not cooperative, was poorly motivated, was very unproductive, was terribly dishonest, or simply did not want to change. The fact that we sometimes succumb to the temptation to think, or at least feel, along these lines is due to a number of reasons and not only to the wish to find a scapegoat.

If we accept the alternative that either the diagnosis or treatment is faulty in case of failure, and conclude that we, the analysts, must take all the responsibility for the outcome of the analysis—all one hundred percent of it—then no responsibility at all rests with the patient. Yet we have learned that the analyst should see to it that the patient feels respon-

* Copyright © 1955 by the William Alanson White Psychiatric Foundation, Inc. Reprinted from *Psychiatry*, 18, 1955, 205–211.

1

sible for what he says and does in the analytic session. So even though I as an analyst might really feel that all the responsibility rested with me in a particular case, I would have to hide this recognition from the patient lest I helped him shirk his part. Perhaps the patient might never ask how much responsibility I felt for the results of treatment. If he asked, I might have good reasons not to answer. Be that as it may, it would be a sad state of affairs if, in the interest of the cure, I wanted the patient to form a wrong opinion about my conviction on this point. My relationship to the patient would be poisoned by this tacit dishonesty.

To dispel this apparent contradiction, it is necessary only to clarify the meaning of the words which I have used. When the patient's illness is diagnosed as one which, in principle, can be cured with psychoanalysis, the failure of the treatment can be due only to the faultiness of its application, which means that the behavior of the analyst alone determines the success or failure. In this sense he has the whole responsibility for what happens. If, for instance, the patient is "dishonest"—or, in nonmoralistic language, if he tells things which he knows to be untrue—that is just another symptom. To say that this symptom sufficiently explains the analyst's failure would be as devious as to say that an obsessional patient could not be cured because he behaved obsessively.

Where does the patient's responsibility come in? The correct answer is *nowhere*. The analyst's behavior should induce in the patient a sense of responsibility for what he says and does, but this principle does not at all mean that the patient should be held responsible to any extent for the outcome of treatment. This principle contains a prescription for the *analyst*, not for the patient. It prescribes a behavior for the analyst which will produce a certain desirable effect: a feeling in the patient that his words and actions are really and wholly his own.

Two questions arise. First, is it generally true of patients that they do not feel at one with their own words and actions and, hence, require treatment to achieve this desirable condition? Second, why is it important to accomplish this objective?

The first question brings up a language difficulty. Certain

phenomena which have appeared in the analyst's field of vision and to which he gradually becomes alert are still without well-defined names; in referring to them, some circumlocution must be used, and one has a choice between being either equivocal or long-winded in one's expressions. The phenomenon I have in mind here concerns the patient's inner attitude toward his own actions and words. My contention is that patients, according to the degree of their illness—however one may determine it—are far less "behind" their words and actions than healthy persons. This is the same phenomenon which is usually referred to by the statement that neurotics are less well integrated than healthy persons. The rifts in the neurotic's personality do not permit him to be "present" to the same degree in his actions and words as are healthier personalities. As a somewhat crude example: A comparatively healthy person will, even when yielding to a severe threat, retain the feeling that he made a decision—that he preferred to do what he was asked to do rather than incur the punishment. A severely neurotic person of a certain type, on the other hand, will be inclined—even when only a request was voiced, unaccompanied by a threat—*to feel:* I have no choice.

There are neurotics who have to experience every major decision in their lives as something completely determined by circumstances. While the healthy person would say that the decision was easy, that the pros by far outweighed the cons, these neurotics say, "Fate decided for me; I had no choice." Both groups might do the same under the same circumstances, might even recognize and weigh the pros and cons exactly alike, but their feeling is different. Other types of neurotics feel, "I did it, but I did not want to do it." Or, "I wanted to do it, but at the same time I did not want to do it." What the neurotic feels about his actions also holds true for the words he speaks. The words are his and he knows it; but the meaning is not quite his—not undisputably really and truly his.

A connection can be found between the phenomenon I have described and the well-known concept of the regressive nature of the neurotic's interpersonal relationships. The neurotic is unable to form a meaningful relationship on the basis of equality or symmetry, keeping his own personality intact and respecting the other personality's boundaries. He wants either to incorporate himself into the other person and lose his own personality, or to incorporate the other person and destroy the other person's personality. When an opportunity for such fusion or identification seems to be offered, every function is drawn into the service of the desire for closeness, in the regressive sense. The expressions of such needs are modified by the fight which the less regressed parts of the personality wage against the primitive desires, so that a plus might be changed into a minus, and vice versa. But the characteristic flavor of the utterances is always the same. What the patient says is not quite representative of *him, his own self,* but something which the hearer experiences as distant, indirect, and artifact, not a straightforward self-expression.

In other words, such a patient does not feel at one with his own words and actions—and this is at the same time the answer to the second question I have raised, of why it is important that he should. It is the analyst's task to make the patient feel responsible for his own words and his own actions, because it is the analyst's task to cure the patient. In more familiar words, it is the analyst's task to resolve the patient's propensity toward archaic relationships, to remove his transference attitude.

If *making the patient feel responsible for his own words* is equal to *curing the patient,* then one must be able to read the equation in reverse. Anything that increases the patient's feeling of responsibility for his own words must tend to cure him. Some excerpts of dialogue between a patient and his analyst might help to clarify this somewhat cryptic statement.[1]

The patient is a 30-year-old psychologist, easily recognizable as an obsessional character, a "bright boy," quite capable in his job, although he complained of a considerable inclination to procrastinate and of other neurotic symptoms. He made it quite clear in his first consultation with the analyst

1. In this presentation I have recounted only those conversations which are particularly pertinent to the subject under discussion. A development such as the one I have traced usually takes many months; it appears here greatly telescoped, and many of the lapses of time are not indicated. The presentation does not claim any authenticity, and is meant not as a documentation of what happened, but exclusively as a demonstration of a possible way of proceeding.

that although he would welcome relief of his symptoms, he was also interested in having the experience of an analysis for professional reasons. The analyst felt no need to enter into a discussion of the respective weights of the patient's twofold motivation and started the treatment. In the third month of treatment the following took place:

PATIENT: Last night I played at the bridge club. But I did not do too well. Usually I come out first or second, but this time I was fourth. I cannot remember that I made any gross mistake; really I played quite well. But, heaven knows why, it did not work. [*Three minutes of silence.*] I just had several thoughts, but I do not intend to tell them. I know I should, but I simply do not want to.

ANALYST: You feel you should tell them but you do not want to?

PATIENT [*Cheerfully*]: No, I *know* I should tell them.

ANALYST: What's the difference?

PATIENT: Oh well, I *know* you want me to tell everything which comes into my mind.

ANALYST: I did not say anything like that.

PATIENT: I know you said nothing like that. You said I could tell what I wanted, but, nevertheless, what you meant was, of course—— [*His voice peters out.*]

ANALYST: You think: The rest is obvious.

PATIENT: Isn't it obvious? Well, what you really meant was that I should tell everything that came to my mind. Maybe you did not mean that. Anyhow, I know I should, but I also know that I do not want to. [*A minute's silence.*] By the way, do you really mean that it would be enough if I only said what I wanted to say?

ANALYST: I can't see how you could do otherwise.

PATIENT: But what would you do if I remained silent for the next three months?

ANALYST: I would regret to have misdiagnosed you so badly.

PATIENT: [*With a grin*] You mean that I would be psychotic? Hm, I understand. You have a point there. [*He changes the topic.*]

At a session three or four days later, the patient returned to this topic. The following conversation was preceded by a silence of about seven minutes.

PATIENT: I have a question to ask and I wish you would give me a straight answer:

ANALYST: You think your question is such that I would feel inclined to dodge it?

PATIENT: [*Smiling*] Exactly. Wouldn't you think it helpful if I would tell you my secret thoughts?

ANALYST: Helpful? For what? For whom?

PATIENT: Hm—let's say for speeding up my treatment?

ANALYST [*His thoughts run as follows: "He is really sharp. This question is a confusing one. Would it, or wouldn't it? If I said yes, it would be as much as telling him that he should say everything that came into his mind; but would it not really help things along if he pulled himself together and brought out his voluptuous sexual phantasies or his wish to have me on his barbecue stove, whatever he may—Oh, the latter, probably, according to the way his question makes me sweat. Oh, hell. Now what's the matter? If I don't know, I don't know, and I can say so. I do not pretend that I can answer every question this man with the I.Q. of 149 may think up." Having made the decision to play straight and to tell the patient that he is not sure what his opinion really is, the analyst calms down and is struck by a sudden inspiration, and tells the patient:*] If you would be able to tell me your secret thoughts, let's say tomorrow, while you could not do it today, I would think that something helpful must have happened in between. Does this answer your question?

PATIENT: No; what you say seems true, but it's not my case at all. It's not that I cannot tell you my secrets; I do not want to. If I wished to do it, I could.

ANALYST: But it seems you cannot wish to.

PATIENT: Of course, I wish——

ANALYST: Wish what?

PATIENT: To tell you—no. Do I, or don't I? Now I feel confused. Let's see. But that's strange; my mind is a blank. I cannot think any more. Darn it. [*A minute's silence.*] I can't think of any damned thing except bridge. Did I tell you I did very badly again? Very badly. I must have made a lot of mistakes. That's what Bill said, and he knows an awful lot. He is my partner all the time. He was not angry with me, or at least he didn't show it. He is a very controlled guy. He said, "What's the matter with you? Are you in love? You've been playing far below your standards for a week or two." I am not in love, but otherwise he is right. He said, "You must want to lose your money." He said it quite friendly, jokingly, though, of course, I lost *his* money too. But I became so infuriated I said, "Shut up," not jokingly I can tell you. Later I felt sorry and told him so. Of course, he said, "It's all right," calm guy as he is. But it was not all right with me, not a bit.

ANALYST: You thought you changed the topic when you could think of nothing but bridge. However, it seems it was the same problem we talked about before. What infuriated you when you had to face it? Did you or didn't you want to lose your money? Do you or don't you want to tell?

PATIENT: Do you really think—I still do not know. Do I or don't I wish to tell? But if I would wish to, then—I would simply hate to admit that I can't.

These excerpts show a development in the patient which I would not hesitate to call progress. The patient starts out by saying, "I know I should, but I do not want to," and winds up with the formulation, "I want to, but I can't." To be exact, the patient has not yet quite reached this second formulation. He is still uncertain; he does not know for sure whether he really wants to tell. But he is certain about one thing: He would simply hate to admit that he can't, should he want to. For simplification I shall assume that this formulation were already valid for him.

When the patient makes his first statement, "I know I should, but I do not want to tell," he assumes then that the analyst has really told him that he should tell, and continues by asking the question, "Would it be helpful if I would tell?" One does not need to be an experienced analyst, or an analyst at all, in order to know that he "really" wants to tell. However, this statement that he really wants to tell, although it contains some truth, is also imprecise and may even be misleading. It tends to make appear negligible the differences between the two mental states of the patient as expressed by his two formulations.

The first formula runs, "I know I should, but I do not want to." When the analyst repeats this formula to the patient, but for some reason replaces the word *know* with the word *feel,* the patient protests vigorously. He probably does it to stress the point that the *should,* as he perceives it, is something pressed upon him from the outside and comes to him by intellectual knowledge, not by immediate inner awareness; otherwise, it would come too close to the meaning of *I want to.* The *I do not want to* has to explain why he does not. It prevents

him from realizing that he cannot and replaces the admission
of this lack of control by an expression of rebellion against
the heteronomous rules—a rebellion which improves his self-
esteem. The patient's position is a tenuous one. Although my sur-
realistic condensation omits much of the intervening work, the
step from the first formula to the second is not too difficult to
achieve. In the example the interventions of the analyst are
nonspecific. A large variety of different remarks in the same
spirit would probably have led to the same result. What con-
tributes most is drawing the patient's attention to the fact that
he did not change the topic, but only the language, when he
switched from his "secret thoughts" to bridge. In the bridge
episode the patient's friend says, "You want to lose your
money?"—that is, he suggests to the patient, *you want to do
something which is contrary to your conscious intention,*
which is just what the patient tries to deny in his talk with the
analyst. Although coined only as a question, it arouses rage
in the patient. It is the patient's protective device to have his
mind turn blank with regard to the original problem in its
proper terms, and to express his feeling about his problem in
terms of the bridge situation, where the analyst is replaced by
the friend. The device allows him to become emotional even
when he talks about his rage. One can hear from his report
how much satisfaction he derives from the description of his
own unreasonable rage and what might be called childish
behavior.

When this device has been brought into the patient's awareness, his mental picture, his construct—one could even say,
his interpretation and integration of his inner position—becomes untenable. He perceives his urge to tell his secrets, and
he has to look for a reformulation of his inner position. It is
interesting and significant that in his new construct—worded
as, "I want to tell, but I can't"—the idea of the heteronomous
should, of which he made so much in his first formulation,
has simply vanished without any trace. He does not even ask
whether there is such a *should.* This idea seems to have been
only a substitute expression for the *I want to,* and has lost all
its meaning as soon as the original, for which it substituted,

has appeared on the scene of conscious formulation. Instead, a new element has made its appearance, the *I can't.*

Part of what I have been discussing appears in another portion of the dialogue between analyst and patient; this took place after some days during which the problem was touched upon by neither the patient nor the analyst. The patient opened the hour as follows, after some minutes of silence:

PATIENT: Maybe you were right. No, you *are* right. This morning, just while shaving, I decided to tell you some of my secret thoughts. Until just before I knocked on your door, I was convinced I would do it. But the moment I entered your office, I knew I couldn't.

ANALYST: We use the words *I can't* in two different meanings, both expressing impossibility. The little boy, eager to show his strength says, "Mommy, I'll carry the bucket for you." He strains desperately at the handle, but the bucket, filled with water, is too heavy for his little body and does not budge. "No, I can't," he says sadly, and this is a proper use of the word. Later, his playmate comes in and asks him to go to a show with him tomorrow afternoon. "Sorry," he says, "I can't. I promised Susie to come to her birthday party." Again he uses the words properly, yet there is a difference in the meaning.

PATIENT: The bucket does not budge. That's my case. It simply doesn't. You see, in your second example, the little boy has a choice, the show or the birthday party. He can pick either one. He can keep his promise or let Susie down; so he keeps his promise; that's fine. I have no choice. The other day I was kidding myself. I can see that now. I simply can't tell, that's all. The bucket does not budge.

ANALYST: There is still one difference between you and the little boy with the bucket that he can't lift. The little boy feels sad.

PATIENT: What was that? I am not a little boy. Do you expect me to cry? [*Five minutes of silence.*] I think all the time of a teacher of mine I had in grade school. I guess she was quite a nice, decent old girl. But there was one thing we were fighting about for a whole year. She wanted me to recite in front of the class. You know, my back to the blackboard, facing all the kids. I could not do that, not for the life of me. Once she spent a whole hour talking to me, telling me that I really could do it, I should not be afraid, I could do it excellently, and so on and so forth. I told her, "No, I can't." But she insisted I could and I would be astonished. The very next

lesson, when the whole class was assembled, she dragged me to
the front, put me with my back to the blackboard and said to the
kids, "Now our dear friend Harry will get over his shyness and will
recite a nice little poem very courageously, and I am sure he will
do it well; now listen." And dear little Harry kept his mouth shut
like a safe-box door for twenty awful minutes while none of the
kids did as much as breathe, and the nice old girl had to say, "Well,
perhaps the next time." But she was all hot and sweating, and it
was her turn to be astonished.

Thus, the patient is again reordering his concept of his own
inner situation. The presentation of the state of mind which he
described in words as, "I would want to, but I can't," is in the
process of being relinquished, too. He cannot keep it up. In his
remarks about the little boy and the bucket he presented his
inability to talk as being equal to the physical impossibility
which the little boy experienced when he tried to lift the heavy
bucket. But he fails to be convincing. His conclusion does not
sound as sad as would befit disappointment. It sounds almost
triumphant. This aspect becomes even clearer in the classroom
story, which he then reports with obvious satisfaction and glee.
His silence in the classroom, whatever it had been in reality,
appears now not as a defeat, but as a victory. The dialogue,
as far as it has been presented here, does not reveal the nature
of the triumph he experienced then, or rather of the triumph
he is experiencing now in telling the story. It could be a triumph
based on his being stronger than the teacher. But the analyst
has good reason to expect something different: The victory is
a moral victory. The patient's satisfaction is not so much
derived from his being stronger than the teacher as from his
feeling that he is better, morally. The mouth "shut like a safe-
box door" means to him the triumphant standing up against
a temptation.

If the analyst were to continue to point out the incon-
sistencies in the picture which the patient draws of his own
view of the problem, the patient would reach a stage where
he would produce a third formulation running like this, "I
would want to tell you my secret thoughts, but I cannot, because I feel it would not be right." In other words, while the
patient formerly compared his inability to tell with the physical

inability of the boy to lift the bucket, he now compares it with the boy's inability to let Susie down. The handicap is no longer a *force majeure* from the outside, but originates in a motivation.

The patient's remark that the boy in the second example has a choice, while he, the patient, has not, is a fallacy, or rather an ambiguous expression which covers two different meanings. The first is that the boy has a choice in the sense of free will. That version has the merit—for the patient's purpose—of constituting a decisive difference between the situation of the boy and his own, at the expense of logic. The other meaning is that what the boy is going to do does not depend on external forces but exclusively on his own motivation. This meaning has the merit of being correct. Its only disadvantage is that it applies to the patient, too. In this sense, he, too, has a choice—namely, the choice between telling or not telling, insofar as this decision depends exclusively on his inner motivation. At the time that he makes this remark, equating his situation with the first example of the little boy and the bucket, he is not aware of his motivation for not telling. He does not feel, *I should not tell*, but is only aware of its effect, the insurmountable obstacle against telling.

The formulation of the third state, "I want to, but I don't do it because I shouldn't," seems to be the complete reverse of the first formula, "I know I should, but I do not want to." This is not quite true when one takes into account that the same words have different meanings in different contexts. The *I should* in the first formula means an external *should*—such as advice given by the analyst—something one can know but does not feel. The *should not* in the third formula means an internal experience of forbiddenness. In a similar way, the *I do not want to* of the first formula is not simply the negation of the *I want to* of the third, but different in the emotional experience which went into it.

The three formulas show a steady increase in directness, expression of experienced emotion, and genuineness. That does not mean that the patient is dishonest in the beginning and later abandons his lies, for at every stage he expresses his conviction as best he can. But a change occurs in what one could call his self-awareness. This again does not mean that he necessarily "knows" more about himself, although this may also be the case. But certainly the patient is more "in" his words or "behind" his words when he has reached the stage of the third formula than at the time when he pronounced the first.

The activity of the analyst which brought about the change consisted of remarks which were not intended to transmit knowledge of any kind, but were geared to draw the patient's attention to certain flaws in his reasoning or his thought structures. This way of proceeding was effective with *this* patient during the period which I have presented. I do not mean to say that this same manner of communication would have succeeded with every patient. One of the characteristics of this patient which suggested the described method of intervention was his high sensitivity with regard to sloppy logic in his own thinking. With another patient this method might not be effective at all, and other ways would have to be found to create in the patient awareness of the artifacts which keep his defenses intact.

Thus while the essential responsibility for the outcome of treatment is the analyst's, I have tried to show how the analyst may function to help the patient to feel increasingly responsible —that is, increasingly "behind" or at one with his own words and actions. The three formulas voiced by this particular patient as he came to feel increasingly responsible, in this sense—or rather, the developmental stages that these formulas represent—appear in many patients. I do not suggest, however, that they are ubiquitous, even among patients of compulsive character structure; nor do I suggest that the specific method used in this case would generally bring about the progress which these three stages represent. But I do believe that the general attitude of the therapist which can be abstracted from this example is the essentially helpful one in the treatment of neurotic disorders. With this patient, I do not think that anything could have been gained if the analyst had tried a short cut and had asked the patient to tell his secret thoughts, transferring to him the responsibility for this element of the treatment. The patient's "I do not want to tell" was just as valuable a communication as the revealing of his secrets could have been, and the work invested to make him pass through the three stages of increasing responsibility and self-awareness was a worth-while expenditure, both for the patient and for the analyst.

The Universal Symptom

of the Psychoneuroses

A SEARCH FOR THE CONDITIONS
OF EFFECTIVE PSYCHOTHERAPY

This work describes an approach to psychotherapy which I found satisfactory.

The description is given in what one could call a *heuristic* manner: i.e., by telling the story of the development of a psychotherapist.

Observations made in the course of therapeutic activity are related in interaction with thoughts about the nature of neurotic disturbance and about the conditions required for effective therapy.

I have drawn freely on recollections of my own development and have—even more freely—changed things around, whenever, by doing so, I could hope to make the presentation more instructive. The sample interviews are not intended to serve in any way as documentary evidence. They are only meant to illustrate the thoughts and observations reported. The reader is therefore advised to accept this history, from a factual standpoint, as fiction.

The work is addressed primarily to fellow therapists who are struggling with the elusive concept of psychotherapy and the many bewildering and paradoxical aspects it presents.

However, it does not presuppose specialized knowledge and might be of interest also to the layman.

The Concept of the Universal Symptom

PREHISTORY

It was five years now since G—, a man in his late thirties, had begun in private practice.

Interested in many subjects, he had studied in several fields without ever feeling sufficiently absorbed to make a final commitment. All of a sudden, faced with the need to make a living, he seized the first job offered him, in the administration of an industrial concern. Without any experience in business and lacking any technical training, he started at the bottom as a kind of living calculating machine in a small office.

G— brought to this work the virginal enthusiasm of one who has spent much of his life studying in *l'art pour l'art* fashion. His life previously had been as remote as possible from the urgent, concrete problems of the workaday world. His lack of any specialized training in the fields dealt with by this little office proved an advantage. The very strangeness of the world in which he found himself—an enormously complicated, not very well integrated organization, a microcosm of people unlike any he had encountered before—kept his interest and zeal alive for a period of years. Promotions, garnished with unhoped for salary increases, lent the job the appearance of an attractive adventure.

Reaching the level of assistant chief, G— became very useful to his immediate superior who, in spite of his intelligence, abhorred mental effort.

Yet the stimulating effect of these new experiences did not last. While work in the office increased, the problems G— faced gradually dwindled. Challenging new tasks became scarce. Organization took the place of inventiveness. There was no question any more whether he could cope with the world of industrial administrators: win approval; overcome his diffidence, the rivalry and jealousy; and earn a decent living. He was liked by some, disliked by others, but anyway taken for granted and accepted. The company was prosperous; its position was unshakable, and, according to its tradition, one who ranked among the medium strata of the hierarchy like G— could count on staying on the payroll for a lifetime.

After two years of hard work and gnawing uncertainty about his suitability for his job, G— thought he could now enjoy success and the security associated with it, but he was already developing signs of a growing depression. Strangely enough, this change of mood was unnoticed by him or his office associates.

Previously, his after-work hours and weekends were easily filled with interesting activities; now his life outside of the office became problematic, disorganized and empty. Adding to his bewilderment was his painfully depressed mood, incomparably more evident outside the office than inside.

Day after day he got up after an almost sleepless night feeling miserable and gloomy, traveled to the office in an unhappy brooding mood, not knowing how he'd manage to get through the day without arousing attention. Yet, the moment he mounted the steps to the entrance hall of the vast building and waved a greeting to the uniformed janitor, he felt a peculiar change occur. Without any conscious effort his face brightened, his listless step became firm and vigorous. He would exchange some banter with his colleagues and greet the employees who worked in his section in a cheerful voice. He would keep the secretaries busy by taking care of the outgoing mail with a furious thoroughness. When no work of any kind could be dug up, he would immerse himself in books with a feeling of numbness which hardly ever left him till the bell indicated the end of the workday. His automatic, spurious cheerfulness then disappeared like a ghost on the stroke of "one." It then became clearer that the joy and satisfaction of the job was fading to the degree it had lost its character as a test, an experiment.

This state of affairs lasted, with some fluctuations, for the better part of a year. Then he spent an evening with a married couple, both good friends, whom he had not seen for a long time, since in this period he had increasingly avoided people who had been close to him. G— could not remember later how the evening went and what he said to his friends. He knew that he had talked about his job and probably about his dissatisfaction when suddenly one of his friends said:

"But you are in the midst of a depression, aren't you?"

This word had a peculiar effect on G—. It was nothing unusual for him to make this comment about somebody else: "He is depressed." And occasionally he had said about himself: "I feel depressed."

If his friend had said: "You have been depressed for quite a long time," he would probably have nodded, feeling that the friend had no more than paraphrased what he himself had expressed.

But the use of the noun "depression" took him aback. It seemed to throw a completely new light on his state of mind. He had been tempted to answer immediately: "Oh, no, not at all!" but recognized at once that this was not what he thought. Somewhat sheepishly he had said: "Well, yes, I suppose you are right. I feel in an impasse. I do not see how this can go on and on, and I do not see how to jump out of it."

The friends had suggested that G— give some thought to the possibility of psychoanalytic treatment, a method which was just beginning to become known in the city where G— lived.

G— was fairly well acquainted with psychoanalytic literature but never had met an analyst or anyone who had undergone psychoanalytic treatment. Though greatly impressed by the "Freudian theories," he had never even thought of this much discussed therapy in connection with himself. His friends knew even less about it, but they knew of someone who apparently had been cured by an analyst. They promised G— they would investigate the name and address of the doctor involved in this case.

In G—'s parental home it had always been considered a virtue to give new ideas a fair chance, a principle G— readily accepted. To give the new and slightly suspect psychoanalytical treatment a try, therefore, appeared to him quite worthwhile aside from the possible chance of being helped. The glamour of such an adventure helped him to overcome his pride, which resisted the idea of looking for outside help in so intimate and personal a matter.

Because their personalities did not inspire him with confidence, he rejected the first two analysts after consultation. The third spared him the trouble of a decision as he was about to leave the city, but he referred G— to a fourth. This one made a much better impression than any of the others and an agreement was made. The treatment lasted well over four years.

When G— was asked, and he was asked many times, during his years of treatment as well as in his later life, whether the treatment had helped him, his answers varied greatly and became more and more uncertain as time passed. After two years of analysis, things took a turn (unexpected for G— but not too unusual as he learned much later) which made it entirely impossible for G— to form any opinion as to the therapeutic value of his treatment.

His interest in psychoanalytic theories grew steadily in the course of the first two years, culminating finally in the wish to become an analyst himself. To his amazement, he found out that this was not impossible from a practical viewpoint though it would be very difficult. More amazing, perhaps, he found himself fully determined to do what was necessary to achieve this goal. His analyst did what he could to lay bare the neurotic component of this decision; but, whatever merit his interpretations and explanations might have had, they failed to alter G—'s decision.

He appeared one day at the psychoanalytic training institute and presented himself to the president.

The result was surprising. The president not only rejected G—'s application for candidacy but refused even to permit his attendance at the introductory lectures, ordinarily open to anyone who paid the small tuition.

"You are neither a physician nor a teacher, and what makes it worse, you are a patient in psychoanalysis who probably intends to substitute theoretical knowledge for therapeutic self-inspection."

G— replied that his analyst was a member of the institute and should be able, if anyone could, to render a valid judgment on the qualifications of his patient. As this analyst had raised no objections it seemed reasonable that G— should at least be accepted on a trial basis. The president remained adamant in his refusal without even discussing G—'s argument. When G— descended the stairs of the institute his bewilderment was equal to his disappointment.

The training institute was the only one in the country. There was no authority to which he could appeal for a reversal or reconsideration of the president's decision. He knew that he might have a slightly better chance if he reapplied after his continuing analysis had been normally ended. But this was not much comfort as nobody could tell at that time when this goal would be reached. In applying at the institute, he had expected to encounter obstacles; he had counted on a lengthy screening or testing procedure and on attempts to dissuade him. But he could not understand this unconditional rejection which seemingly removed even the slightest glimmer of hope for the future. It was only small satisfaction that his analyst appeared no less bewildered. His analyst knew that the institute's policy tended to discourage non-medical candidates in order to make psychoanalysis, the much distrusted rival of medical psychiatry, more acceptable to the medical profession. But even this information seemed insufficient to explain the rigorous decision. While G— was trying to find personal connections to any one of the older members of the institute in a last ditch effort to learn the nature of the obstacle blocking his entry, he received a letter which lent an ironical note to his unpleasant experience. The editor of one of the two magazines which served the psychoanalytic organization informed G—that a little article G—had sent to the magazine a couple of months ago had been accepted for publication. At this time, when most of the articles appearing in these journals were written by more or less well-known analysts, the acceptance of G—'s article was flattering, and he felt more optimistic about the outcome of his plans. His attempts to dig up a chain of personal links to one or more of the higher functionaries of the psychoanalytic movement having failed, he began considering the possibility of enlisting help from the editor of the magazine. At this juncture, another letter arrived.

It was from the founder of psychoanalysis, Freud, in over four handwritten pages, commending G—'s "excellent paper" as a model application of psychoanalytic theory to the interpretation of literary art. When G—handed this document to his analyst he had the satisfaction of seeing his face light up:

"I am sure that'll do it!" his analyst said. "Don't worry any more about the institute."

In this case the analyst proved to be right. Less than a week later G— received an invitation from the president to visit him at his home. The little man offered him admission to the training institute under the condition that he would devote his talents essentially to research and theory and would see patients only to the extent necessary for his research work. Convinced that his opponent was already in retreat and that this moment was the most favorable one to press his demands, G— thanked the president for his offer but insisted on being granted the opportunity of becoming a therapist.

"If this is your wish," said the president, who did not seem the least surprised or dismayed that his compromise had been rejected, "you have to get the assent of the two other members of my training committee." G— understood that this was a mere formality, as in fact it was, and a few weeks later he was starting to attend lectures and seminars at the institute.

As he was working systematically for his liberation, his boredom and depression disappeared. The monotony of his office work was no longer aggravating. While previously he had constantly tried to enlarge the work of the office, now he was eager to squeeze the necessary routine into the fewest hours, devoting the rest of the time to studying psychoanalytic and psychiatric literature and working on his seminar assignments. His "free" time was filled with his own continuing analysis, with lectures and seminars, and, after a while, with the patients he was seeing under supervision. In these years, G— felt as if by a mere stroke of luck he had discovered a hidden passageway to the true and real life, where one moved without any doubts. The direction and the effort came as naturally as breathing or walking.

Attending lectures and listening to a teacher was nothing new to him. The new element was feeling no impatience or anger when the reasoning did not seem conclusive or was somewhat confused. In contrast to former learning experiences, he went to the courses, not with the expectation of being presented with a flawless piece of theory, but ready to be introduced to an on-going investigation, the results of which were still in a state of flux.

The group in and around the institute, including all of the teachers and students, were keenly aware that they were working on something new and advanced and that their interests and convictions were sharply at variance with those of the vast majority of their contemporaries. Belonging, however marginally, to this group one could not help feeling in the center of some rapidly developing force, the effects of which on all of humanity might be tremendous, though hardly foreseeable then.

One of the most cherished tenets of the institute, frequently put into words by the teachers and always implied, was the idea that psychoanalysis was a natural science; a science in its infancy, certainly, perhaps still in *statu nascendi,* but in its goals and in its pure concern with facts and with the laws of nature governing these facts, equal to any fully developed science like physics. Any claim that psychoanalysis had a philosophical or metaphysical background, that it constituted a *Weltanschauung,* defined an ethical attitude or something comparable to a "faith" was forcefully denied and spurned as a deplorable sign of intellectual weakness. With this tenet, G— was in full agreement even long before he joined the institute.

However, though one could keep the psychoanalytic doctrine entirely free from "normative" principles and any declared philosophy, the way in which the student of psychoanalytic psychology was led to look at the human mind, its history and development, its illnesses and sufferings, its victories and failures, could not help influencing the student's outlook on life, molding subtly but decisively his *Weltanschauung.* Two very different features, inherent in psychoanalysis, were most responsible for this effect. There was, at the one side, the necessary basic assumption of so-called psychological determinism and the endeavor to show the lawfulness and strict interrelatedness of all mental phenomena, including those, which like dreams and phantasies, one had considered as the very epitome of irregularity, the production of pure chance.

At the other side, there was this new and unique way by which the laws which govern the mind's working were actually traced. No matter in what abstract conceptualization psychoanalytical theory had culminated, every part of it showed still some imprint of its creator's passionate interest in man and the vicissitudes of his inner life. Listening with untiring attention to the patient's weird, confused and confusing stories for hours, months and years and trying with inexhaustible patience to find meaning in the chaos was the indispensable method by which Freud made his discoveries and established the basis for his theories. Not only this method was transmitted to the students. Some of the mental attitude, the devotion and the desire which made the application of this method possible, was transmitted; the deep and elementary concern with human life, with his fellowman's sufferings and pleasures, strength and frailty, blindness and vision.

The student's attention was drawn towards an impartial scrutiny of hidden and long-neglected elements which enter into the texture of human life, which the strict rules of social convention had banned from being discussed with due recognition of their significance and actual power. What the "purified" language of a taboo-ridden literature had alluded to in playfully jocular baby talk of the nursery or in dehydrated latinized terms of the medical textbook appeared now for the first time in centuries in its true vitality. The functions of the human body were no longer separated from their emotional impact on the mind. While no new ethics were preached, no rules of conduct proclaimed, the students' image of human life changed and with it their attitude toward it. The respect for the factual was extended from the reading of scientific instruments to the observed expression of affect.

Another unique characteristic of psychoanalysis which influenced G— and his fellow students was its dependence on the spoken word. Psychoanalytic treatment had achieved an improvement in patients for which no other therapy had dared even to hope; no medication was given, no diet prescribed and no surgical instrument applied. The analyst's quiet, patient remarks spaced out over the years, well formulated and correctly timed, alone constituted the remedy.

It was impossible now for G— to tell how far his own analysis had freed him from neurotic disturbance and how far the drastic improvements he noticed in his well-being were due to the fact that this treatment had also acquainted him with a field in which he had an immediate and lasting interest, the field in which he was to have a consuming interest for a lifetime.

After four years, G— was graduated and given permission to begin private practice. What had seemed a long time in the beginning appeared very short in retrospect. This achievement was very satisfying, but it presented G— with a new problem. The expenses of the training had eaten up most of his savings so that he could not afford to give notice to his employers without first having some paying patients. He could not open a practice as long as he had to spend most of his time at his job. Luckily, a private mental hospital invited him to join its staff as an assistant psychoanalyst, with the promise that he would get further supervision and that the hospital might refer patients to him at some later time when he might wish to establish his own practice. This offer seemed fair enough and G— accepted.

The year he spent in the hospital was fascinating but a very trying experience. The hospital, in an experimental stage, did not last for more than a couple of years. Insufficiently supplied with funds, it could not be selective with regard to patients. The patient population was the reverse of homogeneous and most were much too difficult to treat, considering the little experience the few therapists possessed.

G—, as was natural for one who had just graduated from school, in the beginning overrated the competency and mastery of his chief and his senior colleagues, or rather underrated the newness and adventurous character of the experiment in which they all were involved. It was a painful disappointment for him to recognize, during months of excitement and rapid revelations, that they were, in fact, fighting a losing battle in a situation far beyond their control.

While the theory which they applied seemed sufficient to explain and illuminate many of the weird events occurring every day in inexhaustible variety, it was obviously less than adequate to allow for correct anticipation of developments, let alone for taking preventive steps.

The spirit of the staff was excellent. Everyone worked much longer hours and with much more intensity than one could have expected. Everyone was ready to help anyone else with advice or any other assistance. As nobody was entirely sure of what he was doing or of what procedure would produce the desired results, every attempt to modify methods and adapt existing rules to newly gained experience found encouragement or, at least, serious attention. Any appearance of improvement in a patient was eagerly hailed as a promising sign of the effectiveness of the therapy. Praise was freely given to the therapist. However, lasting favorable results were few and far between. The number of managerial problems for which no satisfactory solution could be found was steadily increasing. Patients who seemed to profit from the treatment left the hospital as soon as they could manage, bored by the lack of activity and repelled by the behavior of the intractable, more disturbed patients who walked around like ghosts or managed to get riotously drunk. These latter did not respond to treatment at all, but stayed on and made the atmosphere of the institution oppressive. At the beginning of G—'s year at the hospital, the staff felt harassed but also proud of being pioneers on the frontier of psychotherapy.

But after half a year had passed, they became more and more despondent, sarcastic and bitter, finding it harder and harder to maintain a spirit of optimism. They no longer felt like pioneers facing the hardships of an adventurous patrol into virgin country, but rather like tired soldiers in a rear guard action, staving off from week to week the inevitable retreat from their position.

It was with melancholy relief, towards the end of the year, that they learned that the hospital was about to be closed as a financially untenable venture.

Whenever G— looked on this first experience with psychotherapy as a full-time job, it made him wonder how he had managed to live through this nightmare without any serious damage; but he also felt grateful, knowing the experience had opened his eyes to the vastness of the unknown region into which his new vocation was leading him.

The transition from employment at the hospital to work in private practice went smoothly, with no serious practical problems. In comparison with the infinite and ever-changing difficulties of life in the hospital, work in private practice appeared blissfully concentrated, well-defined and steady. All the managerial tasks with which a hospital staff has to deal, and for which G—'s training left him entirely unprepared, disappeared; he could devote all his energies to applying what he had learned to the problems of treatment.

For several months G— felt quite happy. It was highly interesting to observe and listen to his patients. He found out that they not only said what was expected, but confronted him with new facets. As to his own role within the therapy, he mostly seemed to know how to respond to their behavior, and felt quite capable of discovering the hidden meaning they unwittingly expressed by a large variety of disparate remarks. Almost all his patients appeared satisfied with the treatment and some responded with signs of improvement.

But things did not stay this way. Though there was no lack of patients, the happy confidence with which G— had embarked on his work waned. In almost every case, he felt like a wanderer who, setting out on a well-marked path that had run straight for a long time, enabling him to look back at any moment and see the stretch he had covered, had lost his sense of direction. Symptoms that had disappeared showed up again; in other cases nothing seemed to change at all, and while the patients expressed no doubts and appeared regularly for their appointments, G— felt more and more uncertain about the value of what he was doing.

In the beginning, he could draw security and confidence from the awareness that he was following closely the rules and regulations laid down in his training. He had been taught that even the most therapeutic behavior on the part of the therapist would not necessarily bring about visible changes for the better within the first six months. Accordingly, G— had not felt disappointed when the desired result was slow in coming. But, as time passed, he noticed more and more how much he had to rely for his confidence on what he had learned during his training and how little on genuine conviction. This was a sad state of affairs and G—, who had looked forward every morning to his working day, found himself hesitating when stepping into his office, even felt relieved when an hour was canceled. He even wondered whether his trouble was indicative of a permanent lack of capability or was due to a necessary adaptation period with which every beginner in practice had to cope.

After more weeks of intense discomfort, he thought of a remedy that seemed so simple and obvious that he marveled at his own lack of imagination in not having thought of it before. He called one of his better-known teachers and asked for supervision. His request was granted immediately. The teacher showed all the understanding and sympathy that he could have hoped for. The next day, G— went to the teacher's office, his courage revived, feeling immensely relieved that he could submit all his qualms and doubts to an expert.

Of the ten patients G— was treating at this time, there were only two with whom he felt reasonably at ease. Of the eight others, he chose the newest one, whom he had seen for only thirty hours, as the subject of his consultation with his famous teacher.

The patient, a highly gifted, energetic personality, had talked readily about himself right from the beginning and what he had to tell was interesting and colorful. G— remembered it all vividly and could present it without too much effort. He described to the attentively listening teacher how the patient in his first hour (as in every later one) had thrown himself on the couch and had immediately started to talk in a loud almost commanding voice, like someone who has made up his mind not to waste a minute. What he told was a part of his life history. He clearly depicted everything that had seemed significant to him. There were the braveries of the adolescent, the dire tests to which he had put his courage and his will power, the weird rituals with which he had taken possession of

rented rooms in the city, or of abandoned dilapidated huts
when he had spent some vacations in the country. There were
passionate feuds, friendships and religious experiences, oaths
of allegiance sealed with blood, sexual orgies inspired as much
by the need to rebel as by the urge for sexual gratification;
heroic acts of loyalty, cruel severing of close attachments
followed by tragedy, once by the suicide of the partner. Strewn
in were visual impressions sketched in few words but with an
intensity of verbalization which revealed the mysterious significance which they had had for the patient. There was, for
instance, the picture of a stable door opening at sunrise and
the glorious color of the radiant reddish hind quarter of a huge
horse reflecting the first rays of the sun. But whatever the
object of the patient's report, it was always given in the same
harsh, loud, merciless voice, devoid of all sense of shame, of
pride, or regret, or satisfaction with the recollected event. G—
felt that he was succeeding fairly well in describing the patient's behavior, occasionally imitating his manner of speech
and his clipped impressive gestures.

The teacher looked serious and thoughtful, occasionally
shaking his head in astonishment. After G— had stopped
speaking, the older man, with a thoughtful look still on his
intelligent face, continued smoking his huge cigar in silence.
G— felt some comfort that at least the master therapist did
not seem to think that this was no problem at all but had to
consider for awhile how to approach the case. Finally, the
experienced therapist removed the cigar from his lips and
asked, wrinkling his forehead: "The man is a homosexual?"

G—, surprised by this question, said: "Not to my knowledge."

"Have you asked him?"

"No, of course not."

"You should ask him. Look, there is this glorified horse's
ass, there is the dream with the attackers behind the dreamer,
the patient's attempt to paint himself in the nude in order to
keep something of his own personality unchangeable by time
and aging; did he not mention Dorian Grey's portrait? Well,
you see, he gave you a hint. He probably wanted, unconsciously,

to confess what appeared to him as the great sin, homosexual
behavior, compared with which nothing else, not even the
suicide of his jilted girl, seems to matter."

G— had felt confused. He could see that there had been
many allusions to homosexuality in his patient's story—probably more than in the talk of other patients. But what good
would it do to ask him whether or not he was a homosexual?
He had found other features of this patient's behavior
much more striking, much more unusual, much more promi-
nent; for example, the tone of voice, like that of an army
captain reading the riot act to his company.

He sighed and voiced some of his doubts. The face of the
teacher showed a little benevolent smile: "You feel embarrassed to ask about the patient's homosexuality?"

"Yes, I do," said G— meekly, "it seems awkward to me."

The voice of the older man became even more friendly:
"You know, we all have a problem with homosexuality—more
or less; this might make it embarrassing for you to mention it
to the patient; but there is really no reason to be embarrassed.
Such things are simply facts. He would have no reason to be
offended. Ask him this question and the case will become
clearer, I think, and you will feel on firmer ground."

G— felt inclined to say that he was more confused now
than before. But he doubted that this would lead to any clarification. After all, he thought, this man has a tremendous experience in years and years of work with patients. I have to
give him a fair chance and simply try to follow his advice.

When, during the next interview, an opportunity arose to
ask the suggested question, G— did so. The patient did not
seem to mind. "No," he said, "if you mean homosexual activities or conscious homosexual wishes or phantasies, I cannot
think of anything in this line. Once, when I was seven, I had
what you could call a 'crush' on an older boy and wished he
would put his hand on my head as I had seen him doing with
another youngster. He did not and the thing blew over."

G— felt relieved that his somewhat forced move had no
apparent ill effect on the treatment. He recognized that his
consultant had been right at least on one score. He had been
wrong to expect an embarrassing situation to result from this

question. Therefore, it was possible that he himself was more prejudiced against homosexuals than he would have thought.

However, the hoped-for clarification also had failed to appear. He was glad that the patient had to cancel the next appointment, giving G— a chance to see the teacher again before he would have to face another hour with the patient.

When G— reported what had happened in the last interview the teacher seemed puzzled.

"Are you sure," he asked finally, "that the patient told you the truth?"

"Sure?" said G—, hesitantly, "well, as far as I can judge—absolutely!"

"Look," said the teacher. "Of course, we can't know, but didn't it strike you as peculiar that the man told you about the crush he had on the boy, a thing he knew perfectly well you would not consider as a sign of homosexuality in his present personality? Doesn't it look like an attempt to appear scrupulously honest just to mislead you and make you believe in his general denial? At the moment, I guess you can't do more—but wait and see!"

G— was impressed with the teacher's reasoning. True enough, the skeptical, experienced therapist had a point there, which G— had overlooked. Sauntering home through the deserted streets, he wondered whether he had not formed an entirely wrong idea of what psychotherapy should be like. Disconcerting as it was, he had to admit that the patient might possibly have lied to him, that it might possibly be, as the teacher suspected, that the story of the "crush" was a maneuver; the patient had acted naive and innocent in order to hide his real desires and actions! But then he asked himself what he would have thought if the patient had simply said: "No!" Would such a monosyllable have sounded more convincing or less. His thought dissolved in vague speculations which appeared limitless and without direction.

He continued his weekly consultations with the expert, feeling less excitement than he had experienced at his first visit but also less anxiety. The visits were always pleasant. The teacher was imperturbably friendly and patient. His remarks were sensible, sometimes very clever and illuminating.

However, they referred more to the patient's character, his symptomatology and his history than to the way G— conducted the treatment. He expressed the opinion that G— was not doing too badly with the patient: he should not expect too much of a few months' treatment in a case that was certainly not a simple one; he should feel content that he had a chance to learn and not worry so much about the slowness of progress. What seemed hazy now would appear in sharper contours with the passage of time, and so on and so forth. G— appreciated this encouragement highly as he felt very much in need of it. It was comforting to know that in the eyes of the expert he had moved, by and large, in the right direction, that what he had done was closely in accord with the principles of the school and could even consider himself a well-liked student of the respected teacher. At times, however, he knew that he would have felt more relieved if the teacher had criticized him sharply, showing him how wrong he had been and opening to him entirely new views and ways. It was with mixed feelings, therefore, that he learned one day that these consultations would end as the teacher had decided to leave the city.

A month after his last consultation, G— had an opportunity to talk to another young therapist whom he had met frequently during his training and who was also in private practice now. G— described his scruples and worries and found that the colleague had gone through quite similar pains and showed great understanding of G—'s uneasiness. He acknowledged gratefully the help he had gotten from another one of their former teachers, less brilliant in terms of publications and eloquence but all the more devoted to individual supervision. Under the influence of his colleague's enthusiasm, G— decided to follow his example.

A few days later, he was in the other expert's office describing again his experience with the "not simple case." The teacher, covering his chin with his hand, listened carefully and attentively as the first one had done. When G— had finished his exhaustive description, the teacher chuckled a bit and in a warm, friendly manner remarked: "The measles, you have got the measles, a children's disease. Don't worry, that's natural, you know. That's the very thing I would have expected.

What is it that you tell me? You feel at sea, you feel frustrated, uneasy, worried, uncomfortable. That's the result of the incomprehensible way your patient is barking at you; incomprehensible, that is, unless you assume that your state of frustration in all probability is not the mere result of the patient's behavior but rather the purpose, the aim of it. You see? Children's disease, simply children's disease. You did not recognize the negative transference and as you did not recognize it you could not interpret it properly for what it is, see? Don't bother whether your patient is homosexual or not; that does not matter at the moment. But interpret his negative transference and you will see how things change; how things change in due course."

This sounded plausible enough to G—. He felt that he had learned something more tangible than anything told him by his first supervisor. But there was something still unclear.

"Well," he said, "I feel frustrated all right. But I cannot say . . . I do not feel that the patient is barking *at me*. He is barking, this word is perhaps not too strong, but I cannot feel that he is angry with *me* or mad *at me* . . . so I do not know."

"Of course," said the teacher, rubbing his hands together as if he wanted to indicate that things went exactly according to plan, "of course! It is transference, it is a transferred emotion he is not even conscious of."

This was still not quite clear to G—, but as he felt he could not even formulate the vague question that was on his mind, he shifted to a more concrete approach.

"Perhaps you can give me an example of what I can possibly say to him?"

"Sure; you will understand, of course, that you have to pick the appropriate moment. You have to start from the surface as you know. You avoid anything deep and limit yourself to a merely descriptive remark."

"For instance?"

"For instance: You are barking at me! You say it calmly but firmly. You do not say it as a criticism or in any emotional way, you simply state the fact. Understand?"

"In a way," was G—'s not too enthusiastic agreement. His heart sank. How could he say—"You are barking at me!"—

when he did not feel at all that this man was barking at him.
But, perhaps it would be enough for the beginning to say
simply: "You are barking."

The teacher had a lot more to say and it was in itself
interesting to listen to him. But when G— thought of it in
connection with his patient he felt miles apart from him. He
was finally glad when the hour was over and he was sitting
in his study again where he could think over his latest experience. How can I hope to ever understand my patients, he said
to himself, if I am so incapable of bringing about a real understanding between my teachers and myself? Though I can
understand the words they use and their sentences make some
sense, they seem to see a world of reality I cannot recognize.
Their thoughts are familiar only as long as I am considering
theory and do not concern myself with the question of what to
do with my patients.

This consultation was not the last he had with this friendly
teacher nor was this man the last one he consulted. He was
amazed how different these people were—how differently they
saw his troubles, and what a variety of different recommenda-
tions they offered. What, during his training had appeared as
a fairly consistent theory leading of necessity to a certain
course of action, became more and more vague, ambiguous,
obscure and undefined when applied to one of his cases. G—
went through periods when he felt very disappointed, discouraged, even despondent. At other times he could find some
comfort in the thought that, maybe, supervision was not the
real answer to his predicament. Supervision, consultation and
advice can help only limitedly. There must come a time when
each therapist has to see for himself, to think for himself
and find the right decisions in his own heart.

That sounded heroic and made it possible for G— to continue his work in a more cheerful mood. But the comfort did
not last long. It was fine as long as his treatments seemed
to go well, or, at least, as long as he felt he knew what to do;
then he was convinced that the long series of consultations
with his teachers had not been in vain. Every single one had
conveyed something to him, a mode of looking at things, a
new formulation, a sensitivity for certain phenomena in the

patients' behavior, a question he himself had never raised; and he felt grateful for these contacts. But when several of his treatments or all of them seemed at a standstill, when his words fell flat and did not seem to reach the patient; when the patients condemned him for being rigid, authoritarian, doctrinaire, fumbling, heartless and unsympathetic (and in some degree he could not help agreeing without being able to do anything about it), he cursed his teachers for what he called their evasiveness. Their very patience and smiling tolerance made him wonder whether they were hiding a secret from him. Did they hold him incapable of understanding their theory or unable to apply it sensibly without wanting to say this clearly? Or had they got used to a much less effective therapy than he expected and wanted him, by some means or other, to find this out for himself? Why didn't they understand that he suffered not so much from the lack of visible improvements in his patients as from the lack of orientation of his own activity in the sessions?

These periods of hope and despair endured for quite awhile and in time he became acquainted with other young therapists and learned that they too oscillated between contentment and worry; that they too were groping for rules, for orientation, for principles, for criteria of therapeutic and non-therapeutic behavior. They came together, complained about their failures, described with pride and sometimes with bewilderment their successes, engaged in heated discussions, joked and bantered and tried to look at their confusing task from every possible angle. And while G— did not find that he gained more clarity on the basic problems of therapy, at least, he found comfort in the awareness that he was not the only eager and ambitious student who felt bewildered by his experiences in his job.

The sharp pain of despair during his first year in private practice gradually became blunted to a more steady attitude of skeptical resignation. Under the impact of the endless succession of disappointments, triumphs, failures and new hopes, he formed the conviction that there was a sound and satisfactory core in his endeavor, enough to keep hope and courage alive. This inspiring view, however, was marred by the melancholy recognition that he was unable at any particular time to locate this dependable element within the complex, entangled, vexing mass of phenomena which for him represented therapy It was, he sometimes said to his friends, as if he had to hand out the monthly pay to his employees, taking the money out of a large sack which contained real dollar bills as well as a lot of counterfeit. "I cannot tell the one from the other; I know some will get the real thing, others will receive nothing but valueless pieces of paper. And I never will learn *when* I did what I should, *when* I gave true value and *when* I cheated and betrayed the receivers' trust."

A NEW QUESTION

It was in G—'s fifth year of private practice that he read through some of his notes giving the content of his initial interviews with patients. The last section of each note indicated in a few sentences the patient's complaints that had allegedly motivated him to seek psychotherapeutic help. The last eight of them ran as follows:

(1) Please do not misunderstand; I am not sick but I want to be analyzed in order to understand myself better.

(2) I have to get rid of this addiction at all costs. It ruins my life; it destroys my family. This treatment is my last chance; I know it. If it fails, I have to kill myself.

(3) There is nothing wrong with me, except for my impotency—sexual impotency, I mean. If you could help me to overcome that, I will be the happiest man alive.

(4) I come to you because during the last year I suffered from anxiety attacks with increasing frequency. It reached a point where I had to stay away from work, and I don't know what will become of me if I lose my job.

(5) Everything was fine before our child was born, but since then, sex has become repulsive to me. I try hard not to let my husband know that this is so, but he feels increasingly dissatisfied and unhappy. I love him dearly; if I were to lose him, that would be the end of me.

(6) Well, I am here because my friends tell me I should try psychotherapy. Honestly, I don't see how it could possibly help me. I can do my job. I earn a good salary. My wife is a

fine girl, as good as they come. My kids are good, healthy, normal kids. Only, life appears so meaningless to me, boring, empty. I feel it would be irresponsible to commit suicide, but I wish I would die soon. Honestly I do. Do you think you could do something for me?

(7) Well, Doc, what do you think about homosexuality? I think it's all right. But our damned society makes life miserable for me. I am sick and tired of being an outcast or of pretending that I am "normal." Can you help me to accept my social isolation in a better spirit? I do not think that you can make me over into a happily married, law-abiding, family-raising simpleton, of which type there are already too many, *do you?*"

(8) Our family doctor insists there is absolutely nothing he can do to help my insomnia. He flatly refuses to give me any more drugs. I am completely exhausted; I am tired every single minute of the day. He says it's all nerves, but something has to be done about it. He suggested that I try psychotherapy. I am ready to try just anything.

Reading them over, one after the other, G— felt impressed with their dazzling variety. As he realized later, they were hardly more different from each other than the complaints of any random choice of neurotic patients. Yet, as it happened, the diversity within this little collection startled him and triggered off in his mind a chain of thoughts that had a decisive influence on his work for many years to come. His thoughts were somewhat like this:

Strange that I never wondered about that motley assortment of complaints and appeals. How could anyone dare to recommend for all of them the same remedy: psychotherapy. And yet, I myself felt no qualms about doing just this. Even now I find in my heart's heart the conviction that, if anything, psychotherapy would be the answer for all of them. That implies, by necessity, the belief that all these different people with all their different pains, symptoms, and grievances must have something very basic in common. For "psychotherapy" is not the name for a set of different activities or methods—at least not as I do it. And if the same procedure is supposed to be a cure to all these different ills one cannot assume this to be so by chance. One must believe that all neurotic disturbances spring from the same root, no matter how manifold their outward appearance.

Well, this is pretty immaterial—as generalities usually are. What *would* be important is a certainty about the basic condition necessary and sufficient for the existence of neurotic disturbance. True enough, the theory G— had learned included concepts of intrapsychic entities and suggested that a certain configuration of these assumed forces and factors determines illness. That was fine as far as it went. Yet it bothered G— that this common root of all the different forms of neuroses did not show up. Or rather, that it showed only in the therapists calling them by the same name and applying to them the same treatment as a sign that they saw a similarity and kinship among them. Couldn't there be a principle holding that, if there is really some significant inner feature common to a group of people, at least one outward observable feature (however hard to spot) should be detectable in all of them? That sounded good; too good to be true. It seemed almost more a product of wishful thinking than a defensible hypothesis.

Yet, in spite of this self-critical, resigned comment, G's mind felt vibrant, with an unusual excitement. While his thoughts dwelled on these and other highly abstract speculations, his memory was in feverish activity, racing through a large number of very concrete recollections. A series of observations, culled from the whole period of his psychotherapeutic work, emerged in his consciousness in rapid succession. They did not arise from every one of his patients. They were not all equally sharp and vivid; yet the totality seemed to illuminate one important aspect of what he had experienced throughout his practice. G— had some trouble in defining and expressing what it was that made this sequence of disparate recollections into one image of great impact. Uncertain as to which general concept would tie together all these distinct elements, he began to collect whatever descriptive terms came to his mind.

Patients, he thought, did not talk straight. They were never completely, never wholeheartedly behind their words. Listening to them required a very special effort. No, that was not the right expression. Listening to them caused some inner struggle, almost as if one had to listen to two speakers talking simultaneously. There was a strange duplicity about their communications. There were words and sentences and whole stories which were quite understandable and made sense in themselves; but the accompaniment of the tone of voice, facial expression and gestures interfered subtly and sometimes grossly with the total communicative effect. It deflected the interest of the listener away from the content of what was being said and kept it tentative, uncertain in grasp. It seemed also that accompanying this distraction of the listener's interest was a lack of unity between the patients' interest in speaking and the forcefulness with which they spoke. Even when they used strong language, when they raised their voices and gesticulated violently, G— had felt frequently that the over-all impression lacked punch.

Though G— found himself getting a firmer grip on the essence of the phenomenon he was trying to define, he still had not discovered a concept that would fit exactly. It certainly could be described as a disturbance of communication, and although this seemed a valuable first step toward a sharp formulation, it was still too broad. He could think of other disturbances in communication that were in no way characteristic for neurotic patients and of an altogether different quality from the phenomenon that interested him.

He decided to leave the problem as it stood for the time being, but looked for a name to identify the phenomenon in question. After some wavering he settled on the word "duplicity," the everyday use of which seemed vague enough to allow its use in a new and much narrower sense.

If his audacious assumption could be confirmed, if one could find more evidence to substantiate the phenomenon of "duplicity" as a true *universal symptom* (i.e., a necessary and sufficient condition for the existence of mental disturbance), then impairment of communication was probably more intimately connected with mental disturbance than any other symptom. G— felt very elated by the mere thought of such a possibility. It seemed to him that here was a chance to learn something new and decisive about the object of all of his efforts.

Before continuing the history of G—'s views on psychotherapy and especially on the universal symptom, it would be helpful to present the reader with some examples of the interviews on which G— based the concept. The selection of cases (5), (6) and (1) is not a random choice; the order of presentation is deliberate. The numbers refer to the eight initial interview notes reviewed by G—. In these samples, the universal symptom of duplicity presents itself in different forms and with an increasing degree of subtlety. (However, there is a subjective factor involved, inasmuch as one therapist might be more sensitive to a special form of the universal symptom than another.) Furthermore, I have excluded examples where the universal symptom becomes recognizable only after one has listened several hours, where its recognizability depends to a more than average degree on the purely acoustic impression one gets from the patient's voice, its pitch, melody and intonation. The examples give a description of approximately what happened during the first hour of treatment, i.e., the session *after* the initial interview. Where the behavior of the therapist is described, I do not want the reader to assume that I am necessarily in agreement with it.

Case A (number 5): Here is the case of the woman who is afraid to lose her husband's love because of her aversion to sexual intercourse. She has come ten minutes early and now seems very eager to talk. In fact, she starts before she even has time to sit down in her chair.

"Well," she says, "the last time I was here, I told you that when the baby was born and the eight weeks had passed and my husband wanted to have intercourse with me, I was surprised to find that I suddenly felt I would rather not. When I come to think of it, it was not as sudden as that. I am sorry; I am afraid that I misrepresented the facts. I was still in the hospital and the nurse had brought me the baby. It was the first time he drank real well and went to sleep, and I felt very content and felt like sleeping too, but of course I stayed awake in order not to inadvertently hurt the baby during my sleep. Then I thought that we had decided not to have another baby for the next two years, and I felt relieved because I figured— so we won't have intercourse for a year and a quarter, and, I thought, that's something like a long vacation. And then, all of a sudden, I became aware how silly that was. There is another thing which I feel I should say. You asked me last time whether the baby was planned, and I said 'yes, we planned it.' But when I came home, I felt that was not quite right. I mean we did plan to have a baby, but we always thought it would be a girl. And now, it's a boy. I do not know whether you understand what I mean. Of course, one can't plan to have a girl baby, because one cannot do anything about it. But can one say it was planned if it is a boy? Of course, I don't say that we are disappointed, or did I? I mean, I am not disappointed, but maybe George is. George is my husband. Perhaps he is really disappointed with the baby. I don't mean with the baby. He wanted a baby very much, but he wanted a girl. Did I say that? Maybe I should not have said that he is unhappy about *me*, but rather with Ed, the baby. But then, what could *you* do about that? I feel, when I said that about the vacations, I mean in the hospital, you know, that I would not have to have inter- course for over a year, you might think that I did not enjoy intercourse. I did enjoy intercourse. I only thought that if I did not get pregnant for two years, I wouldn't have to worry whether it will be a boy again and whether George would be disappointed again, though, of course, I know that it would not be my fault. But he might think that it *is* my fault, because he said the other day: 'Wives are usually wishing for boys, aren't they?' Please do not think that I meant to say that he really meant something by saying that about wives. That sounds silly. Of course, he meant something. Can you understand that I am afraid that he meant *me*? One should not take any odd remark that seriously, or should one? Of course, I do not want to say that he really thought of me when he talked of 'wives.' I mean *consciously*. But he could have thought about me sub- consciously, couldn't he? I said I wished to have a girl, didn't I? But how can I know whether I wished to have a girl, or rather wished to have a boy? I am not really disappointed with Ed. Ed is really such a cute little thing. If it were not for George, I would not be disappointed. But when I say this, what I am really saying is that I *am* disappointed. Isn't that terrible? What did this poor little child do? I really did not tell you the truth; I did not want to lie; I did not want to conceal anything. Of course not. Then you would not be able to help me. I know that. But I know that I could not live without George. I simply could not. Of course I couldn't."

Here the patient starts to cry with hurried toneless sobbing that sounds so much like sniffling that the therapist is for a few seconds in doubt whether she is really crying or only on the brink of sneezing. But the abundance of tears which are rolling down her cheeks and dropping into her lap removes that uncertainty. The therapist, vaguely concerned that in the next moment she may burst into uncontrollable yelling and then collapse, is just on the point of saying something to break the spell, when the patient, jerking her head violently, interrupts herself. The tears subside instantly, and with a voice that conveys nothing but annoyance, she says:

"I am wasting my time. I am wasting my hour. And then there is the maid. Did I tell you about the maid? She comes once a week. She should do the cleaning, but she doesn't know how. So *I* do the cleaning, and she watches Ed. I don't mind doing the work. No, I don't. I can work much faster when she looks after the baby. But she is such a silly girl. She is giggling all the time, and that upsets the child. Babies should be kept quiet. I tell her that over and over, and she, she giggles! She giggles and blushes and shrieks, and poor Ed gets terribly excited. I explain it to her. I do not shout. I talk as calm as I can. Maybe I am not so calm. No, I *was* in the beginning, at least in the beginning. But, this stupid, senseless person. But maybe that is immaterial. I shouldn't talk about that. I know I shouldn't."

I skip what the patient said during the remaining part of that hour and continue with the beginning of the next hour.

The patient appears in time but feels obviously less hurried than in the previous hour. After sitting down she seems to hesitate a moment, and says, then, with a sigh:

"Well, at least I have started treatment, so I feel a bit more hopeful. I have gotten some sleep last night. Things do not look quite as bad as they did." After this little reflective remark, the patient rearranges her posture in the chair like someone who after exchanging some niceties indicates that she is now getting down to business, and says:

"I am thinking of the maid—Lily, you know. I am afraid I gave you the wrong impression last time. I told you, or maybe I did not tell you, but I should have, that she was recommended to me by George's mother. George is my husband. Of course, one should not upset babies so much but should be quiet in their presence and avoid loud noises; but maybe I would not mind her giggling as much as I do if I had not intended to ask Lisa to come help me out. Lisa was not sure that she could come every Friday, because she has to help her father in the store—Friday, you know, is the busiest day. Mother, I call her Mother, but she is George's mother as I told you (she wants me to call her Mother, so I do, though I do not like it too much). Well, Mother felt I should not take someone who was not sure she could come every time, and as she thought so highly of Lily, I finally felt I could just as well take Lily; but in a way I resented it. No, I did not resent it, or at least not that much, only after I noticed her giggling and how much it irritated the baby. Perhaps I should not say irritated, but it excites him. I felt that Lisa would handle him much better. Besides, Lisa knows how to clean house, and she would have had nothing to do with the baby, and I could have told her just what to do in the house, and I would know that it would be done just the way I wanted it to be done. So, you see, maybe I should not have started to talk about Lily at all, and my talking about her is simply a waste of time. I really should tell you that I feel I said something horrible about George the last hour, or didn't I? Oh, sure I did. I am afraid I gave you a completely wrong impression. How could I say that George is disappointed with Ed? How could I, really?"

Case B (number 6): He is a tall, well-built man about forty years old, and looks as if he might be a good athlete, except that he draws in his head with a slight inclination to one side, allowing his arms to hang down from his shoulders as though suspended by strings. His eyes are kept fixed on one point or another, apparently seeing nothing, like the expression of one who wants to determine whether the pain in his jaw originates in the first or second molar. He walks somewhat hesitantly toward his chair, stops in front of it, reaches first in one, then the other pocket of his jacket, looks around the room, then down to the chair, and finally sits down. He remains silent for a couple of minutes. Then he smiles fleetingly in the direction of the therapist without quite looking at him, and says:

"Well, yeah, I am supposed to say something I guess. Where shall I start? You will probably say it doesn't matter. No, it doesn't I suppose. There is a little town, K, fifty miles north of Lake P. You won't know it; it is not worth knowing, though in a way it is a regular little town, nothing especially wrong with it you might say. Only that I was born there, and that was not exactly the fault of the town either. My parents meant no harm —did what others had done before them—good, hard-working people, so to speak, dead set on making some money, but strictly within the rules of the game—but strictly within the rules of the game." He repeats this last with no recognizable reason, while his eyes take on a blind stare and rest on the doorknob as if he would expect to find there some inspiration or stimulation for what he might say next. A minute or two passes. His muscular hands reach into his pockets while his forehead wrinkles. He opens his mouth, sighs and falls silent again. Another minute passes.

"Mind if I light a pipe?" His eyes, still fixed on the door-knob, away from the therapist, can hardly have noticed the small consenting gesture of the therapist. Anyway, not without effort, he pulls out a pouch, a pipe and a match box and proceeds without haste to fill the bowl and light it. This he does with the movements of an experienced smoker, but it looks as if he does something which needs great care and concentration. Suddenly, while he seems completely absorbed in the business of lighting his pipe, he starts again:

"They owned a hardware store, *the* hardware store; our hardware store. It said HARDWARE STORE in large black letters. But there you could buy every damned thing which could be bought at all in the little town. My father inherited the store from his father and worked there. My mother worked there. My mother's uncle worked there until he died. My brother Milt

worked there and my sister Ann, and Sue, a second cousin of
mine, and my father's half-brother Joe when he came back
from overseas. They did not make much money, though all of
them slaved like hell and hardly took time off for meals. Only
little Vic did not work in the store, heaven forbid. Little Vic
made good grades at school. Little Vic was such a gifted child.
Little Vic had such a good head on his shoulders. Little Vic
was such a Godsend and knew the names of all the presidents
of the United States backward and forward. No, he was too
good for this kind of work, much too good. Poor Sue! She did
all the bills and the statements and all the forms and blanks
and lists. It did not come easy to her. She had no head for
figures, and she had poor hands for writing, and she was no
good at anything else either. She had to do the same things over
and over to get the numbers straight and the writing readable.
Poor Sue! She had to fill in a form for the sales tax; she did it
eight times in a row and it never came out right. She put the
wrong number in the wrong place. She would leave out an item
which should have been included and would put in one which
had nothing to do with sales. She misspelled every other word,
and when nothing else had happened, she would spill ink all
over the finished work. She sobbed and she cried and worked
night and day, trying one pen after another, and when nothing
would help, in sheer desperation and misery she would dare to
suggest that perhaps little Vic—little Vic, the arithmetic genius,
little Vic, the miracle speller, little Vic, the calligrapher—could
do the thing for her, just once, just this one accursed time.
Poor Sue! She was straightened out, she was enlightened as to
right and wrong, she was given a piece of everybody's mind.
She got her beating, until she felt that she was the meanest,
laziest, most selfish little bastard that ever tainted the earth
with her evil, sinful mind. O yes, she believed it, just as the
folks believed it and Uncle Joe and brother Milt and sister Ann;
indignant little Vic believed it more even than anyone else, little
Vic who was sitting in the corner with his books, studying hard
so that he would become a lawyer or maybe a governor one
fine day and redeem the honor of the family and maybe buy
the choicest lots in the cemetery for splendid graves for poor
Daddy and dear Mom, with another square yard or two for

Milt and Ann and a polished tombstone that would last to eternity."

He pauses and looks into the bowl of his pipe, as if something strange and unexpected is to be seen there. With a jerky movement, he takes a pencil out of his breast pocket and presses down the ashes. He frowns, inspects the inside of the bowl for a second time, looks up at the ceiling, sighs again, and while he seems to scrutinize the place where the ceiling lamp is mounted, he shakes his head, and says:

"They were not bad people. One could not say that. When, some years later, poor Sue was smart enough to contract a serious illness, her fatal illness, as a matter of fact, they called one specialist after another. They took her into our house. They nursed her and cared for her and tried to comfort her, saying not a word about the expense, though the store did not go well at this time. That is, it never did go well, but at this time, the long, slow decline had already started when people for one reason or another preferred to go six miles over to L-ford where a new buying center had been built, that worked with more capital or something, and customers became few and far between. No, they were decent people as a matter of fact and deserved the polished tombstone they finally got, with all the gold-lettering and flowers and stuff. They were decent people—straightforward, honest, well-intentioned, you might say—not even narrow-minded. Not even unfriendly or grouchy. That is the sad part of it. I cannot complain. Maybe I wish they had been cut-throats or thieves or miscreants or chiselers. But how could I? It doesn't make sense. Maybe I do. But even if I did, what is the use? They are dead and buried and well decomposed now under their impressive monument with the gold lettered palm leaves, the dates and names, and the 'requiescat in pace.' In a way, they got what they wanted; in a funny way, mind you. Little Vic, he made his grades, made his grades all right. He passed every examination. He grew to be five foot nine and a half inches tall. He did not become a governor. No, that he did not, thank goodness. But he went to the best engineering school in the state and got his diploma and honors and stuff, and he found a job and worked his way up and was able to buy the shiniest tombstone old Dick Middleman had to sell,

with all the inscriptions in gold, 48 cents the letter. There was
nothing missing in the funeral service, and the sermon was the
longest ever spoken by any eloquent minister in K. People cried
and used their snow-white handkerchiefs. Only little Vic who
for quite a time now had measured five feet nine and a half
inches, with his black tie and dark blue suit, holding his dark
blue hat with both hands onto his belly, who had paid without
regret for this dismal splendor, could not enjoy it. He did not
cry, did not sob, left his silken, monogrammed Sunday-after-
noon handkerchief where it was, showing a bit from his breast
pocket, and thought only of his hands which had become numb
and cold and of how he could manage not to drop his hat. And
then he thought that at some time, at some point, even a
twenty-five dollar sermon had to end and that then all would
be over. Well, smart as he was (while he had not become a
governor, he had become an engineer, a run-of-the-mill one, but
well paid), he was right in this assumption. After sometime
the sermon was over; the last prayer said. The hole in the
ground was filled with dirt. And little Vic felt—that's it. Now
I can start living. But he was wrong, absolutely wrong. He
couldn't. It didn't work. It simply did not work. It didn't. My
fiancee (we were already engaged then), courageous, skinny
Diane said:
    " 'Vic, what's the matter? Are you sick? You look simply
awful. Do you feel that bad?'
    " 'No,' I said, 'I don't feel awful, don't feel sick. I don't *feel*,
that's all.' That *was* all. That *is* all."
    He smokes for a while in silence. Then he adjusts the
mouthpiece of his pipe. He looks at it several times, adjusts
it again with skillful and, at the same time, odd-looking movements and falls to brooding. Five minutes pass. Then with
another long and critical look at the mouthpiece, from which a
thin line of grey smoke emanates, he says casually:
    "I had borrowed the money from my boss. It took me a year
to pay it back. This was six years ago." He sits back and remains
silent for another six or seven minutes. Then he looks at his
wrist watch. "Time is up, I guess," he says with a ghost of a
smile. "Bye, Doc." He gets up, and without a further glance at
the therapist walks through the office and out of the door with

his long, halting steps, his head between his shoulders kept at
a slight angle.

The therapist remains sitting in his chair, wrapped up in
the patient's story. He thinks and even whispers the words:
"Amazing, amazing!" He feels highly involved, interested and
sympathetic. Only, on the fringe of his mind, a faint suspicion
seems to be hovering, as if he should have done something
which he had failed to do.

Case C (number 1): The young man who comes next is slender
and delicately built. He enters the office with a smile. He has
a high forehead, large attractive eyes, and a sharp nose.
Towards the chin, his face seems to shrink. The mouth appears decidedly too small.

He is the one who wants "only to understand himself better." In front of the chair where he sat during the first interview, he makes a small questioning gesture with his left hand.
The right one he carries in his pocket, raising the right shoul-
der and keeping the right arm close to his body.

The therapist says: "Will you sit down?"

The patient sits down and crosses his legs. He pulls his
jacket down so that the collar lies in the right position. He
closes his eyes for a moment, looks then at the therapist and
smiles again. Half a minute passes in which the therapist opens
a new box of Kleenex and attends to his nose. The patient
moves uncomfortably in his chair.

"Should I start now?" he asks, slightly irritated.

The therapist looks up at him as he drops the used tissue
into the wastepaper basket.

T: Start, with what?
P: I mean with talking.
T: As you like.

The patient looks puzzled. He leans back in his chair, but
only slightly, more to indicate that he is waiting than to make
himself more comfortable. Again half a minute passes in
silence.

P: Excuse me. I think I did not quite understand what you
meant. Do you want me to talk or don't you?

T [*lighting a cigarette*]: Neither the one nor the other.

P [*looking bewildered*]: Well? Oh, I see it's up to me?

T: Certainly.

P [*after some abortive attempts to say something*]: I was just thinking—in fact I thought the same that I thought while I was waiting in the anteroom. I thought, what am I going to say first? I could not think of anything. Then I saw the newspaper on your little table. I could decipher a headline. "Where Are We Going?" And I thought: "What if I should memorize this article and then recite it when I got in here?" I could have done it. I can easily memorize things. [*He looks with an expression of expectation at the therapist. When the therapist says nothing, he frowns and rubs his eyes.*] I am thinking now of my first day of school. My mother brought me there. I was wearing a new jacket. In the breastpocket, I had a new pencil with an eraser fitted to it with a little metal ring. I put this pencil between my teeth and tried to dent the little metal ring. I can almost experience the taste of the metal right now. [*Pause.*] My mother said: "Don't bite your pencil. Put it away." She meant, of course, I should put it back into my pocket, but at the moment, I thought I should throw it away or something. If there had been a table nearby, I would have put it there. But there was none. We were standing in the middle of a very large room, maybe the dining room of the school or the gymnasium, and I looked around and felt helpless. I held the pencil in my hand, arm outstretched as far from my body as possible. My mother did not understand what the trouble was, but she took the pencil and put it back into my pocket, and I almost felt like crying from relief.

I have deliberately refrained from stating hitherto the features in the cases just given that form the symptom of duplicity. I know that giving the three samples without comment leaves the reader, possibly, somewhat in suspense, uncertain whether he recognizes the common element in the three examples, the same phenomenon which G— called "duplicity." Perhaps the reader could not even see anything in common among the three samples. In neither case would I regret having created some doubt, confusion or even disappointment in the reader's mind. The thesis that a truly universal symptom exists and that the phenomenon (which G— at this stage tried to describe under the name of "duplicity") *is* a universal symptom, is of far-reaching consequence and basic for G—'s developing views on therapy. It is therefore important that the reader become fully aware of the inherent difficulties of this concept. It can only be of advantage for his participation in G—'s development when at this early stage his skepticism is aroused. He may well ask himself if G— has not become the victim of a half-baked generalization which forces him into distorted observations. He would only be experiencing the same doubts which haunted G— for a long time.

I will now try to disclose the phenomenon of duplicity in the foregoing examples. I will not explain it or venture a hypothesis as to its origin, purpose or function. I only want to do the equivalent of what one does to make the hidden dog in the mystery picture visible—blackening its outlines with a pencil.

CASE A. The patient's talk appears very clear as to its intention. The patient had said during the initial interview that her aversion against intercourse had appeared suddenly, and to her surprise, eight weeks after the delivery of her child, when her husband wanted to have intercourse with her and she refused. She wants to correct this statement, to the effect that her aversion against intercourse had manifested itself much earlier; in fact, soon after the birth of the baby as a faulty and apparently wishful calculation. Her thought was that by their decision not to have another baby for the next two years they had implicitly agreed not to have intercourse for fifteen months. The wishfulness of this faulty thinking was confirmed by the fact that she had thought of these fifteen months as a vacation. So far one can follow her without difficulty. But when she comes to the point of saying, "There is another thing . . . ," the listener is baffled.

In her preceding eager talk about what she called her "misrepresentation of facts," she aroused the expectation that her amendment of her former statement would be of some importance, at least in her own eyes. By the way she drops the subject and picks up another one without making sure that the therapist understands the "implications," if there are any, she gives the impression that her interest in the rectification has vanished as soon as she has finished her report; or, perhaps, more to the point, that she had been interested only in the rectification and not at all in the circumstance described in her rectified version.

Without paying attention to the puzzled expression on the face of the therapist, she talks about "the other thing" which she feels she should say. This other thing is again the rectification of something she had said in the initial interview. She feels doubt about her affirmative answer to the therapist's question whether the baby had been planned. Her doubt about being justified (in calling the baby "planned"), since they always thought it would be a girl, seems completely absurd. One might be tempted to call it a sign of thought disorder; but only for a moment. In the next statement, the patient remarks correctly that nobody can plan to have a baby girl. This implies that the question could not have been whether they had planned to have a baby boy but simply whether they had planned to have a baby, and should have made it clear that her answer in the affirmative was correct. But the patient does not seem interested in following this line of thought to its reasonable conclusion. She rather makes an effort to maintain that, at least in some sense, the baby was not planned. The listener can agree with that and feel that he can follow her statements, piecing together the following essential facts, i.e., facts which *he* would consider essential in the situation.

The patient's husband, George, had wished so much for a girl baby that he now feels disappointed. The patient not only notices his disappointment but, rightly or wrongly, feels that her husband is blaming her, assuming that she, like "all women," had wished to have a boy and thereby managed to get one. At the very least, she feels he is blaming her for not sharing his disappointment. The patient herself is not unhappy that her baby is a boy; she is unhappy because of her husband's disappointment. The listener could readily sympathize with a young mother's bitterness over the fact that her husband cannot enjoy a newborn child because of its sex. Yet, her confused way of talking distracts the listener continuously from the very facts she seems eager to emphasize. While she is, or at least seems to be, mortally afraid that George's disappointment may lead to an estrangement she appears even more interested in selecting the right words, in not misrepresenting the facts, in not misleading the therapist and in not wasting her hour. She expects to be misunderstood where there is no justification at all for such an expectation. The listening therapist feels almost relief when she, somewhat abruptly, but with some intensity asserts that she "could not live without her husband," and starts to cry in an apparently reasonable reaction to her fear of estrangement. Here, at last, the patient appears consistent in her attitude and her words. Yet, again, the listener finds himself distracted and baffled. Her crying sounds like sniffling, and though the tears keep rolling over her cheeks, her emotion seems shallow. With the jerking of her head, the expression of sadness and fear vanishes as abruptly as it came, and her voice betrays nothing but annoyance and concern with time-economy. And with the same eagerness to be accurate, to say the right thing, and the same readiness to question and amend every single sentence, she talks about her maid, Lily.

Listening to this type of talk, the therapist might be initially inclined to form the following "gestalt perception": The description of the patient's fears and worries with regard to the threatening estrangement, he might perceive as the figure, or to use an acoustical term, as the melody; the expressions of doubt about the correctness of her presentation and the frequent "side-tracking" remarks, the unnecessary questions, amendments and apologies, as background noises. The listener, therefore, will tend to focus his attention on the story, "the melody," and disregard as far as possible what appear to be random disturbances, emanating from the chaotic background. As time passes and the random noises do not diminish, the listener needs more and more effort to maintain his gestalt perception and might feel frustrated and in consequence, irritated. However, it might happen as a result of the continuous struggle with the background noises that the listener's gestalt perception changes. The random noises may lose their random character and may appear as elements of a melody, for what before was perceived as melody will fade into the background. This new view which leads from irritation and inner struggle to a new gestalt perception is what G— had experienced frequently while listening to patients, and recurred almost regularly after he had formed the concept of the universal symptom of duplicity.

CASE B. While in Case A the patient's story is a confusing one, jumping from one element to another, petering out in one place and then starting all over again later, putting a strain on the listener to follow, in Case B the patient's story is really a *story*. It takes its course with certainty and with a kind of artistic forcefulness of style, easily holding the listener's interest. When the therapist in this example is deeply moved by the narrative and so much under its spell that he barely notices the end of the hour and the departure of the patient, we may doubt that this reaction is the most desirable one but it is certainly at least understandable.

The beginning of the patient's talk seems very casual. "Well, yeah, I am supposed to say something, I guess." These are his first words after some minutes of silence. He continues naturally enough with the question: "Where shall I start?" But this question is obviously a rhetorical question. He does not wait for the therapist to answer. He gives the answer himself: "You will probably say, it does not matter! No, it does not, I suppose." And then he starts his narrative.

From the first sentence on, up to the last, the story moves with imperturbable determination, in strange contrast to its casual introduction. The storyteller does not show any haste. He drives it home; he is in no hurry. He takes time out for little sarcastic remarks that do not contribute to the events he is going to describe. He is not afraid of repetitions nor does he avoid minute details. He pauses in the middle for minutes, his whole attention apparently devoted to his pipe.

He is sitting in the office of a therapist whom he has met only once before. He is in his first hour of therapy (whatever that may mean to him); his story could be understood as an enlarged and broadened restatement of the "complaints" he had stated only laconically in his initial interview:

"Life appears meaningless to me, boring, empty!" These terse words are now replaced by a very colorful description of the patient's childhood and home situation leading up to the impressive scene of the funeral where he, probably for the first time in his life, formulated the fateful sentences:

"I don't feel. That's all."

In spite of his dilatory side remarks, repetitions and detailed enumerations, his story is the opposite of a rambling, leisurely, thoughtful, or emotion-driven account of the historical background of the patient's present plight. It is not epic. It is rather dramatic. The listener does not feel induced to follow with sympathy or compassion the unfortunate experiences of the speaker. He feels caught in the iron grip of a powerful hand and pushed along a winding path irresistibly until he faces the dead end, the stone wall of absolute finality. Instead of feeling that this patient was sharing the tragedy with him, the listener felt assaulted, struck by a blow.

The few close-mouthed remarks with which the patient prepares to take his leave underline the effect of his story. He did not talk to someone, he accomplished a job. When the job is finished he falls silent, waits to the end of the hour and walks out with a brusque goodbye.

The therapist is amazed and disquieted. His discernment of the patient's universal symptom did not go beyond its first phase, namely the irritating uncertainty of the gestalt perception. He still tries to see the patient's childhood, his suffering and bitter disappointment as the melody, and the dynamic power that forces him, the listener, into a state of helpless amazement as the background noise. At which point the therapist's gestalt perception undergoes the change is, of course, unimportant for the existence of the universal symptom. Its distinguishing characteristic is to be described not by what shift in the therapist's gestalt perception actually occurs, but by the fact that it tends to induce a shift.

CASE C. This short specimen of the young man's talk in his first hour of treatment is again very different from the two other cases. There is neither the painful eagerness nor the irritating pointlessness of the woman's talk or the bitter determination and imperturbability as is the case in the story of the engineer. What the young man says comes out fluently, is easy to understand and appears polite and civilized. One can easily imagine that a therapist could listen to a good number of similar recollections or little phantasies without experiencing any uncertainty with regard to his gestalt perception. How-

ever, after some time, a certain quality of the patient's talk
will begin to make itself felt as a cumulative accretion. Then
the therapist's gestalt perception will start to oscillate.

The young man with the receding chin is *talking in quotes.*
It is not by chance that within the short period of the talk,
three times he introduces what he is going to say by: "I just
thought . . ." or: "I was just thinking . . ." He is not really
talking *to* the therapist but *in front of him.* One could say he
produces specimens of thought, phantasies or recollections to
hand over to the therapist. He seems to consider himself the
subject of a psychological experiment, and what he says seems
less directed to a conveyance of something than to making a
pointer move over the dial.

I hope that with the help of these examples and comments,
the reader will have gained a better grasp of the type of phenomenon G— was subsuming under the name of duplicity. I
will now continue with my narrative.

THE UNIVERSAL SYMPTOM
REPRESENTS THE ILLNESS

The difficulties and inner struggles G— experienced in
connection with his concept of the universal symptom did not
derive entirely from the fact that it was not always easy to
observe. This new idea which he found so elucidating and
promising led also to a series of disappointments. As soon as
G— felt reasonably sure of the soundness of his conceptualization, he expected it to grow into an important addition to the
existing theories of psychotherapy. He had no doubt as to the
next step he should take in order to reap the fruits of his discovery; he should formulate a neat, precise definition and
dynamic explanation of the new concept. But this goal, which
in the beginning appeared very clear and not even too difficult
to attain, proved to be highly elusive. It was, of course, easy
to define the universal symptom as a configuration of behavior
present in all neurotic people and absent in those reasonably
healthy. This formulation, however, left undecided the problem
of whether the one phenomenon, the symptom of duplicity,
was the only one or whether there were perhaps others which

also had a claim to being called universal symptoms. G— noted with some bewilderment that he had originally anticipated the existence of only one universal symptom. Whether this was true or not, G— soon realized that it was impossible to deduce from the concept of the universal symptom the uniqueness of the phenomenon which could be subsumed under this concept.

Fortunately, there appeared to be a chance that a very accurate examination of the phenomenon of duplicity would bring forth evidence to establish its unique importance as the universal symptom. The outcome of such an examination G— imagined would be a reduction of the descriptive terms he had used in characterizing the phenomenon to more basic, dynamic terms. Such a reductive analysis of the phenomenon, he hoped, would demonstrate that the universal symptom had a closer relationship to the real root of mental disturbance than any other symptom. It would, therefore, shed some light on the nature of mental illness and consequently help to determine the factors needed in therapy.

G— made many attempts to find a formulation to match the image he had in mind. But the results were unsatisfactory. It did not seem too hard to explain the universal symptom in dynamic terms. Several formulations appeared promising but none really seemed to have any advantage over the others, and all of them finally were dismissed as arbitrary, adding nothing new to his understanding. The only impressive thing was— and remained—the phenomenon as such; every explanatory construction he could think of appeared as needless as a pebble on the road. With these uneasy doubts, he decided half-heartedly to stop searching. There was a confusion of mind he felt quite unable to clear up. "Maybe," he said to himself, "I do not even know what I am searching for." This thought too was disconcerting.

Some weeks later he hit by chance (as it appeared to him) on an exciting thought. It was just after he had finished his last hour of the day with a patient he had seen for six weeks and whose case had caused him more worry and thought than any other. There could be no doubt that this patient suffered from a very tangible disturbance. But to G's amazement he also appeared to be completely free of the universal symptom. He talked fairly fluently, intelligently and with obvious animation, and there seemed nothing in his behavior which one could call spurious, nothing which could be termed *duplicity*. However, G— had found it increasingly difficult to follow his stories. He noticed that he had started to feel hesitant when he had to call this patient into his office.

During the last week, G— had been assailed frequently by the embarrassing question whether his discomfort in seeing this patient originated just from the fact that this man's case seemed to disprove G—'s concept of the universality of the universal symptom. "Is it possible," he asked himself, "that the trouble I have in keeping my attention on his talk is simply due to my aversion to finding evidence accumulate that my promising discovery is in danger? Of course, it *is* possible!"

When the last hour was at hand, G—, tired after a long working day, called the patient in mechanically without bracing himself as he had done against the uncomfortable period during the last couple of weeks. When he greeted the patient and sat down in his chair, he wondered if the look of resignation on his face might escape the patient's attention. "So what," he thought. "There is as little point in hiding my mood from the patient as in hiding it from myself. Maybe I should stop seeing this patient. My personal limitations are bound to show to a different degree with different patients. So why should not this patient tax me beyond my capacity?"

However, to all appearances, the patient noticed nothing unusual. He started, as always, in his vivacious manner and fixed his clear blue eyes straight on the therapist's face, as if to make sure of his undivided attention. These eyes were like hands holding the therapist in place. The well-formed sentences, underlined by frequent "you know" and "you see" which were fired at the therapist in rapid succession reminded G— of the gestures of a buyer who anxiously puts down dollar by dollar to make sure that the seller counts with him and will finally hand over the goods. G— was so much taken up by this sudden impression that he said nothing for the rest of the hour.

Even on his way home, he thought again and again: "Oh, I see, this patient's stories are not *told* to me; they are handed to me as the price for whatever therapeutic incantations he expects in return. So, maybe, the universal symptom really exists and is truly universal." Then the following thought came to him: "Assuming the universal symptom is a reality, exists in every neurotic and disappears with recovery, then the task of curing any mental disturbance would entail the removal of the duplicity of communication." At this point two thoughts occurred almost simultaneously in G—'s mind:

One thought was a recognition that he would feel immensely relieved when he could devote all his attention to the universal symptom of duplicity and convince himself that this was compatible with effective therapy.

The second thought concerned an observation that seemed to open up at least the theoretical possibility of doing something to remove the universal symptom.

G— had asked himself, some time earlier, what his patients might possibly have in common in spite of the great diversity of their complaints and indications of mental disturbance. When he was able to find an identifiable gestalt of duplicity in their behavior, he had felt enthusiastic. The existence of a universal symptom promised to confirm the basic unity of all mental disturbances, and allowed one to think of all psychotherapy as guided by a simple basic principle. This prospective gain in the theory of therapy, which might lead to improvements in the technique of therapy, seemed to justify his enthusiasm. But G— had not realized that his enthusiasm had sprung from yet another source, a more personal one. Long before he had formed the concept of a universal symptom, he had encountered with some of his cases the conflict of whether or not to overlook what he later called the phenomenon of duplicity. He had not found an adequate expression for his confusing conflict until one day he thought of characterizing it as involving the "transformation of the therapist's task."

For this conflict, the following example was typical:

G— was listening to Doris, a girl in her late twenties, who told him about an experience in her adolescence. She had alluded to this event several times in the past in a somewhat mysterious manner, as if to indicate that it was a turning point in her youth, if not in her whole life. Although she usually began talking immediately upon entering the office, this particular hour she began by being silent. Keeping her head slightly bent, she looked furtively several times at the therapist, bent her head even further and started to open her handbag. She said:

"I have decided to tell you. . . . Do not mind, if I cry. I know, I have to tell you, anyway." She extracted from her bag a handkerchief, folded it carefully and dabbed her eyes. "I never thought I would ever tell anybody about it, not even you. It was awful." Here she looked questioningly at G—, and he could see the tears in her eyes.

"You say nothing. Of course, you never say anything. Maybe it was not so awful, maybe it was just an ordinary thing that happens to everyone, or at least could happen to anyone. Perhaps, it is not even worth mentioning?" She sobbed for a few seconds. Then she again applied her handkerchief carefully, shook her head vigorously, as if to make herself stop crying, and said very loudly, almost shouting:

"It was terrible. I was fifteen when it happened, just a little girl. It was in the beginning of the summer vacation. Lucy, my sister—she is eight years my senior, and was then, let's see, twenty-three. So it was a bit more than a year since she had married Bruce. She called me and said that she was going with Bruce to the country house of our Aunt Maud and could she take me along. Lucy was always so eager to do something nice for me and to give me a good time. If she only had known. How could she know, really? We drove out to Aunt Maud's beautiful house; the day was perfect. But why do I have to tell you every detail. That's silly. I could just say . . ." The patient who had sat in her chair very erect, her eyes looking at the window well above G—'s head, now slumped in the chair. It seemed to G— that she was looking at his face from under half-closed eyelids, and, surprisingly, with a smile.

"Anyway, after we had had lunch with Aunt Maud, Lucy and Aunt Maud decided to take a walk to the little forest. Bruce wanted to try the grand piano in the living room and I . . . I had the impression that Maud did not want me along, so I, too, stayed behind, on the terrace under the trees with a book I had taken from one of the shelves . . ." Her voice trailed off and a little silence ensued.

G— was quite certain that the story would wind up with

Bruce making some amorous advances to his attractive sister-
in-law. Whatever had happened, she must have been left with
guilt feelings and in a state of terrible confusion. G— remembered that about three years later the marriage of Lucy had
ended in divorce, because of Bruce's extra-marital affairs, and
that his patient had always talked of Lucy with admiration and
compassion, using words which seemed strangely overdone.
But while this thought flashed through his mind he felt that
in spite of the tears and her apparent inner struggle about telling or not telling, her mind was not really deeply concerned
with her story. She seemed much more interested in creating
suspense, impatience, and impressing G— with the courage
of her resolve to reveal her "secret," in spite of her shame and
embarrassment. He felt a strong urge to say something about
the histrionic elements in her behavior, something like: "You
want to show me how hard it is for you to talk about this
experience and how courageous you are to be able to do it." Yet
he knew, or believed he knew, what her reaction would be. She
would fly into a rage, abuse him, accuse him, and then clam
up for hours and hours as she had already shown she could do
when her feelings were hurt. Conversely, if he said nothing
and waited a bit longer she would certainly tell the whole story,
with all the details, and she might be right when she said that
this had been a turning point in her life. It would probably go
a long way to explain the mixture of pity, inordinate admiration, and condescension she revealed when talking about Lucy.
It might also explain, at least partially, the absence of any
social life outside of her family, her spinster-like existence, and
even her sister's contempt for men. Wouldn't it be a pity to
jeopardize the gain of such valuable material, when only some
minutes of patient waiting might bring it forth? And for what?
Just because G— felt irritated with her vacillations! Wasn't it
natural for her to look for sympathy in telling how she had
been instrumental, as she might believe, in the destruction of
her beloved sister's marriage? And wasn't it understandable
that she wanted some recognition for her courage in volun-
tarily undergoing this ordeal of confession?

But in spite of these arguments, another voice in G—'s mind
was not so easily silenced. It talked rather more loudly and

with increased vigor: "Let's assume one would sit in silence and wait for her to continue her story. Let's assume she tells exactly what you anticipate. Would this constitute fair and honest behavior? You know quite well that she wants to impress you, to please you, maybe to squeeze out some encouraging remark. But you act as if you were taking her story at face value, as if everything really is what it is made to look like—while you *know* it is not. Would you not feel like a hypocrite listening piously while inserting an interested question, nodding your head at the proper place, making a mental note of every 'significant detail,' but ignoring what stares you in the face, what is calling constantly for your attention, and, indeed, concerns you more than any disturbing action unscrupulous Bruce might have taken, or any shame and guilt poor Doris might have experienced?"

This inner controversy went on long after the patient had finished the story and the hour was over and done with.

Again and again G— felt inclined to formulate some moral condemnation for what he called the "conservative" attitude, the one which disregards what the patient "did" with him, or did for his benefit, and which is content merely to focus on the "information" in the patient's talk. To G— the latter seemed simply dishonest. However, as soon as he had thought in these moralistic terms, he knew that his virtuous indignation was entirely out of place. He told himself: "What else is my obligation but to do the job I contracted to do, help her to get better. I did not promise to tell her all my thoughts. Just keep your observation to yourself—that's all! That wouldn't be lying! And even if it *were* lying, wouldn't I lie if this could possibly cure the patient?" This sounded plausible at the moment, but after a few hours its validity began to fade away.

He discovered that the job he felt attracted to do could not be described merely as helping another person get well or better. What attracted him was much more than that. Not only was he exclusively interested in doing psychotherapy, he had also to admit to himself that he felt drawn to do psychotherapy in a certain way and not in any other. That was surprising, and all the more so since he could not define what it was that he wanted to do. He only knew that, in this *one* case, for example, he regretted that he hadn't interrupted her to discuss her efforts to impress him with her eagerness to hold nothing back.

It was disquieting to have an urge to behave in a certain way, practicing therapy, yet not being able to find a general formulation for the *type* of interaction he felt drawn to. It was even more disquieting that, to the contrary, he *did* find an argument which seemed to force him into the opposite direction. He thought:

"Regardless of what I want to do, it should fulfill the condition that it is helpful to the patient. In order to be helpful to the patient I have at least to *understand* him as a necessary precondition for whatever action I might take. I cannot expect to understand the patient if I do not know enough about him; therefore, I have to try to get as much information from him as I possibly can. It follows, therefore, that I was right not to interrupt this girl in her story with any remarks about her way of behaving, due to the risk of hurting her feelings and, as a consequence, losing the thread of the story temporarily, if not forever. Indeed, this case proved the value of not interrupting."

When Bruce sauntered out on the terrace and suddenly put his arms around Doris and started kissing her, she wriggled out of his embrace and ran down into the garden. He followed, caught up with her, and a second struggle ensued which was only interrupted by the noises they heard from the house. Bruce let go of her arms and she stood frozen a few steps away from him, mortally afraid somebody might find them.

Isn't it clear that if she really wanted to get rid of Bruce's advances she would have run into the house where the maid was working and whose presence would have protected her? Running into the garden was, in effect, an invitation to Bruce to renew the exciting struggle at a place where they were safe from detection. Without being aware of it, her feeling numb with terror when they heard voices from the house revealed her true wish: not to be interrupted. From these details of her story, it became clear that she felt, if not downright sexually excited, at least immensely flattered by Bruce's amorous attentions, and must have felt very guilty toward Lucy. This sense of guilt must have been reinforced when Lucy's marriage broke up, just because of such behavior on the part of Bruce with other female accomplices. And all this explained the patient's perpetual readiness to serve her sister as nurse, maid, baby sitter, in complete disregard of her own plans.

This argument in favor of an attitude in therapy oriented towards getting as much information as possible had seemed unassailable to G— and, at the same time, it made him feel sick at heart, for all its logic could not subdue completely his urge to act differently.

Accordingly, G— persisted in seeking a justification for his indestructible desire to practice psychotherapy in a new way. At least logically, he held, the existence of a truly universal symptom allowed the equation of the therapist's task with the sole objective of removing the universal symptom. Therefore, if a direct attack on the universal symptom could succeed, his struggles and conflicts would be over.

This vague and lofty promise which G— still felt inclined to brand as "wishful thinking" became more concrete, solid and respectable by a *concomitant* thought based on the observation that patients seemed never to be aware of their own universal symptom. No matter how obvious it had appeared to G—, even the most self-critical, the most intelligent, sensitive and psychologically interested patient, seemed completely blind to his own duplicity. In this aspect, the universal symptom seemed unique, and was unlike most other symptoms. The patient who trembled for fear every time she walked through a dark room volunteered readily the admission that, of course, there was not the slightest reason to expect any bad man lurking in the darkness. The obsessive compulsive who after touching his right ear felt an insurmountable urge to touch the left one immediately, affirmed spontaneously that, realistically, nothing untoward could result from omitting this second gesture, only he could not avoid doing it. The agoraphobic patient who could not leave his home would readily admit: "Well, I never fainted on the street and, maybe, I never will. But what keeps me in the house is the idea that I will faint walking on the street among people. Isn't it crazy?" Yet the most bizarre case of "duplicity" remained not only unnoticed

by the patient, but G— had found it extremely difficult to
make him see it vividly enough to elicit an expression of
surprise.

In view of these observations, G— felt inclined to formulate, tentatively, the hypothesis that the universal symptom
can only exist as long as the patient is not fully aware of it.
Assuming that this hypothesis is correct, the way to work on
the removal of the universal symptom was clearly indicated.
It would be necessary and sufficient to bring it to the patient's
attention.

The first objection to emerge in G—'s mind to this formulation was, naturally enough: "This cannot be right, it
would be much too simple." Yet, the little experience he already
had in *drawing the patient's attention to the universal symptom* seemed to contradict this objection. G— realized that this
task was far from being as simple as its formulation.

Reaching this stage G— felt overwhelmed by the newness
of his formulations and the impossibility of foreseeing their
implications and consequences. To avoid being swept away
by his eagerness to find what this new view entailed in terms
of actual therapy, he forced himself to retrace the steps he had
followed in his last conclusion and to check again on the
solidity of his entire construction.

His suspicion turned immediately to the logical trick (as
he called it), permitting him to derive from a simple hypothesis
(duplicity as a universal symptom) a completely new prospect
for therapeutical outlook. Logic was not likely to produce anything really new; if it seemed to have performed such a miracle
one could not be cautious enough in examining its soundness.
Yet G— discovered soon enough that in his case, too, logic had
not performed miracles, and had not even devised a new way
of practicing therapy. If he accepted the hypothesis that the
appearance of the symptom of duplicity was a necessary and
sufficient criterion of mental disturbance, the conclusion that
"removal of the universal symptom" was identical with cure was,
and remained, very trivial. All the new and revolutionary truth
was already contained in his hypothesis. This hypothesis,
though based on observations, was, of course, a generalization
far beyond empirical findings. Whatever confirmation one

could hope to get for it could consist only of the *improbability* of coincidence in observed correlation between the degree of mental disturbance and the appearance of the universal symptom. Of course, the improbability of coincidence would increase in relation to the number of patients observed.

Although this prospect of optimum confirmation looked somewhat flimsy, G— knew that his distrust was not justified simply by the fact that any possible confirmation depended on a probability consideration. No empirical science could operate without relying on probability judgments of the same type. The vulnerable factor was rather the determination of the existence in any given case of the universal symptom and, even more importantly, the necessary differentiation between higher and lesser degrees of the symptom.

Disquieting as these thoughts were, G— decided to shelve them for the time being. He felt—though not without trepidation—that he had already made up his mind to reorient his therapeutic work in accordance with his view that the illness could be equated with the duplicity symptom. The immediate problem was therefore determined by the questions: How could one make the patient aware of his universal symptom? What would be the patient's reaction? Was it really possible to confine treatment to just this one type of intervention? Was such a reduction of the patient's "diet" not equivalent to emotional starvation? Could it keep the patient's interest alive, not to mention the interest of the therapist?

G— could see no way of finding an answer to these questions except by actual experience in therapy. Mere intellectual effort could not prove the validity of any therapeutic method. He realized that his theoretical speculations could not do more than remove the theoretical obstacles which had kept him from trying what intuition urged him to attempt. They could do no more than lead to the removal of prejudices. No sooner did this simple truth dawn on him than he remembered with dismay that he had not yet found a solution to the problem of the reduced information that might result from the changed relations with the patient. Of course, G— thought, one could not be sure that the information he would be able to get by following his approach would actually be insufficient for an understanding of the patient. This reasoning was not very reassuring. For quite a while the whole issue was very confused. Suddenly G—'s suspicion turned towards the principle he had always taken for granted: that his understanding of the patient would grow in proportion to the accumulation of information. This was true *only* if one took "understanding" to mean "understanding the present as connected with or determined by the past." The principle lost its "obviousness," if one took "understanding" to mean "empathic understanding of the patient's actual, present behavior." It now raised the question, in the light of these two meanings, whether the undeniable importance of understanding in the second sense was not by error attributed also to "understanding" in the first sense. Indeed, these two concepts referred to very different mental activities.

G— felt that this distinction, never clear in his mind before, was of a far-reaching significance. "It might very well prove to be the pivot-point around which my approach to psychotherapy has turned from one direction to another."

History, even this small, limited history of G—'s views of psychotherapy, can hardly function without dividing the continuous flux of events into periods, characterizing certain elements of time as turning points. Such a procedure enhances the neatness of the gestalt to be elucidated, but is always at variance with reality which has a dislike for sharp borders and arbitrary functions. So it has to be taken with a grain of salt when we say that G—, after the foregoing developments, entered a new phase of his therapeutic activity, and really embarked on the project of putting his intuition to the test of experience.

Theory and Practice in Interaction

HOW TO START: THE FIRST DISAPPOINTMENT

Not long after deciding to reorient his therapy, G— accepted a new patient and was loooking forward to working in accord with his new concepts right from the start.

It was on the day before the patient's first appointment
that G— realized suddenly that his new way of thinking could,
in all probability, have an effect even on the very beginning
of treatment, on his own first moves.

When he asked himself how he used to start a treatment,
he was not too sure that he could tell. In the beginning, of
course, he had done what he had been taught to do in his
training. He had given the patient a general idea of how
psychoanalysis worked, explaining that it followed from this
theory that the patient had to cooperate by observing the "basic
rule." That meant the patient had to say everything that came
to his mind no matter how he felt about it, whether he considered it true or false, smart or stupid, polite or impolite.
Every instructor, after recommending this procedure, had
warned his students to make the introductory explanation "as
short as possible" and not engage in a drawn-out discussion of
the theory of analysis. G—'s own experience soon convinced him
of the wisdom of this warning. Most patients accepted the basic
rule without objections or questions and those who challenged
its rationale could not be satisfied by any explanation and had
to accept it finally on faith anyway. Like many of his fellow
students, G— decided early in his private practice to drop
completely the introductory exposition of psychoanalytical
theory and to start each treatment with a statement of the basic
rule. This practice seemed satisfactory for a while, but not for
long.

During all his struggles, from the beginning of his therapeutic work up to the time he had formed the concept of the
universal symptom, G— had attributed his professional dis-
satisfactions to the difficulty of *applying* psychoanalytic technique. He was not critical of psychoanalytic theory as such.
When he suffered from doubt, it was doubt of his own skill and
understanding rather than doubt of the soundness of the
method he tried to apply. Only on one point were his scruples
essentially theoretical. He was dubious about the formulation
of the basic rule and had given much thought to revising it in
a logically unassailable manner. He was distressed that no
formulation he could devise seemed quite satisfactory. At first
he had besought the patient's obedience to the basic rule as a

necessary condition of successful treatment. But, as he had learned from his teachers and confirmed in his own experience, no patient obeyed the basic rule consistently for any length of time. As some treatments had been successful in spite of this, G— was forced to conclude obedience to the basic rule could not be a necessary condition.

In one attempt to side-step the difficulty, G— modified his statement as follows: "You can assist the treatment by doing your best to obey the basic rule." And, for a while, this was what G— told his patients. Yet, he was not too happy with this version either.

He could not decide whether what mattered for the treatment was the amount of effort on the part of the patient to obey the basic rule or the degree to which this effort was actually successful. However, this seemed a minor problem when a much more serious doubt was raised by a patient who, to all appearances, not only took the basic rule very seriously but also seemed perfectly successful in obeying it.

Talking at neckbreaking speed this patient produced an unending stream of "free associations" where interjections, quotations, unfinished sentences, profanity, unexplained names, absurd phantasies and unintelligible complaints about entirely undefined physical sensations kept chasing each other in a perfect chaos which left the therapist baffled and utterly confused. G— was little comforted to remember that this ghastly phenomenon had been described in the analytic literature and "explained" as a case where obedience to the basic rule "turns into resistance."

G—, in experimenting with himself, found that whenever he tried conscientiously to voice "as best he could" everything that came to his mind, without regard for logic, coherence or intelligibility, his production was not too different from his patient's. Not every patient who tried to obey the basic rule produced similar gibberish, because most patients unquestionably interpreted the basic rule in a restricted way; namely, say everything that comes into your mind as long as you can expect the therapist to understand what you are saying and skip the rest.

For a while G— made further attempts to formulate this

modified prescription more neatly, but every new formulation seemed to require new protective clauses and conditions. With each failure, he became more and more disgusted with the compulsive, hairsplitting character of this pursuit. He could see, of course, that any special choice of words with which he made his initial announcement of the basic rule would not likely have much influence on the course of treatment. On the other hand, he knew that his inability to find precise words for what he wanted to convey to his patients indicated some very basic confusion, the existence of an unsolved theoretical problem.

To carry on his practice satisfactorily, he finally settled on a compromise by perfunctorily alluding to the basic rule and avoiding any stress on its importance.

As the time approached for the "first hour" with his new patient, G— again asked himself how he would open the session. He found to his surprise and satisfaction that the whole problem connected with the basic rule had disappeared. If the basic hypothesis of his new approach was valid, if no patient could help displaying the universal symptom of duplicity in one way or another, there was no sense in recommending any type of verbal or non-verbal behavior as being more conducive than any other to successful therapy.

"This sounds pretty radical," thought G—, "and it seems to imply an even more fantastic solution to the problem of starting the first hour. I may say 'hello' to the patient. But that is all!"

Yet G—'s elation over the beautiful simplicity of this answer was suddenly dampened by the thought: "But what if the patient remains silent? If he says nothing at all, how can he display duplicity?" This was indeed a baffling and crucial question. Its significance was by no means limited to the beginning of the first hour of treatment. Some patients said little or nothing in the first weeks or months, others became silent later somewhere in the course of treatment. Would it be necessary to urge them to talk?

G— could vividly recall the many painful hours spent with such silent patients. They did not sit comfortably in a relaxed posture during their silence. They did not look through the window at the sky with quiet pleasure. They never picked up a newspaper from the table close by or took a book or letter out of a brief case to read. They never did anything people do when bored. In fact, these silent patients never actually seemed bored or in need of entertainment. They were tense and often remained immobile until they began to speak. On their faces was a sulky or contemptuous expression, a stony imperturbability or a look of grim determination. Their eyes were usually fixed on one spot on the carpet or they just stared provocatively at the therapist. The silent patients were not simply mute; rather they were intent on doing something which consisted of doing nothing at all. Their silence did not seem due to the lack of a desire to talk but the result of conflicting forces.

It finally occurred to G— that this persistent silence was, indeed, another form of duplicity. "There is absolutely nothing," he further reasoned as uncertainty faded, "that must be demanded from the patient for treatment's sake. The whole responsibility for the therapy rests with the therapist! To ask the patient to talk is as unreasonable as to ask him to be healthy. If the patient is inhibited from working, it is my task to make it possible for him to work; if he has an inhibition against talking, it is my task to make talking possible for him. For these 'silent' patients, talking cannot be a necessary condition for successful treatment, but my treatment should be a sufficient condition for their becoming able to talk."

With these thoughts, G— arrived at the conclusion that the new orientation did not, indeed, require him to give any initial instruction to the patient. It also did not imply that if a patient remained silent the therapist had to react with silence.

G— was delighted that he would not have to worry any longer about the vexing problem of formulating the basic rule. He did not yet know that his success with this problem necessitated a further step in his development, or that his repudiation of the basic rule was only the first deviation of a future, more general, divergence from basic classical doctrine.

His confidence in his project was greatly enhanced by the discovery that the precepts which were to govern it had already led him to an unequivocal decision on the way to start treatment. With a new sense of security and expectation, he looked forward to the next day, when he would be able to test his ideas with the raw material of a new case.

The patient, a well-mannered, intelligent young man, close to ending his college education, had consulted the therapist because of what he called "attacks of anxiety." He had added that this expression was, perhaps, not correct since the extreme mental discomfort he suffered periodically was not real anxiety, and he only used the word for want of a better one.

Physical examination by his family doctor and by a specialist had failed to provide any explanation or to reveal any organic disorder, and both physicians had, not without hesitation, suggested that he should "try" psychotherapy. The patient, however, showed no hesitation and the agreement was made.

At the appointed hour, the patient appeared and entered the office with a polite smile and an expression of controlled curiosity on his face. He exchanged greetings with the therapist and sat down in a chair. The therapist closed the window and took a chair *vis-à-vis* the patient. A minute passed in silence.

P: May I ask what the therapy will consist of? I mean, what is the procedure?

T [*casual*]: Say whatever you want.

P [*raising his eyebrows and with a gesture of polite doubt*]: You mean, there will be only talk?

T: Yes, only talk.

P [*after a short pause*]: What do you want me to talk about?

T: There is nothing I want you to talk about. You may say whatever you feel like saying—if you do not feel like saying anything, that's just as well.

P [*after a short pause, with slightly lowered voice*]: Analysts, I understood, tell their patients to say everything that comes to their mind; your prescription is different. Isn't that so?

T [*keenly aware that there is something wrong with the course of this interplay without knowing exactly what, he is as reluctant to say "yes" to the patient's question as to say "no"; but neither does he like saying nothing; somewhat belatedly and sheepishly*]: Yes, indeed.

P: Well, I would like to talk a bit more about my anxiety or whatever I should call it.

And, so he does.

G——, after the hour is over, feels that he bungled the beginning of the hour, though, fortunately, by mere chance, no
discernible damage was done. He reviews his discussion with
the patient. He remembers that he almost blushed when the
patient said: "Your prescription is different." He thinks, "What
irked me was, of course, the word 'prescription.' It *sounded*
like sarcasm. Whether he meant it as sarcasm or not is immaterial. The sad truth is that my statement: 'Say whatever you
want!' *sounded* like a prescription. Indeed, it *was* a prescription
but an empty one. 'Say . . .' is an imperative. Why did I use
the imperative, if I only wanted to tell him that I did not intend
to prescribe anything?

"Oh, I know, when he asked me: 'What is the procedure?'
I understood, and probably rightfully so, that he meant: 'What
am I supposed to do?' Obviously, the suggestive power of this
question was too much for me. He asked for a prescription and
a prescription I had to hand out, though it was only the empty
shell of one, its content being zero. I answered the patient's
first question with self-contradictory nonsense. What a start!
I ordered him not to take orders. I was so eager to lay down
the rule of 'no rule at all' that I did not really listen to what he
said. Nor did I take sufficient care to be understandable. What
was his next remark? Oh, I remember, he said, 'You mean there
will be only talk?' Now I feel almost sure that this young man
knew as well as I that I would not give him medication or
massage and that his question, 'You mean, there will be only
talk?' was a kind of escape from embarrassment. He probably
felt bewildered without knowing exactly what made him feel
that way. When I then said to him, 'Yes, only talk,' he let it go
at that and did not seem to be surprised at all. But he asked,
as if it were a new point which had to be clarified, 'What do
you want me to talk about?' When I then, belatedly, told him
that there was nothing I wanted him to do, as I should have
done to begin with, he did not react to it as he probably would
have, if he had heard it earlier, and had understood and believed it. He waited politely till I finished, as if he thought to
himself: 'I should not have asked him this general question,
for this provokes him to react with the same rigmarole he gave

me when I asked my first question. Let him have his whim; it's a meaningless formality. As soon as he is through with it I will do better and be more specific.'

"And so he did. For, when he said, 'I want to talk a bit more about my anxiety,' he did not lower his voice at the end as one does in a statement but kept it at the same pitch as a sign that he meant to ask a question. If he had not been too polite to express his real feelings, he would have said, 'Well, whatever you mean with this strange formula—that there is nothing you want me to do—please tell me in plain English is it all right if I talk a bit more about my anxiety?'

"All this escaped me because I was concerned so much more with what *I* was going to do than with what my patient said."

G— was amazed by the unexpected difficulties he encountered in making his first moves in the project.

G—'s critical afterthoughts to the foregoing dialogue made it clear that he had failed to carry out his plan as intended and showed him how his own curiosity, excitement and self-consciousness had hampered his making real contact with the patient. However, even the report of these afterthoughts gives an incomplete picture of the difference between what he did and what he, however vaguely, had intended to do.

At this point his plan was clear only as an abstract concept, the method of implementation remaining quite vague. It would, therefore, be desirable to try to imagine how this first treatment hour with the same patient would have gone if G— had then possessed the attitude he was later to acquire as a result of his experience in the next few years. Unrealistic as the following play of fantasy may be, it will, nevertheless, shed some light on what effects G— had been striving unsuccessfully to attain. A comparison will then be made between the two versions, almost line by line, and the significant changes in G—'s behavior pointed out.

SECOND VERSION.
P: May I ask what the therapy will consist of? I mean, what is the procedure?
T: The procedure . . . ? I am not sure that I understand you fully, but if I do, I would say: There is no procedure!

P [*smiling politely*]: Oh, of course, I meant only: What do you want me to do?

T: That is exactly what I thought you meant by "procedure."

P: I do not understand. [*20 seconds silence.*] I mean . . . of course, there must be something I am supposed to do. Isn't there?

T: You seem certain that there is something you are supposed to do here.

P: Well, isn't that so?

T: As far as I am concerned, no.

P: Well . . . I . . . I . . . I do not understand.

T [*smiling*]: I think you understand what I said but you cannot quite believe it.

P: You are right. I really don't think that you mean it literally.

T [*after 10 seconds pause*]: I meant it literally.

P [*after an uneasy silence of 60 seconds with some effort*]: Is it all right if I say something about my anxiety attacks?

T: It seems impossible for you to believe that I meant what I said.

P: I am sorry . . . I did not mean to . . . but, indeed, I am not sure at all that I really . . . excuse me, what did you say?

T: I said: It seems impossible for you to believe that I meant what I said.

P [*shaking his head slightly as if irritated*]: No, I mean: Is it all right for me . . . [*he looks up and when his eyes meet those of the therapist he starts laughing.*]

G— is right in being sharply critical of his answer to the patient's first question in the first version: "May I ask what the therapy will consist of? . . . I mean, what is the procedure?" He recognizes that he did not really listen to what the patient said. G—'s answer, "Say whatever you want," responds to the patient's question as if this question were clear-cut and precise, while, in fact, it was groping and vague. The answer, also, with its prescription-like character, was self-contradictory. If the patient meant to ask (as he says he did in the second version), "What do you want me to do?" he certainly did not come straight to the point. The terms he used seem to suggest that he wanted some general information on the technique of therapy. The word "procedure" in this context even has a slightly ironical overtone. One can assume that the patient, respectfully awaiting the therapist's initiative in complete silence, felt uncertain what was going to happen and whether or not he himself was expected to do something or other. Yet the question he finally asks evades any expression of his embarrassment and doubt and sounds rather impersonal. In the first version, G— ignores this indirectness and artificial impersonality and takes the patient's question as a welcome cue for what he himself is eager to say: "Say whatever you want." In the second version, G— responds to the ambiguity in the patient's question. He does not pretend to have read the patient's mind and to have recognized his wish in spite of the peculiar wording. Instead, he lets the patient know that he is not sure he understood the question. His answer is conditional: ". . . but if I do I would say: There is no procedure."

It would not be surprising if G—'s second version answer was considered pretty obscure. Many would think that G— could hardly expect the patient to make sense of the statement: "There is no procedure."

"Why doesn't G— make an effort to be more explicit?" some will ask.

It is true that this second version answer does not explain unequivocally what "no procedure" entails. But G— is no longer interested in instructing the patient as he was at the time of the first version. From the viewpoint of G—'s theory there is no need and no place in the therapy for instruction, introduction or a lecture; not even for the announcement that there *are* no requirements. G—'s answer is a real response to what the patient's words convey to him and reflects their ambiguity.

The patient's next remark reflects a recognition that his first question was misunderstood and that he had now found more suitable words for it. "I meant only: What do you want me to do?" is certainly clear enough. Yet his introductory words, "Oh, of course," sound strange. They make it appear that he knew exactly what the therapist understood by the word "procedure" and that he, the patient, was in full agreement that there could be, of course, no procedure in this sense of the word. But, if the therapist did not mean the word "procedure" as a "prescription" for the patient's talk what could he have meant? The patient's agreement seems somewhat hasty, more intended to acknowledge whatever misunderstanding had occurred than to express an opinion.

G— again is in no hurry to dismiss what was said before or to answer the newly-formulated question as if nothing had preceded it. He does not know what went on in the patient's mind that prompted his statement, "Oh, of course!" and he does not hesitate to say that he is puzzled. "That is exactly what I thought you meant by 'procedure.'" The patient is taken aback. He probably understood G—'s remark quite well and his quick response, "I don't understand!" is only a cautious expression of the bewilderment caused by *what* he understood. He needs 20 seconds for the decision to express squarely what he thinks. "I mean, of course, there must be something I am supposed to do, isn't there?" Here again G— does not feel impelled to state or restate his views immediately. His interest is not so much focused on the fact that the patient expects to be told how to proceed (a fact which is not surprising) but rather on the *firmness* of the patient's belief that there is something he is supposed to do. Accordingly, he underlines his observation: "You seem certain that there is something you are supposed to do here!"

The patient feels, of course, that the therapist, by repeating the patient's own words, is expressing some disagreement with the thought they express. But he hesitates to accept this fully. He clings to the idea that there might be some misunderstanding on the semantic level. He says, "Well, isn't that so?"

G—, for the first time, now feels certain of the meaning of the question and answers it immediately. "As far as I am concerned, no!" The patient's reaction, "Well, I . . . I . . . I do not understand," is again not so much an expression of doubt of the sense of the answer but rather of disbelief in the reasonableness of its content. G— perceives this clearly. "I think you understood what I said but you cannot quite believe it!"

A summary of the changes in G's behavior from the first to the second version, up to this point, discloses the transition from a limited and selective attention to a greater receptivity to the significant elements in the patient's verbal and non-verbal behavior. Only in the second version is the patient's duplicity

reflected in the therapist's response. This change of attitude in
G— results in a change in the nature of the entire interaction
between him and the patient. While in the first version the
dialogue seems to prevent a meeting of the two minds, in the
second the patient and therapist are approaching each other,
to the point of even discovering that they hold different opinions on the requirements of psychotherapy. An examination of
the remainder of the dialogues shows that in the second version, the result is even richer than one would envision from the
first part.

After G—'s last remark, taking the ambiguity out of the
patient's use of the word "understand," the patient agrees. "You
are right." This infers, "I, indeed, cannot believe that there is
nothing I am supposed to do here." It seems that both now are
talking about the same idea. Yet the patient's next words,
continuation of his affirmation, "You are right," introduce a
new uncertainty. "I really do not think that you mean it literally." The therapist, somewhat taken aback, needs a moment
to assure himself that there is no meaning to his statement
apart from the literal meaning. He has the vague impression
that the patient's remark is an attempt to say, in a polite
manner, "I do not believe you, you are pretending." But as the
impression is indecisive, he says simply: "I meant it literally."
This statement throws the patient into an uneasy silence. Its
definitiveness leaves him "up in the air" or "to his own devices."
Besides, the very fact that he finds himself suddenly involved
in an exchange of real opinions (instead of merely formal
conversation) makes him uncomfortable. Something like an
inner struggle fills the time of his silence. It is uncertain what
kind of thoughts accompany this struggle. What he finally
says might suggest a decision to drop the whole confused
issue and come down to business. The patient says, "Is it all
right if I say something more about my anxiety attacks?"

But the therapist recognizes that the patient did not really
drop the issue. Though the patient now expresses the wish to
talk about his symptoms, he asks whether it is all right for him
to do so, implying by this very question that he expects the
therapist to discriminate between therapeutically desirable and
undesirable topics, and again indicating his belief that the

therapist did not really mean what he had said. At this stage of his development, G— is neither eager to hear more about the patient's anxiety attacks nor exasperated by what he would have termed, at an earlier stage, "the futility of the preceding discussion." His response is a direct reflection of the patient's duplicity, which, neither decreasing nor increasing, has become less subtle. "It seems impossible for you to believe that I meant what I said."

The patient's display of confusion has all the hallmarks of "duplicity." It is neither "pretending" in the usual sense of the word nor completely genuine and straightforward. "I am sorry . . . I did not mean to . . . but, indeed, I am not at all sure that I really . . . Excuse me, what did you say?" G's answer shows again his perception of the patient's duplicity. The patient's next reaction strikes the listener as an abortive effort to maintain a lost position by desperate means. Shaking his head slightly, as if irritated, he says, "No, I mean: Is it all right for me . . . ?" His voice is uncertain and weak, almost a whisper. When his eyes meet the eyes of the therapist he starts laughing. In this moment a mutual understanding occurs, far more complete than at any time before. Neither patient nor therapist could probably put it into words, nor does either feel the need to try. It is not unlikely that the patient, still laughing, would stammer, "I don't know what I am laughing about."

Although version two is obviously a fiction, since a therapist could hardly treat the same patient twice for the first hour of his treatment, the spirit and course of version two are similar to many "first hours" about two years after G— had started on his "project."

Such hours frequently left G— with mixed feelings. They imparted a sense of satisfaction and accomplishment, as if "things had gone well," but when he compared them with his theory, he still could doubt whether he had really lived up to his original intentions. He could see that he had been well aware of the patient's duplicity and had in some way responded to it. He could also see that in response to such hours the patient's duplicity had sometimes receded, at least for short stretches of time, from minutes to, maybe, a couple of sessions. Yet, when he asked himself whether he had actually made the patient aware of his duplicity, to the extent that the patient recognized and acknowledged its existence and its nature, the answer was "no!" In fact, it hardly ever happened that the patient said anything roughly equivalent to, "Oh, I see now, my talk was simultaneously inspired by two conflictions."

This was confusing. It was even more confusing when occasionally the patient *did* say something which could be understood as an acknowledgment of his duplicity.. These apparent acknowledgments failed to create in G— the immediate sense of satisfaction he experienced in hours when nothing of this sort happened. It seemed almost as if the strict application of his theory, entailing the attempt to "make the patient aware of his universal symptom," was less satisfying than a behavior less aim-directed and theory-conscious. No wonder that these observations tended to fill G— with grave doubts as to the validity of his basic assumptions.

Another cause of concern for G— was the question whether events, like the second version of the little dialogue, as satisfying as they were, really were indicative of an irreversible step, however small, in the patient's progress to health. Certainly, the initial distance between the two had lessened. The early painful tension was relieved as indicated by the meeting of their glances and the patient's irresistible laughter. But was this merely a pleasant interlude, or did it create a helpful insight within the patient's mind? Was it at least a sign that such an insight had been achieved?

Again G—'s theory failed to provide a convincing answer.

A SECOND MISTAKE: INTENTION
VERSUS THEORY

This section will describe other aspects of G—'s development in the first two years of his project. It will show, with the help of the more dramatic case of "little Vic" (case B), how G— worked and by trial and error reached a promising approach to his patients which gave him a sense of ease while, at the same time, it ran counter to his expectations.

In the process of tempering the structure of theory in the fluid of actual experience, the gestalt of his whole project

underwent a subtle change. New observations continuously in-
filtrated the very concepts that formed the components of his
basic hypothesis and altered their meaning almost unbeknown
to him. Frequently, his project appeared to him not so much a
plan *he* had conceived and which he was wittingly adapting to
his growing experience, but almost like a creation with a life
of its own, that grew according to an innate pattern and with
which he had to live as well as he could.

The device used in the previous section will again be used
with the case of little Vic to imagine how G— would have dealt
with the same patient in exactly the same moment of the patient's life and at a different point in G—'s development.

The sample hour (refer to pages 41–46) should be considered as the first version, preceding in time G—'s start with the
new project. The second version (which will follow immediately) should be thought of as occurring only a few weeks
after the start of the project. It runs like the first up to the end
of the patient's narrative, except that now the reader must believe that there are about fifteen minutes remaining of the
hour.

While in the first version he had watched—like a spectator
in a play—the unfolding tragedy of the patient's life, in the
second G— does not lose sight of the fact that the gifted nar-
rator is a patient who is here with him for treatment.

Towards the end of the narrative G— feels half inclined
to remain silent. He is curious how the patient will extract
himself from his immersion in history of the past and make
the transition into the present. He says nothing after the patient
finishes his little pointed dialogue with Diane at the cemetery
and silently watches him inspecting his pipe. But when little
Vic finally adds the dry short epilogue, winding up with the
remark, "This was six years ago," G— feels an urgency to
speak up.

G—: What you told me during this hour seemed to me a kind
of condensed life history. It gave a picture of your childhood and
adolescence as they appeared to you in retrospect after the death
of your parents, and up to today. It is the life of a well-endowed
child who has been singled out from the rest of the family by his
parents as the one who would and should have a chance to enter

a higher social stratum. So they gave him the privilege of being exempted from participation in the daily struggle of earning a living. Yet, this privilege was at the same time an exclusion from the group and from its life, and overburdened him with the duty to make up for it by achievement. Well, this came across to me from your talk and it seemed understandable and convincing enough. However, in the way you told the story another intention seemed to come to the fore, beyond the intention to tell how much you have suffered and still are suffering from being condemned to superiority. There was something forbidding in the artistic perfection of your manner of telling the story and left no room to doubt that you felt without hope of finding relief under any circumstances. I felt you were intimating to me in an indirect but very impressive manner [*quoting*], "Look, though I came for help, as I felt I should as a man of this century and of a country where people believe in the doctor, deep down I know beyond any doubt there is no help for me."

P: I did not come to entertain you. If I had known for sure that you could not help me, as you suggest I did, I would have been a complete fool to have come at all! But after your flattering suggestion it seems to me that I have been a fool to have come with *some* hope, however faint, that you might be able to help me. [*30 seconds silence*.] Is that all you have to say?

The therapist feels miserable. He had put himself into his speech and had felt that he really expressed what he thought and had expressed it convincingly enough to be justified in expecting at least something of what he had meant to convey would get across to the patient. Instead of eliciting a sign of recognition, a smile, a widening of the eyes, a thoughtful look or an interested question, he had produced a complete misunderstanding. He had hurt his patient's feelings and given the impression that he had scolded the patient for being foolish!

He already sees the patient pick up his pouch and matches and leave the room with a bitter, contemptuous glance at the therapist. What can he do? Should he say: "No, no, that was not what I said, and certainly not what I meant. I did not say that you felt *hopeless* but only that you *talked* as if you felt this way. Can't you see the difference?" But he already knows what the patient will say in return, "Now, when you have seen that your wise remark has shattered my hope, you want to take it

back and act as if you had said something else; you play with
words to pull the wool over my eyes!"

G— feels bitter. "All my attention, my sympathy, my
understanding, my thoughtful and sensible speech, was wasted
on this hardheaded, belligerent prophet of doom, whose mind
was made up in advance to distort every word I would say!"
But something in this thought strikes G— as weird, and—
suddenly, as if the light has changed—the whole situation
takes on a different appearance. He knows, for instance, that
his "sensible sensitive" speech was a freakish composition of
true feeling coated with a false unctuosity meant as a *captatio
benevolentiae*, a bribe of flattery and sympathy to make the
essential truth more acceptable. "Oh, now I know that my introduction with the condensed 'illuminating' description of his
childhood was only intended to buy his favor and had nothing
at all to do with what I really had to say. And when I finally
talked about his skillful plea for hopelessness . . . I somehow
adopted his solemnity. I talked dignified rhetoric instead of
plain English."

Yet, instead of feeling more despondent because of his cowardly approach, G— feels relieved and almost cheerful. And as
G—'s whole emotional reaction, which takes so many sentences
to describe, used up less than a second of actual time, he is
immediately aware that the patient is not only still sitting in
his chair but has also asked a question, inviting further communication.

G— [*while his face brightens*]: Your question seems to confirm
my impression that you are inclined to say "black" when you feel
"dark gray"! [*He pauses a second but when the patient raises his
eyebrows a little he continues.*] Well, you would hardly have asked
me what more I had to say if you were as thoroughly convinced of
my inability to help you as your . . . well, very sweeping remark
suggested.
P [*with some irony*]: "Black! Dark gray!" What is the difference?
Things are bad enough as they are, and that is a fact!
G—: They must be, I assume, otherwise you wouldn't be here!
P: They sure are!
G—: But the hour is up. Do I see you Thursday?
P [*after a short hesitation*]: I'll let you know!

"There is no telling whether he will come or not," thinks G—, after the patient's departure. "But there is a good chance that he will. When I asked him about the next appointment I am pretty certain he intended to say, 'Yes, of course!' But he felt it would be out of style to be that positive; so, as a kind of face-saving device, he left it open. His rambling phrases about 'black' and 'dark gray' and 'what is the difference?' in spite of the ironical smile he put around his lips . . . they were . . . just words . . . they did not make sense. Compared with the skillful, derisive harangue with which he demolished my silly declamation, they sounded clumsy and ineffective. A smoke screen to cover retreat!

"What did I say that weakened his position? Was my comment that he says 'black' when he means 'dark gray' more convincing or better expressed than what I said before? Or was it my insinuation that the fact that he remained in his chair and asked me a further question was not compatible with hopelessness? I could think of any number of biting, derisive answers he could have produced to put me out and which were not harder to find than his vituperative distortion of my speech that threw me into despair.

"Admittedly, my initial speech was cautious, 'pussyfooted' maybe, but it was not tactless or offensive. Why did this speech arouse a potent outburst of rage while my later somewhat blunt and aggressive remark brought forth a lame and almost reconciliatory reply? This is all very mysterious!"

Later, not too long after the time at which the imaginary second version could have taken place, G— came to ask himself the explicit question: "What would an ideal therapist do? Would he try to anticipate how the patient might react to his talk and adjust it accordingly?"

This seemed a reasonable and proper thing to do, if one talked with a purpose in mind. "Yet, wouldn't this preparation in advance result in talk that would sound stuffy and academic, resemble bribery or diplomacy? Can one even be sure of a desirable reaction at which to aim?"

The debate with himself continued: "Am I to sugarcoat the bitter pills to make the patient say, 'Yes, you are right, doc!' Or should I make my remarks as pointed and frank as possible to achieve full impact? Don't worry about the patient's reaction but rather say what is needed to show up his duplicity? On the other hand, wouldn't it be wrong to be indifferent to his reaction since this will certainly affect how well I succeed in my purpose to help, to cure, to improve to the extent I can?"

But the patients came and the hours went. Other questions occupied G—'s mind, driving out the confusing, unanswered questions mentioned above. He felt hopeful or worried, successful or incompetent in irregular sequence and only sporadically did the old, vexatious questions reappear to provoke new, frantic attempts to formulate satisfactory answers. Always in vain.

The following third version of little Vic's first hour of treatment corresponds roughly to G—'s way of conducting treatment a couple of years after he started his project and a few months before new thoughts about the nature of psychotherapy crystallized in his mind.

In this version G— starts speaking at the same point as in the second; i.e., after the patient finishes his little epilogue with, ". . . this was six years ago!" and several minutes have passed in silence.

G—: In your story you introduced each person with his name and with some indication of his position in your family. But one person you introduced with only his nickname, and in a way that had me puzzled for quite a while before I felt certain that you were alluding to yourself.

P: Did I? [*On his face appears the ghost of a smile.*]

G—: I understand yours is a rhetorical question. You are not *really* uncertain whether or not you did what I said you did. When you used the form of a question, "Did I?" you wanted to say, "This is hardly worth remembering, though, as a matter of fact I remember it." But then you smiled a very, very faint smile, as if something had struck you as slightly amusing and as if this amusement was just a bit embarrassing.

P [*says nothing, but his dark eyes meet the eyes of the therapist for the first time; his facial expression is inscrutable. The next five minutes pass in silence.*]

G—: The hour is up. I'll see you day after tomorrow?

P [*very short*]: Right!

G—: Goodbye!

P [*nods, gets up and walks to the door; he turns his head slightly and says, before his eyes become visible to the therapist*]: Goodbye!

The therapist in his first remark to the patient focuses on one single detail of the patient's story. It is the detail that impressed him more than anything else the patient said as an artistic device to convey to the listener the speaker's grim finality. It seems impossible to him that the patient would not remember immediately this high point of his story. Of course, it is not the high point with regard to the *content* of the patient's presentation. With the life history of the patient as frame of reference, the high point is certainly the funeral scene. But, if the frame of reference is what goes on in the therapist's office between him and the patient, the subtle and cunning introduction of the patient's nickname, unknown to the therapist till then, is the most striking element. G— describes this element and adds that he felt puzzled for a while, as he, in fact, had been. He does not ask the patient, "Why did you make me perplexed?" which could only force the patient's attention away from the "high point" and distract him by the need to produce an answer. The very fact that he singles out this one element without any attempt to draw a conclusion or to prove a point conveys G—'s perception to the patient much more directly than the elaborate speech in G—'s less experienced version.

The patient's close-mouthed reaction shows immediately that what G— said had caught his interest. In his somewhat uncertain remark, "Did I?" he does not even pretend that he cannot remember. If less had happened within his mind than what happened when the therapist reminded him of the "high point" he would have had no trouble in finding clever words with which to lash out against the therapist's "pedantic fuss about an oversight of minute significance." But, as stated, something was set into motion inside of him and his mind was busy with an experience he could neither name and express, nor deny and forget.

It is doubtful how much the patient understands of G—'s remark on the rhetorical nature of the patient's question. However, what the therapist says about his smile seems not lost on

him. The rigidity of attitude he showed throughout his narrative has given way. In telling his story with its twofold message,
his appearance was that of a man with a single and well-defined
purpose in mind. Now he appears thoughtful, puzzled and not
too certain of his direction.

In the course of approximately two years from the beginning of G—'s "project" to the time into which these second
and third versions of the previous sample hour fit, the rift
grew steadily between G—'s actual behavior in treatment hours
and the type of behavior his theory seemed to call for. After
hours like the one with little Vic, G— was frequently amazed
not only that he had deviated from his original plan but that
he obviously used criteria in disregard of his theory in evaluating a therapy hour. While according to his hypothesis he
should have been concerned only with whether the patient
gained any insight into his duplicity, he actually felt content
with an hour to the degree in which mutual understanding
was achieved. "I behave," said G— to himself, "as if all that
matters is that I have had a good talk with the patient," and
he blamed himself that he did not resent this fact as sharply
as he felt he should.

On the following pages are described two more treatment
hours of the same period as the third version of little Vic's first
treatment hour. They will be little Vic's second and ninth hours,
respectively.

Between the first hour and the second G— has several
times reflected on his experience with this patient, trying to
anticipate how the next hour might run but to no avail. Nothing
emerged from these cogitations that seemed to fit this patient.
It appeared unthinkable that little Vic could possibly do anything but talk about the hardware store, about poor Sue's
unsuccessful and unrewarded efforts, about the precious tombstone with its gold lettering, the interminable sermon, the
numb fingers clutching desperately the dark blue hat and the
unredeeming end of the funeral scene.

The patient arrived on time. In the waiting room, without
returning the therapist's greeting, he rose from his chair and
crossed into the office with the same hesitant, uncertain steps
as before, which brought him not quite in front of the chair

but somewhat to one side, where he stopped. His eyes wandered over the whole room, as if he were uncertain where to turn next. But then, with left hand on his forehead, like someone who tries to wake up, he looked down at the chair and moved around it so that he could sit down. Without looking at the therapist, who already sat in front of him, he spent a minute or two lighting his pipe and remained immobile for a while except for his lips, which opened from time to time to allow the smoke to escape.

Then he threw a short glance halfway in the therapist's direction, jerked his head, as if he had just now discovered the presence of another person and took the pipe from his mouth.

P: I came straight from the office. I'll have to go back there after this hour, but before I go back I have to see some people, look over a plant. So I took the service car. Old man Brenner insists that we do not use our own cars for business appointments. God knows why! His forget-me-not blue Pontiacs look awful. But I will hand it to him, he makes his mechanic keep them in excellent shape. I did not like the color and felt silly to alight from such a sparkling display of chromeplated tin and bad taste. Keep your oil, gas and tires, I told him when I first came years ago. I'll take my own car and won't charge you for anything. But he made such a fuss. Maybe he thinks that everybody reads the chrome copy of his terrible handwriting *Brenner Incorporated* at the edge of the fender. I finally said, "O.K." I was sitting in one of the service cars at the intersection of Shelton Avenue and Almond Street. Almond Street is fairly narrow and has a curve just before entering Shelton. There I was sitting and waiting for the light to turn green, when I suddenly heard a bang and got such a push that my foot slipped from the clutch. But my right foot was on the brake and so the motor was killed. At least that kept the car from jumping into traffic. Instinctively I started the motor again. At this moment the light came on. I knew I was late. I was just about to start, when I saw a hand on my open window and I heard the man say: "I am very sorry I bumped into your car. Your bumper got dented. I *am* sorry!" "Never mind," says I. "Are the cars clear from each other? Can I drive on?" But he was so confused he did not hear what I said. He said: "I am insured. Will you take down the name?" I said: "I am in a hurry. Never mind the dent. Are the cars clear?" Was he deaf or what? He did not hear me and held on to my door. "Don't make a fuss," says I. "If a cop comes along it will take 20

minutes." But he stood there like a dope. So I yelled, "Take off
your hand!" and immediately stepped on the gas. I was furious. I
wished he would fall and break something, not because he had
bumped into me. No, but because he didn't understand and
wouldn't take his hand off the window. When I parked here I
noticed the left end of the bumper was bent in and the fender
scraped. Even *Brenner Incorporated* had been torn loose at the
one side. But this I don't mind, really. On the contrary, I wished
there had been even more damage. I wouldn't have minded, if it
had been my own car. The man was maybe around fifty. He wore
gold-rimmed glasses and had kind of a pudgy face that looked
grief-stricken and bewildered. Poor idiot! Maybe he didn't see very
well but why couldn't he let me drive on, instead of bothering me
with his damned insurance? I don't like being late. I don't know
whether I really don't like being late, but I certainly don't like being
delayed. He didn't fall; he swayed a bit because he couldn't let go of
the window fast enough. I do not know how I managed to see that
he didn't fall, but he didn't. I must have looked back or perhaps I
saw him in the mirror. He was jolted but quickly recovered his
balance. There is a newsstand downstairs in the hall. If I hadn't
read the morning paper during my breakfast I would have bought
it and read it down there in the car. What is the point of being on
time, after all? But what is the point of anything? So it's just as
well. [*3 minutes of silence.*]

   G—: I see; you are careful not to be misunderstood. You felt
angry with the old gentleman and wished him to fall down, not
because he was careless enough to bump into your car, but because
he delayed you in his anxiety to take responsibility for the damage.
You are here in time, not because you wanted to be on time but
because you hate to be delayed and because you had read the
morning paper during breakfast.

   P: That's what I said. [*The therapist remains silent. The patient
shrugs his shoulders as if to dismiss the issue.*] Anyway, I am
punctual. I might leave late, but I always manage to make up for
it. I know, it's silly. It's hardly ever worth while to risk your neck.
[*Under his breath*] But how does one find out?

   G—: Find out? I do not understand. Find out what?

   P: Find out what is worth while. [*A minute's silence.*] From
here I drive over to L. E. F., a machine tool plant. The name's
different, but it's owned by Brenner, Inc. They are reorganizing
their types of products and there is a heated struggle between two
groups of engineers and high executives about the amount of

standardization of parts that would offer the optimum economy. It's a very complex problem. Besides all the technical and economic and market angles, there are also the highly personal interests of several department chiefs involved. And the main office (but this is only another name for old man Brenner) wants a neutral report on the pros and cons of the two conflicting projects. Well, I know approximately what's what, and will come up with a reasonable proposition on the thing within a week or two. The main office will make its decision, and that's what it's going to be. That's the type of job I've been doing most of the time in the last two years. In a peculiar way I know how to do it. I go ahead; I know exactly what I will have to do next, what information to get, what statistics to consult, what figures to look into, whom to ask and how to ask them what. And I know the main office will think that the report is exactly what they wanted and will pat me on the back and say, "Thank you for the intelligent job." But what I do not know is: What am I working for? Is it this pat on the back, or is it a good report, or is it the prosperity of Brenner, Inc., or is it just the counting and figuring and combining, the interviews and conferences, the doing of nice graphs and schemes and tables and the proper phrases, the therefores, the whereases, the whole trimmings of neutral observation, objective reasoning? Is it making appointments and keeping them to the minute, making neat little notes under the proper heading in an elaborate filing system, or is it simply the money, the salary, the raise, security, a savings account, a new car, a trip around the world? When I think of such questions (and I cannot help thinking of them whenever I am not just too busy to think), I feel nauseated. Do I work for my family, my wife, the kids, for the grandchildren I might have some day in the future? Or do I work for my own funeral, so that Diane without worrying about the expenses, can arrange for a respectable ceremony; that the speakers may complain a valuable member of the community has passed away all too early from his devoted family? This thought is nauseating, too. The split second in which one actually dies seems so insignificant, uninteresting, really dull. And for that silly happenstance should I spend my whole life working, worrying, planning? No, not I! [*A minute's pause.*] Well, what I say in so many words is nothing more than a repetition of what I told you in our first interview. Life is empty for me. And it seems a damned silly expectation that you are going to make it more interesting. Don't you agree?

G— [*taken by surprise by the patient's sudden question, but*

happy that he finds himself ready with a quick answer]: I do agree.
It would be silly if I tried to make your life more interesting. The
only thing I can try, is to make you more interested in life. [*But
this sounds too glib and almost like a play with words. He dis-
misses the answer. But now he feels under some pressure to find
another answer to the patient's question, which seemed so casual
and yet so urgent that it was impossible to remain silent.*] When
one makes a strong, drastic, far-reaching statement one sometimes
adds a question like "Isn't that so?" or "Don't you agree?" politely
affirming that one does not feel so cocksure about it as not to
admit the possibility that the other guy may have a different
opinion. Your question, "Don't you agree?" was not of this nature.
I rather feel that you wanted me to say either *yes* or *no* to your
statement. I do not know whether you would have preferred the
"yes" or the "no." But it seemed to me that you wanted me to
commit myself, one way or the other. And this question of yours,
though expressed in as few words as possible, seemed to me the
very climax of what you said during the hour. I mean it seemed
that in your talking you worked up towards this question and
conclusion, towards this concluding question as it were.

P [*with a frown*]: This might be so or it might not be so. But
no matter which is the case, you evaded the question.

G—: Indeed, I did not answer it. That is, I did not answer it in
words. But I am sitting here. I am not getting on my feet to say:
"Sorry, I have to give up. I feel I can't help you." Nor, for that
matter, do you get up, saying: "Excuse me, the situation is hopeless. It was a mistake to come and see you." So, while you worked
up towards this question and though you are interested in eliciting
an answer from me, your interest is not in finding out what I think
or in getting my opinion to weigh against yours.

P: So, what *is* my interest then?

G—: I cannot know. I only see that there *is* an interest of yours
in addition to and different from the interest to get well. [*Five
minutes' silence.*]

P [*staring at the inside of his palm*]: So, I take it, you don't give
up, do you?

G— [*quietly*]: Correct. The hour is up.

Not too long ago an hour like this one, undramatic, and
one in which he had made hardly any contribution, would have
left G— very disquieted. Now G—'s first thought was not, "What
did I accomplish?" or, "How did I do?" Now he was only con-

cerned with the patient's behavior, which was markedly different in this second hour from what it had been in the first. The patient had not dwelt in the mythical past where unchangeable events had taken place but had jumped into the present where things were still happening, time was passing and changes might occur. He had mentioned the little street accident and had talked at some length about his job which occupied most of his waking hours. No matter whether this shift would have occurred anyway or had been brought about by G—'s attitude in the first hour, it certainly was something favorable. Hardware store and cemetery had given way to "Brenner, Incorporated." However drab his present life appeared in the patient's eyes it *was life* and not memory.

Notwithstanding the encouraging aspect of this move from the past into the present, the patient had not abandoned his claim to hopelessness but had made it, perhaps, even more impressive.

"Look," he had said, in effect, "I am not a dope like poor, stupid 'pudgy face.' I am quite capable of doing the things I want to do. I am always on time even if I leave too late. I may speed and behave quite recklessly and cruelly, but I get away with it, because I know exactly how to do it. I fill a position requiring a lot of skill, alertness and technical knowhow. I am indispensable to my boss and know perfectly well that I merit every cent of the high salary he is paying me. So, you'd better dismiss the idea that you can patch me up by teaching me better working habits—how to get up in time, how to be more conscientious or how to please my superiors. I know all that and more. You don't have to cure me of accident proneness. I have no accidents that any human skill could avoid. In all probability I make more money than you do. Understand, I have everything I could wish for but it doesn't please me a bit. Can't you see that you have nothing to offer to a person like me? Won't you please admit that the thing I'm in need of is not among the goods you have to sell? You'd better confess your incompetence right away, and give up acting like a charlatan who promises more than he can produce."

Reviewing what he had done in the face of this veiled but vigorous attack or plea, G— feels, "Well, nothing spectacular."

However, he can credit himself with having stood his ground. He had not entered into a futile argument and had not been distracted from the main theme by the peculiar features the patient had revealed when talking about the street accident. He kept his focus on the main theme and intention of the narrative which came to the fore in the final question, "Don't you agree?"

G— concentrated his attention on this question. What he had said was not very skillfully expressed. When he started to speak it had not been clear to him what he was going to say. His thoughts had developed in the process of talking. His first idea had been that there was something strange about the patient's question. G— almost thought it might be an expression of politeness, a misplaced politeness, certainly. But this did not seem a plausible assumption and G— rejected it. He then acknowledged that the patient had really wanted the therapist to answer. But again, this could hardly be true in the sense that the patient wanted to know G—'s opinion. G— was certain the patient knew that the therapist was not ready to give up. He then tried to describe the patient's intention with the words, "You wanted me to commit myself." Although G— felt that this was quite relevant, the expression seemed to fall flat and G— did not elaborate on it. In his last statement he limited himself to the observation that he sensed an interest in the patient that he could only describe negatively as being different from the interest in getting well.

It had been a fight, a struggle, a matching of forces. In retrospect G— was aware how much of an effort it had taken to stand his ground. He smiled without knowing that he was smiling. What was the outcome of the fight? A defeat, a victory, a draw?

"So, I take it, you don't give up, do you?" This was the patient's final question. A skeptical question, even a sarcastic one, but, on closer examination, not much of a question at all. And its sarcasm was somewhat weak; it was a disguise and not a very effective one for something like humor or even warmth. It left the therapist with a feeling of contentment. "Maybe it was a draw with a plus sign behind it?" He suddenly knew that the patient had understood precisely what he had meant with his laconic "Correct!" The mild irony it contained could not have escaped him and yet he had let it pass without comment. "Maybe, it will help, maybe it won't," G— thought. "Who knows? But there is nothing I can do but stick to my guns and hope for the best."

Project, theory, his worries and doubts about it seemed forgotten—for a while. The following interview, the eighth or ninth, occurred approximately two weeks after the one previously reported:

The patient enters with a frown on his forehead. He hardly greets the therapist, walks to his chair and sits down. Seemingly absorbed in thought he pays no attention to the therapist, remains for a long time in the same position and only the fingers of his right hand are drumming almost noiselessly on the upholstered surface of the arm of the chair. Twelve minutes pass in complete silence.

G—: You indicate that you are immersed in thought and almost not aware where you are. [P *grunts. It is uncertain whether this means agreement, or expresses only irritation.*]

G—: You kept the little noise you made halfway between a questioning "huh?" and an irritated snort.

P: Does it matter?

G—: I think it must matter to you to keep it that uncertain.

P: So what? [*Three minutes pass.*] So what?

G—: I don't understand what you are asking.

P: You understood that I said, "so what?" didn't you?

G—: I did.

P: Silly conversation. Don't you understand what "so what?" means?

G—: Not in this case. When you said it for the first time I understood you to be expressing your discontent with my remark. But I do not see what you want to say with the repetition.

P: Your remark seemed very pointless to me.

At this point the therapist feels uneasy. His first intention is to answer: "So I understood. My remark seemed pointless to you." But this reaction suddenly appeared very formalistic. Up to this point he had said what he felt like saying without hesitation or any misgiving. Even now he does not think that his remarks were really pointless. Only the remark he had planned to make seemed "wrong." It looked like a trick one might use to exasperate an opponent in order to win out in the battle of words. He realized he was pretending not to understand when he really understood. And though he did not understand completely what the patient was driving at he certainly understood more than the intended remark would indicate. Thinking this he suddenly smiled.

P: I don't know if you smile contemptuously because I can't appreciate the profundity of your cryptic words, or benevolently, because you are ready to condescend to enlighten me . . . but for the time being I find them pointless and silly.

G—: I smiled because I found that we both were hedging, probably in different ways, or with different motives. When I said, after our lengthy initial silence, "You indicate that you are immersed in thought and almost not aware where you are," nothing profound was in or behind this remark. What you said in the meantime, especially your "so what?"s, made more definite the impression which prompted my first remark. It seems to me that you expect something from me; I don't know what. And, yet, you seem unwilling to ask for it in so many words or, if you cannot name what you are expecting and waiting for . . . for some reason you refuse to say even that much. I think you want me to take the initiative.

P [after thoughtful silence]: Well, suppose I do want *you* to take some initiative . . . After all, *you* are the expert; I am the patient. *You* imply, if not in words, at least, by your very presence in this office, that you see our meetings here as potentially helpful for me. So you must have some idea what has to happen here if I am to be helped. I think you must know by now what my trouble is. I told you all I can about it. If there is something more you must know, well, you can ask me and I will tell you if I know an answer. But what is the point of my introducing you to the intricacies of Brenner, Inc. and its workings? What good would it do if I were to tell you that nothing has changed, that yesterday, just as on all the days before, I see Diane looking at me with a brave smile searching for any minute sign of change, never asking a question, as if she were afraid that any word might shatter her brittle hopes? Well, I say nothing either. I try to smile back as well as I can—not too much, not too little—no news from the Western front. Absolutely no news.

G—: When you say, "no news from the Western front," you

are repeating, in essence, what you told to Diane with your carefully measured smile. But you say it also to me; you say it emphatically and repeatedly in spite of your question "What good would it do to tell you that nothing has changed?" It reminds me of Marc Antony's "It is not meet you know how Caesar loved you."

P: Is there anything wrong if I let you know that nothing has changed?

G—: Of course not. But you would hardly be so intent on saying and repeating it merely because you knew it wasn't wrong.

P [irritated]: What was that? . . . what did you say?

G—: Let me say it more explicitly. In all the preceding seven or eight hours you started to talk about something, be it Brenner, Inc. and your job activities, your hometown, your parents, the hardware store, your daughter Felice, your boy Elmer, your old lawyer friend or your contempt for bridge, almost every single hour you ended up with a restatement of your complaint. And in some way the word "complaint" does not seem quite right when you speak about the emptiness and purposelessness of life. It sounds more as if you were expounding, pronouncing, explaining your philosophy, your *Weltanschauung.* A melancholy philosophy, no doubt, but still a philosophy. The more usual designation might be "pessimistic philosophy." I would not go so far as to say that you try to win me over to it. Still, you confront me with it as if you felt that a mere look at the sad truth would speak for itself. One can be saddened by a bitter and melancholy truth. and still have something like an investment in it. Life is empty and meaningless: all your abilities, all your efforts are doomed to come to naught. Nothing ever changes or is going to change. Nothing remains but waiting for death to come. A sad, a melancholy view, very tragic indeed, but, facing it unflinchingly, facing it without allowing the slightest doubt to creep in . . . well, this has grandeur, this nobility would be marred by a sneaky, cowardly attempt to even as much as consider the possibility that from somewhere a slight alleviation of the harsh sentence could be smuggled in. So you make sure that all its gloomy elements are still in place; nothing has changed, absolutely nothing.

P [after a pause, with a quiet voice]: I do not believe in self-deception.

G—: And your coming here to see me for the purpose of getting help, as you say, comes dangerously close to self-deception?

P: I do not want to hurt your feelings, but as you ask me . . . *yes,* you are right. I think it does come close to self-deception. It does not matter what you call it, my philosophy, my complaint, my

Weltanschauung, my pessimism or what have you. But it's there, it's real, it's the only truth I know of. I understand optimism is one of the basic principles of your trade. Things will get better, if not now, then in the long run. God bless you! It's your job. I can imagine that you would land in the poorhouse if you were not an optimist and didn't preach confidence, confidence in God, in the world, in humanity, and maybe in the miracles psychiatry can perform. That might be a very honorable, a very useful, and if I may say so, a very lucrative occupation. Nothing wrong with it. *Mundus vult decipi.* But, you see, I don't.

G—: I was not aware that I tried to talk you out of your gloomy . . . philosophy.

P: Hm! Whatever the proper words may be . . . isn't that exactly what your job consists of?

G—: You mean: acting as promoter of, or assistant in, self-deception?

P: Correct!

G—: Now I have the impression that you would love it if I would blush a little and say, "Well, indeed, one could call it that."

P [*smiling faintly*]: I would certainly appreciate your frankness.

G—: You make it very attractive to fall in with your suggestion. But I believe I can help you without promoting self-deception. And that is exactly what you believed when you first came to see me. Since then you have changed your opinion.

P: What makes you think that my opinion has not been the same all along?

G—: Would you have set foot in my office if you had been convinced that all I could do for you was to teach you how to deceive yourself? You must have made this discovery quite recently!

P: I don't know what to think of you. [*Chuckles.*]

G—: Well, you might find out.

P: How do I know that it would be worth while? It is definitely a very expensive research proposition.

G—: You *can't* know! It is a risk, as most research propositions are.

P: You are a funny guy. [*A minute's silence.*] But, now listen, life, as I see it, is a very drab and dreary affair. Let's assume I came to you regularly for . . . oh, whatever you say is needed to help me. And let's assume you were successful. Such a thing must happen, occasionally, at least in *your* view. Would I then see life differently? Is that the idea?

G—: Yes, that's the idea.

P: And you really think you can persuade me?

G—: No! But not every new view is necessarily acquired by way of persuasion. When you in your childhood learned that the earth is round like an orange you might have commiserated with the poor antipodes who were forced to walk upside down, with their feet sticking to the ground above and their heads dangling down. Since then you have probably stopped feeling sorry for them. Would you say this was because somebody persuaded you?

P: Oh hell, your analogy doesn't fit.

G—: You are right; it does not fit. It does not fit to the extent that your views on life do not depend, as do your views on the fate of the antipodes, on information and on thinking. I don't think, for instance, that your outlook would change were you to learn that one now had the means to ward off death eternally.

P: On that point you are right. An invention like that would make it ever so much worse! [*Changes his position in the chair and looks thoughtful, his eyes wandering around. Pulls himself together.*] Where were we? What is the upshot of all this? So you do *not* try to persuade me . . . if you mean what you say. But what else are you going to do?

G—: [*Finds his eyes looking at the clock and notices with relief that the hour is almost up. He feels "on the spot." The patient's last question sounded sincere. The sarcasm, the teasing, ironical quality had disappeared. There was a real sadness in his voice when the patient asked, "But what else are you going to do?" It was a good question, very reasonable, and well to the point. How was he, the therapist, going to change the patient's pessimistic philosophy? He had spurned persuasion and ruled out that mixture of observation, information obtained through others, and the logical thinking by which one reaches the conviction that the antipodes are not worse off than we are. So far so good! Yet how could he explain to the patient how therapy operated when he himself had only a faint notion? However, G— felt the urge to say something.*]

G—: This question is certainly not easy to answer. To some extent you must have noticed already what I have been doing in our sessions here. For instance, you will have noticed that what I am saying depends a good deal on what you are doing; and the inverse is also true, of course. I could say, perhaps, that I am trying to understand you and to make myself understood, which is at least one aspect of the job of the therapist.

P: You are very cautious, indeed. So far you *have* made yourself understood.

G—: To go even further in caution, let me say that the hour is up.

P [*smiling*]: Goodbye, Doctor!

G—: Goodbye!

NEW DOUBTS AND NEW FACTS

Not more than the last few minutes of this hour was needed to destroy almost all of the equanimity G— had acquired with respect to the problems of therapy.

He did not feel bad about the hour itself; nor did he find anything seriously wrong with his response to the patient's question about what he was going to do in the treatment hours. Certainly, his answer had not brought out his point very well. He had intended to remark on the fact that the patient seemed to ignore his own experience during these nine sessions and seemed to consider these sessions a mere introduction or prelude to the treatment proper. Instead of saying this and thus pointing to an element in the patient's behavior, he had watered down his original intention. What he had said could be understood as an advice, which indicated that the patient could procure the information he wanted by having a good look at what G— had done in these nine hours. Weaker still was his last phrase, asserting quite unnecessarily, that he was trying to understand the patient and to be understood by him. G— knew that he had been perturbed by his own uncertainty as to the rationale of what he was doing in treatment and that this perturbation had interfered with his original intention, impelling him to say something comforting.

But, while this lapse had not interrupted the communication between him and the patient too badly and perhaps was only apparent because it had occurred so close to the end of the hour, immediately after the session was over, G— was assailed by all the doubts and irritating questions that had accumulated since he had started on his "project." They had never been cleared up in any satisfactory way, and had retired to the background of G—'s consciousness. Now they seemed all at once to storm into the foreground and clamor for his attention, demanding unequivocal solutions. They all centered

around the fact that G—'s activity in his treatments appeared
to deviate markedly from what his theory demanded, and that
he could not wholeheartedly ascribe this deviation to a series
of simple slips, mistakes or errors. While logic told him to stick
to the requirements of his theory, the validity of which could
not be tested in any other way, his innermost feeling favored
the deviation toward which his mode of behavior tended more
and more in therapeutic activity.

Under the impact of this inner turmoil, G— thought: "I
either succeed in straightening out all these vexing problems
before tomorrow or cancel little Vic's next hour. For, as sure
as the sun will rise, this man will insist that I answer his question completely and down to the last detail. What a nightmare!"

It took G— an hour to recover sufficiently from his panic
to recognize the fallacy in his thinking. "Granted that it appears
reasonable for the patient to ask for some information about
the method of treatment before entering such a lengthy enter-
prise, it does not follow and it is erroneous to think that any
explanation could possibly increase his confidence. What I owe
him is effective treatment and not a lecture about its rationale.
But for my own sake I have to find out where I stand."

After overcoming this urge to explain his ideas about
therapy to his patient, G— calmed down enough to compare
carefully the behavior required by his *theory* with that which his
intuition recommended. On one point there seemed to be agreement and harmony: Paying attention to the patient's universal
symptom of duplicity was required by both directive sources.
He then asked himself whether the theory inexorably demanded, as proof that the patient has become aware of his
duplicity, that the patient actually express his awareness. This
seemed, indeed, doubtful. When a workman stands too close
to a crane in operation and the foreman waves his hand
towards him, the proof that he understands the gesture is usually his stepping back, not an exclamation, "Oh, I see now I
am in danger here!" However, this analogy was only of limited
relevance. When G— reacted in one way or the other to the
patient's duplicity, the patient did nothing that fully corre-
sponded to the stepping back of the endangered worker. At the
worst, he continued to talk or to behave in the same manner

as before; at best, he responded in a way in which the duplicity was less pronounced, at least in G—'s eyes, as in the case of the patient who stopped in the middle of his sentence and started laughing. Even in this "most fortunate" case it was meaningless to say that the patient had become aware of his duplicity. Further, it did not add anything to the observation that the patient's attitude had changed for the moment.

"Maybe," G— thought, "the entire theory that the duplicity can be removed if the therapist makes the patient aware of it, is an unsound formulation. There is really no valid criterion for this type of awareness. But if I drop this hypothesis, what remains of my theory? I can possibly reduce the scope of the formulation by the statement that it is helpful, if the therapist pays attention to the patient's duplicity. But that is terribly vague! And how do I know that it *is* helpful? I have not seen a single patient whose duplicity vanished completely, for a short time, yes, but does that mean anything? The most I can say is that in some patients I notice a slight decrease in duplicity. Is that enough? Did these patients improve? The answer is: No, they did not. Others, where no decrease of duplicity was visible, improved moderately. But will this last; will the improvement spread to other areas? Would all the gains—not too spectacular anyway—disappear if treatment were interrupted now?"

The prospect looked pretty gloomy. Should he abandon his project and go back to whatever he had done before? G— considered the pros and cons of such a resolution. But after arguing with himself for awhile he noticed that this was no more than an empty gesture. He knew his decision was to continue. His qualms about deviating from his theory diminished and he was certain that he would rely on his intuition. G— was calm now but far from cheerful when he contemplated the length of time he would have to work in uncertainty before he could hope that accumulating evidence would clearly decide for or against his work.

"I am marching through a tunnel," he said to himself, "and I don't yet know whether there is an exit at the other end."

During the next four or five weeks, day after day, G—'s mood changed in a fairly regular pattern. When facing his patients he felt in good spirits, interested and alert. He lived almost completely in the moment and, unhurried yet intense, did not worry about the results. But when the day's last patient had left, his good spirits started sinking as an endless stream of doubts and questions invaded his mind. On some evenings he buried himself in the scientific literature searching frantically for anything that seemed related to his problems. On other evenings he tried to discuss his thoughts in writing, made notes about his treatment hours and tried to compare the trends of different cases. Occasionally he thought he saw some light but this impression did not last and he finally had to confess that he really did not know what he was doing.

It seemed unbelievable to him that the next morning he would be able to face his patients, attentive and even cheerful, as if all his worries had vanished; but by experience he knew that exactly this was going to happen. Towards the end of this period, G—, disgusted with his fruitless ruminations, decided to protect himself from these torturing evenings and nights by distracting his mind from the confusing riddles of therapy. He called up some friends, accepted invitations for social gatherings and, when at home and free, he immersed himself in the great novels of Dostoevski which, after he had read a few pages, always held his attention completely and made him forget the rest of the world.

Then, two incidents occurred in close succession (not more than ten days apart), which, though small in themselves, made a lasting impression on G—. Their impact on G—'s mind, all the more intense by an element of surprise present in both of them, conditioned him to enable a chance remark, made a month later by one of his colleagues, to trigger off a new line of thinking.

Two patients whose treatment had started only a couple of months after G— had formed and was using his concept of the universal symptom had brought him more doubts and worries than any of the others. He had not only failed to make them both recognize their duplicity, but to the best of his observation their duplicity had shown only a minimal decrease, if any, even though he had seen them now for almost two years.

One of them was a woman, thirty-eight years of age, who

in the initial interview had complained in a very low and monotonous voice how a depressed mood, which had stayed with her more or less since her college years, had deepened during the last three years to such a degree that her social life, always very limited, was now nonexistent. She could not bring herself to accept invitations any more nor could she receive visitors, not even friends or close relatives. She practically never left the house except for an occasional visit to her dentist, when pain became intolerable. Her kind and understanding husband had done what he could to adjust to the relentless demands of her mental disturbance but had urged her gently and consistently to try psychotherapy.

At the time the aforementioned little incident occurred, G— had already spent most of these many months in a persistent and very patient effort to draw the patient's attention to her own behavior in treatment.

This behavior was directed in every possible way towards convincing the therapist that she was coming to him not for her own sake but exclusively for the sake of her husband and her children. Success of the therapy seemed to mean to her only that she would be able to do what she now was unable to do; namely, to fulfill such dread duties as entertaining guests in her home, paying visits to friends and relatives or going shopping. She seemed to expect that "cure" consequently would intensify her misery rather than alleviate it. On this point her certainty was absolute though she insisted that she knew nothing about psychotherapy or how it worked. After the first year of treatment the patient seemed physically somewhat better. Her face was less drawn and had better color. But after another ten months G— could observe no further progress and especially not the slightest change in her attitude during treatment. At the time in question he was invited to a housewarming party where he met a lot of new people. By chance he got involved in a lengthy and lively conversation with a distinguished-looking gentleman who might have been close to seventy. At one point the old man, finding himself unable to address G— by his name, apologized for his bad memory and asked the therapist to aid him. As soon as G— introduced himself the old man stretched out his hand and said with a warm smile: "I am very, very glad to meet you. I am the father of your patient, Mrs. S., and I am very much impressed with the effect of your treatment!"

G—, to his amazement, recognized that the old man spoke in all seriousness. He managed to smile appropriately and mumbled an embarrassed, "I am glad you say so!"

"Of course," continued the other man, who was quick to observe the therapist's reservation, "there is still much room for improvement, but to see her once again moving among people . . . when half a year ago not even *I* was permitted to see her for more than ten minutes a week! I would not have thought it was possible!"

The second incident occurred ten days after the house-warming party, during the treatment hour of a patient who had been referred to G— by a psychiatric hospital. The patient had spent several weeks in this hospital to be weaned from demerol, a drug to which he had been addicted for more than a year. He was thirty years of age when he came to G— but looked much younger.

Every day, in the late afternoon, for as long as he could remember, the patient had experienced a highly uncomfortable state of tension and irritation which frequently lasted deep into the night, keeping him awake. More than a year earlier he had discovered by chance that a small dose of demerol alleviated this painful condition and addiction developed rapidly. Shortly before the end of his hospitalization the afternoon depressions had reappeared. The hospital physician had prescribed a seda-tive which the patient was to take daily somewhat in advance of the time when the tenseness and irritation usually began.

Already in his first hour the patient told G— in a sarcastic banter how much he hated and despised this "baby food" with which he was doomed to cheat himself out of the "real stuff." He proclaimed that in his eyes the only possible goal of the therapy was to "pervert his sense of values" to an acceptance of the "baby food." His eyes looked deadly serious when he expounded this conviction, while his mouth curved in an ironi-cal, contemptuous smile.

This pronouncement seemed to have set the pace for the patient's whole behavior in treatment. "The saving grace in this moral decay," he declared with a melancholy look on his expressive face, "is, of course, my foreknowledge of the true nature of this analytical racket, which claims to cure by means of transference while the only transference which it produces is the transference of the patient's money into the pocket of the therapist. It sentences the patient to eternal virtue but it furnishes the therapist with the wherewithal for unlimited depravity."

"Is it really a comfort," he mused at another time, "to pay a substitute for going to hell in my place while I, always the same old ampule of demerol in my breast pocket, prolong a colorless life by swallowing my mirthless way through gallons and gallons of baby food?"

G— soon felt perplexed as to what to think of these bantering monologues, the irony of which was always overdone and contrived, though at times they were witty enough. After some time they were hard to listen to, though they were more repetitious in tone and style than in actual content which was as unpredictable as the pattern of a kaleidoscope.

At first G— had viewed the patient's glorification of "vice" and his corresponding contempt for the "dullness of virtue" as a mannerism of speech, indicating, in fact, by reversed semantics, fear of the addiction, and he had reacted accordingly. But with the passing of time he felt that this was an oversimplification not fully justified by the facts. G— then found himself compelled to take much more seriously what he had termed the patient's "inverted language." He now interpreted the banter and irony as a means of softening the expression of a really "perverted value system" and not as a means to express fear.

"What his queer talk conveys to me now," thought G—, "is not a skillfully veiled anxiety with regard to a possible return to his addiction but an abhorrence for the dull, virtuous, normal life: a *moral* abhorrence I feel tempted to say."

Though G— found this interpretation very confusing, indeed, he could not help feeling that it was in closer agreement with what he experienced in the hours.

After some hesitation G— remarked to the patient that his peculiar, bantering language seemed to be a device to induce the therapist *not* to take his praise of vice and condemnation of virtue as his real conviction, because he, the patient, felt too shy to admit this conviction bluntly. The patient's reaction was surprising. He responded with eager applause to G—'s remark but accepted it only in a restricted sense, as if G— had referred merely to the patient's language.

"Oh," he said, "you finally noticed my topsy-turvy English. Congratulations! You are real smart! There seems to be almost nothing you would not discover in due course. To show you how much I appreciate your mental effort I'll give you some additional information. This topsy-turvy English is an old, old habit of mine. You could call it an innate habit, if you want to call it anything. It grew up with me. It stood on its head right from the beginning and it's still standing on its head. It has to, because—and this is a secret I will reveal to you free of charge and out of the goodness of my heart—it has nothing but a head, so, what else could it possibly stand on? See my point?"

"I think I do!" said G—. These words referred to much more than the patient's statement; yet what he thought was not yet clear enough for further comment.

The patient continued to talk his "topsy-turvy" English; the therapist continued to describe more and more of its features as soon as they came to his attention. This went on and on and nothing seemed to change. About a year after the little exchange described above the patient started to talk occasionally about a topic that was obviously of great interest to him and to which he had devoted much time and thought. He even had a special expression for it. He called it "the pathology of literature." Under this title he talked of mediocre novels and plays, mostly with the intention of proving one general proposition, which was that any sentence or little paragraph, taken out of such a mediocre piece of writing was enough to reveal all the basic misconceptions of art by which the author was beset. Weird as this endeavor appeared, the therapist had to admit that the patient possessed an uncanny ingenuity at detecting insincerity, pretense, thoughtlessness and inconsistency in the mere position of a word, in the use of an adjective which did not quite fit, the rhythm of a sentence at variance with its content. When he talked about "pathology of literature" his language was precise and to the point and showed only faint traces of what he proudly called his "topsy-turvy" English. Yet, as soon as he left this topic (which he turned to only sporadically), his language reverted to the ironical, the stilted, and the bizarre.

Almost two years had passed since he started treatment. It was winter; and for a week the temperature kept far below what was normal for the season. The patient appeared in the therapist's office rubbing his hands that were bluish white from the cold, and as he strolled over to the chair and flung himself into it, he said: "Well, here I am, shivering all over, but dutifully putting in an appearance at your insufficiently heated office. Last night the furnace of my own little apartment went dead and for all I tried I could not bring it to life. When I phoned the company it was already too late and nobody answered. I knew I had to do something to protect you from the disappointment of losing one of your most promising patients as a victim of winter. I piled everything I had in the line of textile material on my bed and crawled underneath; but to no avail! It was too cold to fall asleep so I tried to read. But I could not do it without exposing my hands and large parts of my poor body to the murderous cold. I was confronted with freezing to death. Then I remembered that there was still the ampule of demerol in the breast pocket of my jacket that I had hung up against the icy draft from the window. Well, *now* you prick up your ears! *Now* the story gets professional, doesn't it? Huh, if you only knew! Patience, Doc, you will learn in time what happened. 'Why?' I said to myself: 'Why? What's the point in making death that uncomfortable? Why not take this sacred stuff and meet the inevitable with a smile? Why not finally triumph over the tyranny of virtue and take the real thing instead of the damned . . .'"

He stopped suddenly, his face showing embarrassment and surprise. He opened his mouth several times but closed it again without uttering a word. A minute passed, a second minute and a third. Finally he sighed and mumbled: "Terrible . . . terrible! You see me embarrassed, Doc, to break the sad news to you. I have to accuse myself of criminal negligence. As far as I know, it must be a month, if not two, that I have completely forgotten to take my baby food! Well, that is a trifle.

What was I going to say? I finally succumbed. Virtue got the better of me! Death turned away in disgust. When the morning came I found myself alive and as dutiful as ever."

G— was not very attentive for the rest of the hour. This was the second incident, occurring, as already stated, ten days after the "housewarming party." While G—, though very much pleased and intrigued by the first incident, had managed to minimize its significance, the second swept away the barrier of cautious skepticism which had made him think of "chance," "misunderstanding," and "simple error."

He could hardly wait for evening, when he would have the leisure to think about these thrilling events which at the same time seemed both familiar, like the appearance of a long-expected friend, and also mysterious and bewildering.

The facts as he could see them were as follows: For almost two years he had worked with both patients to effect the dissolution of each one's duplicity by making them see it. How far he had in actuality followed his idea of exposing their duplicity remained uncertain. He felt sure only of the fact that *he* had been aware of this symptom practically all the time, and had responded to it in some way or other. He was also quite convinced that this symptom had shown only slight changes, if any, in either case, and had certainly not disappeared. But— and this was the exciting aspect of the "incidents"—in both cases something else had changed. The lady had lifted at least some of the restrictions on her social life. (G— now admitted that there was no sound reason to discard her father's favorable report as either the product of wishful thinking or the delusion of a senile old man.) The young addict had, without even noticing it, broken the compulsory habit of taking his sedative, and obviously without the reappearance in late afternoon and evening of his regular state of tension and irritation. In other words, the neurotic features had abated for which treatment had been instituted while the universal symptom on which G— had focused his attention had remained in essence more or less as it had been before.

If this interpretation of the observed facts was correct it was the death blow for G—'s theory. His fundamental hypothesis that the universal symptom of duplicity was inseparably con-

nected with the neurotic disturbance (as a necessary *and* sufficient condition) seemed to be contradicted by this evidence. Of
course, there was one inconclusive element in his interpretation
of the "evidence." Both patients had shown undeniable improvements but it could be questioned whether these were
temporary or lasting, reversible or irreversible. If he could see
them as only temporary his basic hypothesis could be salvaged.

Like any other therapist, G— knew from experience those
deceptive temporary improvements which appear frequently
in the first days or weeks of treatment and greatly impress the
patient, his friends and relatives and also invariably the inex-
perienced therapist who has not been warned by earlier disappointments. Neurotic patients, like their better adjusted fellow
men, feel differently and show a corresponding change of
behavior whenever their life situation changes sufficiently. A
depressed young man forced by circumstances to participate
in a pleasure trip with congenial companions might feel cheerful during the trip but will revert to his depression when the
trip is over or when its newness has worn off. Something similar can happen to patients for whom "being in treatment" is a
new and satisfactory experience which might fill them with
a pleased sense of security. Sometimes, as G— also knew, this
beneficent effect of the treatment situation could last to a remarkable extent, even for years, and, actually, to the very end
of the therapy, when a slow or a rapid reversal to the *status
quo ante* might occur. Of course, in such cases one used to say
that there had been something definitely wrong with the therapy. In his training, G— had derogatorily learned to call these
disappointing phenomena of temporary improvements "transference cures."

When G— examined his two cases of unexpected improvement in the light of whether they were temporary or lasting,
it was clear that the final answer could be supplied only by a
follow-up study of these two patients over years following the
treatment. To the extent that the special features of the observed improvements could be ascertained, they seemed atypi-
cal for the temporary category. They both had occurred a very
long time after the beginning of treatment. In the case of the
lady, she had either not noticed the improvement herself or had

not evaluated it as such. She certainly had shown no inclination to bring it to the therapist's attention.

In the case of the young man it was obvious that he had not even been aware that his need for the sedative had vanished and had only discovered this development weeks after it had occurred. In discovering it during his treatment hour he had not shown satisfaction or triumph but rather embarrassment and a tendency to minimize the favorable result.

G— realized, partly with dismay and partly with joy, that all this spoke heavily against the assumption that the improvements in question were of the reversible type.

How could he reconcile the assumption that these improvements were permanent with his theory? Asking himself this question he was aware that he felt rather satisfied to think of the two improvements as lasting ones even if it meant accepting an argument against his theory.

"After all," he thought with a smile, "there must be a kernel of validity in the theory if my attempts to apply it finally produced some of the desired results if not the *expected* ones. It seems certain that my first image of 'making the patient aware of his duplicity' was illusory. I neither do it nor does the concept work, and the whole thing is ill-defined. Lacking any operational definition for the 'patient's awareness,' my hypothesis was meaningless. I can safely drop it. But what can be salvaged from my theory if there is improvement unaccompanied by any change, decrease, or disappearance of the universal symptom? Well, the theory does not specify any measure of decrease of duplicity or what change in its appearance is proportionate to a given improvement. Perhaps there was a change in duplicity in both cases that I was not perceptive enough to observe. Maybe I expected a drastic change and overlooked or discounted the little there might have been. This offers one possibility for resolving the problem. It does not look very elegant but rather contrived and made ad hoc. Yet, when I examine the case of the young man I can make the point that for months before the improvement occurred there were those hours, when he spoke of his hobby horse, 'the pathology of literature,' in which the absence of duplicity was rather conspicuous. Of course, I did not count this as a 'decrease of duplicity.' I didn't because—well, because he then did not talk about his symptoms or about himself at all! All that talk about the pathology of literature seemed like an evasive maneuver. No, it did not, at least not at the time. Only later, when I asked myself whether his duplicity had diminished and became aware that it always disappeared when he talked about his pet topic. Oh, my God, what did I expect? I was struck by his directness and the expression of undivided genuine interest— and *that* I called an evasive maneuver! How stupid can one get?"

But what about the lady? In spite of G—'s attempt to sift from his recollections the least trace of evidence that her duplicity had changed or decreased, nothing tangible emerged. He knew that his attention had remained on this essential feature very consistently during the whole course of treatment up to the last hour, but as far as he could observe her behavior during the hours, her talk had stubbornly exhibited the same quality of duplicity. If her father's enthusiastic report was correct— and G— could not doubt this any more—it was mainly during the last half-year that her behavior at home, outside of the therapy sessions, had shown a remarkable change! She had not lied to him. Her allusions to her social isolation, frequent in the first year of treatment, to the best of G's recollection had ceased. But as she had never mentioned any increase in her social contacts G— had assumed that the situation remained as it was in the beginning.

Musing over this enigma, G— suddenly thought of the kinetic behavior of two billiard balls lying in touch with each other and both on a straight line with a third. When this third ball was rolled against the pair it hit, of course, only the first one; yet this first one remained immobile while the second one rolled away. The one which was hit did not show any sign of the impact, though it was able to pass the energy on to the second. Although the similarity between the two sets of events was, probably, a very superficial one, G— nonetheless felt encouraged by this analogy.

"I had really no good reason," he thought, "to fear for the life of my theory. This theory is such a meager skeleton; it consists of nothing but the contention that the symptom of duplicity is very closely connected with or representative of the mental disturbance. It must therefore be compatible with an endless variety of facts. It says nothing at all about the way in which the phenomenon of duplicity is connected with all the various signs of the disturbance. Obviously, without thinking about it, I assumed there would be some evident proportionality between degrees of duplicity and the number and severity, or both, of all the other signs and symptoms of the disturbance. This assumption had no other justification than its utter simplicity; and now it is quite clearly disproved. Perhaps the very observations which disproved it are going to tell me something about the most conspicuous missing link in my skeleton theory, namely the connection between the universal symptom and the other well-known and well-studied symptoms of the neuroses."

G— spent much time trying to construct plausible hypotheses to fill in this blank spot satisfactorily. But his efforts were unfruitful. It was not until a month later that he stumbled by mere chance into a new avenue of approach and began to see this mystery in a new light.

Reorientation

AN ABORTIVE ATTEMPT AT CLASSIFYING PATIENTS

For a long time one of G—'s cherished "dreams" had been that finding "just the right viewpoint" for a classification of patients would bring about a marked advance in theory, as well as in practice of psychotherapy. But every system of classification he tried to apply seemed arbitrary and correlated neither with the degree to which the life of the patient was impoverished by his mental disturbance, nor with the difficulties of treatment nor with the probable results of therapy.

Then, one of G—'s colleagues casually asked him whether he too had a high percentage of passive-dependent people among his patients? G— could not answer the question offhand but promised to find out. As soon as he had time available he listed the people he had seen in treatment during past years and tried to give them a rating according to the degree of their passive-dependent manifestation. He did it with some eagerness and with the vague expectation (as he realized later) that rating the patients with a view to their greater or lesser dependency perhaps might prove to be, or approach, a fruitful method of classification.

He took a sheet of paper, drew a vertical line, and wrote the word "submissive" at the top; at the bottom he wrote the word "domineering." Knowing from experience the advantage of starting with extremes, he tried to think of a patient whose behavior, more than anyone else's, suggested the classification "submissive."

That seemed easy enough: For eight months he had been seeing a man in his late thirties who appeared ready to do whatever he understood was being requested of him. Whenever G— had wanted to switch the appointment to another day or another hour the patient's answer had invariably been, "Certainly, Doctor, certainly!" He was always on time, but never seemed to mind if G— were delayed. When, during the hour, the sun came out and shone into the patient's eyes, he never would have dared to draw the drapes and lower the blinds. He sat in silence, painfully blinking and twisting his neck until G— remarked on it. The patient then would respond as if G— had asked him to let the blinds down, "Certainly, Doctor, certainly!" he would say, jumping up from his chair and unhooking the cord. "This way, Doctor? Is that too much?"

Satisfied, G— put down the name Howard Topper at the upper end of his list.

To find a representative for the other extreme caused just as little trouble. Margret Easterbrook, a lady of forty-two, and very active in at least half-a-dozen organizations, unhesitatingly carried her distrust of other people's abilities into her therapy sessions. She had hardly emerged from the waiting room for her first hour when she started to take things in her own hands.

"Hello, Doctor," she said. "One thing I have to tell you. I think it is in your own interest. The sound-proofing of your office door is absolutely insufficient! A drape, you say? Sound-insulating tiles? No, that won't do. What you need is a second door with an air space in between. You should consult an architest! Phone the Home Builders Association, RO 7-1489! You need a pencil? You can't keep the number in mind! So, write it down! Well, that woman patient of yours, I could almost understand every word. Why did you make her cry? Well, maybe she *is* a silly girl; but anyway, you better know from the beginning: you can't make *me* cry! By the way, what brand of psychotherapy are you practicing?"

It seemed only fair to put her name right at the end of the list where it said "domineering." G— thought that now, after this start, it could not be too difficult to classify the remainder of the patients with reasonable accuracy between the extremes. But he had worked hardly half an hour when he recognized with dismay that it was far from easy. Not only was it hard to assess degrees of submissiveness when the persons whose behavior had to be compared were different in personality, background and education, but he found himself more and more in doubt whether to call the behavior of certain patients a sign of submissiveness or the opposite. When, for example, a patient insisted on being instructed by the therapist on what to talk about and showed righteous indignation in being denied such advice, G— felt that it made as much sense to evaluate this behavior as submissive as to list it as domineering. He found himself in the same dilemma in cases where a patient declared with imperturbable conviction that he, the patient, did not know how he felt but the therapist did know, and must know, and should, therefore, tell him immediately. It could be interpreted as being humble and self-effacing or arrogant and demanding.

While this puzzling question seemed to reveal some hidden paradox within the two concepts involved (namely, the concepts of a "submissive" and of a "domineering" attitude) and G— was tempted to discard them altogether, these vexatious terms appeared at the same time to be indispensable as helpful tools of great descriptive power. G— decided to interrupt his attempt at classification and to clarify first the meaning of these two expressions which had the quality of being both familiar and mysterious.

WHAT CONSTITUTES SUBMISSIVENESS?

To qualify as being submissive, G— said to himself, a person has to subordinate his actions to dependence on another's wishes, decisions or opinions. But is this sufficient? Hardly! The bank clerk, for instance, who hands over money at the command of the heavily armed hold-up men is not actually submissive; nor is the patient who stays in bed much against his own inclination simply because his trusted physician advises him to do so, nor is the testator who formulates his will in strict accordance with the suggestions of his lawyer. G—, in his imagination, went through many more cases where people by various motives complied with the wishes or demands of others. Yet, it turned out that in none of these examples did he feel justified in applying the word "submissiveness" as a necessary qualification for the person in question. That seemed strange. Was submissiveness such a rarity?

He thought finally of the typical legacy hunter who fulfills every whim of his rich old relative with an ingratiating smile in order to be amply rewarded after the old tyrant's death. If anyone, such a man should be characterized as a submissive person! But again a doubt appeared: Wouldn't it be appropriate to say that the legacy hunter *play-acts* the role of a "submissive person" rather than that he *is* one?

It was now clear to G— that he had expected to find the distinguishing mark of submissive behavior in a special motivation behind the readiness of the "submissive" to let his actions be determined by the demands or wishes of other people. Yet, however he varied his examples with regard to the motive which makes a person decide to yield to another, he never seemed to find one which characterizes the acting person as clearly submissive. It does not seem to matter whether the motive is love or greed, fear or respect for the other person's better judgment.

It was as if the *decision* to yield on the strength of any motive were incompatible with the specific flavor of submissiveness. What then remains as the characteristic of submissive behavior? A readiness to obey without decision? What a strange

definition! It sounded like the thematic phrase of the *Arabian
Nights:* "To hear is to obey!"

In spite of this apparent absurdity, G— felt that this
phrase *obedience without decision to obey* described very well
the essence of submissiveness. And yet he was scolding himself
for being so pleased with a formulation which, notwithstanding
its descriptive value, seemed too illogical to contribute signifi-
cantly to the clarification of the concept in question.

In spite of his concern with logic, G— had enough experience with psychological riddles not to discard too easily any
formulation which seemed to strike a chord in him.

"Obedience without decision to obey!" Dwelling on this
formula, he looked around for a more concrete image of what
it could mean. It suggested a very intimate connection between
the mind of the person who obeyed and that of the person whose
wishes or opinion gave the directive, a connection which never
could exist in reality but only could be imagined, and is implied in phrases like the German: "Er ist ein Willenloses Werk-
zeug in meiner Hand." (He is like a tool in my hand without
volition of his own.) The imagined relationship between the
two people is such that the separateness of the individual
appears diminished. Though in all other respects they might
be considered "two persons," they have only *one* power of
decision between them. Or, in other words, one of them appears
only as an extension or an organ of the other.

Of course, it would be wrong to say that a submissive
person is one who has no ability to make decisions of his own,
because such a condition is only imaginary, but it would be
possible to define the submissive attitude as one which *pretends*
that the person himself has no power of decision and has to
"take over" the decisions and value judgments of another, as
if the two of them together were forming a kind of mental
Siamese twins. This formulation, as G— recognizes with satisfaction, is free of any self-contradiction. Mental Siamese twins
do not exist and even the concept of such a monster seems self-
contradictory. But there is nothing inherently illogical or self-
contradictory in the assumption that people, under certain
conditions, have wishes incompatible with logic and like to
imagine that they are what they never can be.

The vexing concept of submissiveness seems now somewhat clearer. G— is almost certain that the thoughts he has
developed will be of help in understanding his patients and,
therefore, might have significance in his approach to therapy.
But, for the moment, he is unable to perceive any useful application.

SUBMISSIVE AND DOMINEERING ATTITUDE

Mulling over the phenomenon of submissiveness and the
delusional element he had discovered in it, G— finds himself
confronted with two new questions. The first originates from
the fact that the phantasy image of being "a mental Siamese
twin" is utterly repulsive to him. He feels he can't claim empathic understanding of a delusion as long as he can discover
nothing attractive in its content, however much it might be
overshadowed by repelling features. The second question seems
less crucial yet more urgent: It concerns the counterpart to
submissiveness, namely, the domineering attitude. Comparing
the two attitudes, he feels confused that these extremes which
he had thought of as opposite symmetrical deviations from a
healthy middle appear now much less symmetrical with respect
to mental health. He cannot help seeing the submissive person
—with his delusionary tendency to ignore his own identity—
as "weak," and the domineering person, however unwarranted
his claim and how silly his demands, as comparatively "strong."
While weakness is necessarily opposed to health, strength as
such, no matter to what unworthy tasks applied, is not.

"A politician," G— thought, "who by unceasing effort manages to get into the leading role in every organization to which
he belongs and feels impelled to impose his will on everybody
he can possibly subjugate, might be a man without vision and
higher inspiration and lead his group into disaster; but all this
would not mean that he is a sick man hankering after delusions. And yet, there is something wrong with this reasoning.
When I speak of a 'domineering attitude' I mean something
different from what necessarily goes with leadership. One can't
say that every leader is a domineering person. This would be

just as wrong as calling all of his followers 'submissive.' The follower follows because he has confidence in the leader to serve the right cause; i.e., the cause the follower approves. The submissive is not so much interested in the cause as in *submitting*. What distinguishes the leader from the domineering person is again the latter's preoccupation with his power over others as against the leader's preoccupation with what he plans to achieve by means of this power. This feature, namely, the domineering person's interest in the specific inner attitude of the dominated, is what I have in mind when I use the word 'domineering.' But this word is, perhaps, not well-chosen. In everyday language, it refers more to the actual fact that the domineering man determines the actions of others and not enough to the specific desire of his to subjugate. A better word for my purpose would be 'tyrannical.' The word 'tyrannical' characterizes the person to whom it is applied with regard to mental attitude, not to actual power. The tyrant wants the people he tyrannizes to obey; but obedience in itself is not enough to satisfy him. They should not obey by any rational reason, because they share his goals or are motivated by rewards promised or punishment threatened. They should obey blindly like robots without any volition of their own. He is interested in making demands which are arbitrary and unreasonable, or at least must appear as such to his subjects, in order to make sure that their obedience is not attributable to their agreement with his goals.

"All that means," thinks G—, "is that the tyrant wants to deal only with *submissive* persons. Now, it seems that the submissive and the tyrannical really are true counterparts to each other. Though they play different roles in their interaction, both are interested in creating in their own minds the same delusion. They want to believe in a 'subterranean' connection between the minds of people in such a way that the power of decision is one for both."

This interest in one and the same delusion, which both types have in common, makes it more plausible to G— that one person might switch, within a short time, from submissive to tyrannical behavior, and that sometimes both attitudes seem to be expressed in the same sentence as in the case of patients who insist in a dictatorial manner that the therapist should tell them what to do or tell them what they feel.

G— also realizes that the combination of submissive and tyrannical attitudes in the same person is a well-known fact which can be observed (and has been observed) outside of any connection with therapy. The boss who tyrannizes his employees but is at the mercy of his wife's whims, and the subservient employee who is always of the opinion of his boss, but is a cruel despot to his family, are both standard figures of comic strips and cartoons.

"If only I could understand better what makes this common delusion of *subterranean connection between people* so attractive that even men of high intelligence distort obvious facts and sacrifice logic for the sake of a spurious belief in this product of phantasy! One would think, perhaps, that the tyrannical type is primarily interested in having power over the minds of others; and surrounding himself with persons of the submissive type might be the best way to satisfy this need for power. If it were so, the tyrant would not necessarily share the delusion of the submissive. He would only welcome it where he sees it in others, and might find it expedient to contribute as much as he can to maintain it.

"But this construction leaves the submissive type as mysterious as ever and does not account at all for the presence of tyrannical and submissive behavior in the same person. No, there is as much delusion in the tyrant as in the submissive."

G— recognizes that he feels impatient and almost angry when he thinks of people who want to see themselves as "mental Siamese twins," and he notices that, illustrative as this expression might be, it also carries a derogatory note which does not belong here and is not conducive to understanding. He looks for a less biased description of the content of the delusion. But, it does not seem easy to find one. The following phrase appears in his mind, "The delusion tends to weaken the strict boundaries which separate one individual from the other." Yet he feels suspicious of the word "weaken" which, too, seems to have a derogatory connotation. He replaces the word "weaken" by the word "soften" and feels somewhat silly when he actually observes that this purely semantic change makes the delusion appear less offensive to him. Somewhere in his mind a thought flashes by in which his own insistence on the unalterable or unqualifiable separateness of the individual is tainted slightly with ridicule.

"After all," he says to himself, "there is a certain fascination in the fairy-tale phrase, 'To hear is to obey!' a meeting ground for the submissive and the tyrannical mind. If one could take it as a mere phantasy, disregarding the way in which patients try to give to it a semblance of reality, the idea of softening the boundaries between one person and another would not be unpleasant throughout. It is even, I could say, a generous, disarming idea of loosening one's identity and fusing one's personality with another. 'Fusion' seems an especially suitable word to picture the goal of some patients. I shouldn't really say, 'goal of the patients,' but rather, the goal of which their behavior is suggestive. One could then formulate: *the submissive and the tyrannical elements in the behavior of patients tend to create for them the semblance of a delusional fusion relationship.*

"This formulation would express an important fact, if all patients were either submissive or tyrannical, or a mixture of both. But this is simply not so. There are some patients to whom neither of these terms apply, and I cannot even say that these are the patients with less severe afflictions."

G— feels that he is close to understanding something of vast significance and yet he cannot see in what direction to turn. He thinks again of the patients whom he had found free of submissive, as well as of tyrannical, features, hoping that closer scrutiny might reveal something like a hidden form of just these character traits. But to no avail! Giving up the enticing expectation that an inclination towards fusion-delusion might turn out to be a characteristic common to all patients he attempts to bring it into connection with other symptoms. But here, too, his efforts remain futile. Asking himself what a patient might gain from imagining a fusion-existence as real, he could only see that this delusion might produce a pleasant thrill, which would be pleasant only if short-lived and would otherwise turn into a painful nightmare.

THE UBIQUITY OF FUSION-DELUSION

Tired from the long, drawn-out, frustrating effort of direct-
ing his thoughts to an unknown goal, G— leans back in his
chair and allows his thoughts to wander. After a while he finds
himself thinking with pleasure of a show he had seen a few
years ago. It had been an ice-skating performance executed by
well-trained professionals, embellished by some floor-show
features. Only one number of the program's rich variety had
made a sufficiently deep impression on him that he had mentioned it occasionally in conversations. And it is this number
again which appears in his mind's eye.

The act had been performed by two young men. They were
dressed, not in the traditional black, tight-fitting cardigans and
tricots of the ice-skater, but in ordinary gray slacks, marine-
blue street jackets and brown hats. They also wore the same
type of ties of the same loud red color. They both stood in a
relaxed, casual posture waiting for the music to start. Then
they executed some difficult, complicated figures one after the
other with the greatest ease, grace and precision, well-synchro-
nized without ever having to look at each other. The last vigorous arc they described terminated in a nonchalant fashion; it
brought them back, as if by chance, to the exact location from
which they had started. While the audience applauded the
brilliant performance, they both relaxed, looked with an expression of slight fatigue and complete indifference somewhere
into space and, to G—'s bewilderment, both lifted their arms
lazily and readjusted their ties. G— felt excited without knowing the reason for his excitement.

The music started again, and again the two skaters raced
through their complicated arcs and spirals, pirouettes and
jumps to wind up as at the end of the first number with their
momentum spent in their starting position. While the applause
rose louder than before, they again relaxed, looked somewhere
into space, indifferent, slightly fatigued, and again, almost
simultaneously, raised the left arm with the typical gesture
and looked dreamily at their watches.

G—, of course, by now knew what had happened. What

had appeared to him as a strange coincidence was now clearly seen as a trick—a piece of deliberate and well-rehearsed acting. But his enthusiasm and his fascination were in no way dampened by this recognition. He felt, and remarked to his companion, that it was an admirable and very original idea to extend the synchronization of movement from the performance where everybody expected it, into the rest period where it came as a confusing surprise. His companion agreed readily enough but G— felt that his friend's "very nice, indeed!" did not match his own rapturous enthusiasm; even the words G— himself had used appeared lukewarm to him in comparison with the emotion he felt.

As soon as this recollection has passed through his mind, G— finds himself assailed by a whirling multitude of thoughts, all competing for his attention so that he can hardly manage to keep them apart, and inspect them one after the other in any kind of order.

Foremost in G—'s mind is bewilderment over the fact that it needed this one little piece of memory to call to his attention the significance of untold numbers of experiences, most of them of far greater importance and generality than this small single trick of showmanship which by any objective standard could be called amusing and maybe thrilling but nothing more.

His next thought turns to the trick itself and the special excitement which it had aroused in him. "Certainly," G— says to himself, "when two ice skaters, after performing some vigorous figure skating, feel the need to readjust their ties, this is nothing anybody could get excited about. When they do it in almost the same moment, two alternative assumptions are possible: Either it is mere coincidence, or it is a deliberate maneuver which they had agreed to perform and practiced before. Which of these two assumptions came to my mind when I felt so excited and thrilled? There is nothing exciting about chance as such nor about the synchronization of such a simple procedure which required not even a hundredth of the skill these two men displayed in their skating. The source of my excitement must have been a third assumption, a fantastic one, which seemed tempting not because of its plausibility—it is neither plausible nor even possible—but because of its secret fascination, the assumption that they were not wholly separate personalities but had only one mind between them. That means that I too have a secret desire that 'fusion' be possible. And not only I, everybody is attracted by . . . oh, almost anything which allows for a fleeting impression of—well, of fusion!"

Uniformity of movement and synchronization of movement, if both come close enough to perfection, attract, thrill and fascinate an audience no matter whether or not the movements performed by a single individual would in themselves be pleasing.

A single well-trained soldier going through the steps and paces, the turns and halts of his drill may please the eyes of the training officer; in the eyes of any outsider he looks ridiculous. If a whole battalion moves over the parade ground, all in step, breaking up the large column into smaller groups, all making the turn at exactly the same moment, turning again and forming one long straight line and maintaining this unbroken front, marching and pivoting around and then, on one short signal, freezes on the spot so that all the arms and legs, the helmets, canteens and rifles are suddenly at rest, all in exactly the same position with not even a single bayonet deviating in direction from all the others, then even an ardent antimilitarist cannot help being gripped by this spectacle. And what grips him is certainly not the beauty of right angles and straight lines, but the image . . . or rather the idea of the many acting as though animated by *one* mind.

To bring about this effect on the onlooker (and also in the participant) strict uniformity of movement is not even necessary. It is enough that the movements of different persons are in harmony with each other, and thus, together, form a gestalt. The impression of connectedness, the fusion-effect might even be stronger when the unifying relationship of form is a more complicated one than simple congruity. The artistic group dance where different members play different roles seems especially efficient to create the delusion of fusion-existence. In contrast to the performance of chorus girls where, as in the military parade, the individuality is almost extinguished, the artistic group dance emphasizes individuality of the dancers so that the perception of the mutual relatedness of their movements is delayed and, therefore, is intensified by an element of surprise.

G—, tempted to think more extensively about these phenomena of visually induced fusion-delusion, is yet impatient to turn to a much broader field that has appeared on the fringe of his consciousness, and on which he expects to find more important evidence for a general human inclination towards delusion. At first it is only a word which sticks in his mind and he needs repeated effort, extended over consecutive days, before he can spell out how it applies.

The word is "tradition." If it were referring only to the fact that each generation acquires most of its knowledge and skill from the preceding generations the word would imply no allusion whatsoever to delusional thinking. Indeed, frequently enough the word "tradition" is used in this sober sense in which it merely denotes an observable fact. And yet, it is capable of an extended meaning which puts it into the neighborhood of "blind obedience" and "subterranean connection." Where adherence to tradition appears as a motivating force it brings about (or, maybe, presupposes) the same softening of personality boundaries as those concomitant with submissive and tyrannical attitudes.

Tradition! G— is thinking of the time-honored formalities which governed many functions of the university in his home town. He remembers especially how it was traditional that doctoral examinations took place in the professor's home on a table, covered with a white tablecloth and that wine was served before the questioning started. It was unthinkable that the professor, after having invited his "guest" to sit down and having taken the chair on the other side of the table himself, would open the conversation with anything but the question: "white or red?" This was the tradition. Of course, the purpose of the examination was the same as that of any examination at any scientific institution the world over. The candidate's knowledge and achievements had to be tested. And the professor was free to ask whatever questions seemed suitable to him for this task. He could be lenient or strict, content himself with a few easy questions, or go on for hours on the most difficult topics. But in contrast to this freedom where the real

purpose of the examination was concerned stood the unshakable regularity and conformity as to the unessentials: the
black coat, the white tablecloth, the red and white wine, and
the polite inquiry into the "guest's" preference.

Here, where arbitrariness and personal taste could have
had no effect on the outcome, each individual professor followed the example of his predecessors. Submission to this rule
was voluntary. Nobody was entitled to reprimand the professor
for any deviation. Nor could the candidate contest the validity
of the procedure, if it had not been true to tradition. And yet,
every professor waived his freedom of decision with regard to
the frills and trimmings and abdicated his individuality on this
point. G— is reminded of his two ice skaters and the stunning
effect it had had on him when they abdicated their individual
freedom in the rest period.

The professors liked it, G— thinks with a smile. How could
they help remembering the one unique situation in their own
lives, decades ago, when they themselves were sitting, tense or
excited, in their unfamiliar tail coats at a similarly covered
table, and were to answer the question: "white or red?" In a
way, they were play-acting the past; they were impersonating
their own teachers, or rather, feeling one with them.

Is it not essentially the same desire which makes people
repeat, or at least imitate, the past on occasions which we call
celebrations? This is a vast field. It seems that wherever people
come together, motivated by the sober thought that each one
will serve his own interests best by cooperating with others,
features are introduced which go beyond what is required for
the fulfillment of the original interests but tend to create the
image of a group personality. It appears that there is an always
present interest in "softening the boundaries of the individual"
by establishing the artificial super-individual of the group.

G— thinks back to the time when he worked in the big
industrial firm, and how amused he was when he discovered
that every single employee, from the president to the bellboy,
from the muscular transport worker in overalls to the skinny
youngster behind a calculating machine, referred to the firm
by the pronoun "we." Even the elevator boy, who had been
hired just a week earlier, while opening the door had addressed

G— with the words, "Have you heard, sir, we have bought the Lion Works?" And G—, to his own amazement, had heard himself say to his secretary only a few minutes later, "Have you read in the newspaper, Felice, we bought the Lion Works?" And though he did not know then what the Lion Works were producing, nor that any plan to buy them had existed, he found that his formulation expressed exactly how he felt.

This mysterious interest in finding, or rather imagining a kind of connection between people which goes far beyond the interest in companionship appears in an enormous variety of forms. It might express itself in superficial little signs, as, for instance, when a student fraternity requires its members to perform the greeting in a very special way, or it might induce masses of people to submit their actions and judgments, even their very thoughts, to the dogma of their leaders or prophets. It could very well be that at least one motivational source from which religious behavior and teachings stem is the desire for an indestructible connecting link which is independent of the vicissitudes of life.

G— is impressed by the new and unfamiliar color in which so many very familiar phenomena· appear when seen in a new context. His observation of patients with which he had started this train of thought has receded into the background. He does not think any more about possible applications to the theory of therapy; he is completely absorbed in thinking through the confusing multitude of instances, which all seem to belong to the same theme but are not easy to bring into any kind of order.

A question is stirring in his mind which he can formulate only vaguely: Does this desire for fusion, for the softening of personality boundaries, aim always at fusion with the largest number of people? And if this is not so, what determines in one case the limitation, and in another the trend towards union with all of humanity? Before G— can decide whether this is a sensible question or not his attention is deflected from this problem and attracted to a phenomenon which seems to present a very special case of "desire for fusion-delusion." "A peculiarly clear-cut case," G— feels inclined to call it.

Several times in his life G— had met persons who were

interested in telepathy and similar phenomena. The experiments to which he had been invited occasionally, and which were undertaken to prove the existence of telepathy, had always failed to produce convincing results and G—'s initial curiosity with regard to the alleged phenomena had vanished soon. Yet, all the more he had felt puzzled and even fascinated by the behavior and mental attitude of the people who took the opposite view; i.e., who were highly impressed by the same experiments, and devoted much effort, time and money to the study of what they called "occultism" and "parapsychology," or—more recently—"extrasensory perception."

The most challenging problem for him was the fact that scientists of name and fame, people who had evinced a most critical mind in their own field of research seemed to lose all power of discrimination and sense of proportion when it came to evaluating alleged evidence for the occurrence of occult phenomena. With amazement, he looked at the printed testimony of several of his university teachers, some of them well-known the world over, in which they confirmed without reservation that at certain séances where very bewildering apparitions had occurred, no deceit had been possible, while, according to their own description, not even the simplest precautions had been taken to exclude crude methods of cheating. But, perhaps, the case of some other scientists was even more instructive. These were men who stated flatly that the occurrence of telepathy was proved by the strictest scientific methods and only ingrained prejudice kept the bulk of their fellow scientists from seeing the truth. Writing in a style which avoided any expression of exhilarated triumph or surprise but merely sober acceptance of undeniable facts, they proceeded to claim reality for the phenomenon of "precognition."

After many exhausting discussions G— recognized that the interest which animated the apostles of occultism was different from that which was active in any other kind of research. It seemed that its main goal was to prove that phenomena of the peculiar kind which constituted "occultism" really existed. To show them in any connection with known facts, or already established laws of nature, seemed far less important. G— even got the impression that in spite of efforts on the part of the occultists to establish some regularities, and to examine the conditions under which the cherished phenomena appeared, they actually delighted in the fact that what they claimed to have observed did not allow for even a tentative explanation.

"It seems," he once said to an ardent partisan of telepathy, "that the name of your science, namely, occultism, has been chosen not because it studies the unknown, the hidden, the occult (this would not distinguish it from any other science), but because it studies what will and should remain hidden." The occultist smiled at that and admitted that the name "occultism" was a historical relic smacking of superstition; he preferred the name "parapsychology." "You prefer it," replied G—, and it came as a revelation to him, "because the word's second part is the name of a respectable science—psychology —but your innate honesty gets the better of you, you qualify this respectable science by the preposition 'para' which means something like 'irregular,' 'deceptive,' 'weird.' "

Again the occultist laughed: "As a matter of fact," he said, "this word too is somewhat outdated; among my colleagues it is becoming usual to speak of 'extrasensory perception!' "

But G— felt all the more confirmed in his view. "Well," he said, "this name, I must admit, indicates that you and your colleagues succeeded somewhat in your fight against honesty, but not completely!"

"How is that?"

"Oh," continued G—, "you might interpret the word extrasensory perception to mean a perception which does not depend on any of our well-known physical sense organs. Yet, for every uninitiated listener, the word conveys the concept of a perception which occurs without the help of any physical sense organ whatsoever. And I have a hunch that it is the overtone of this meaning which made it attractive to people who felt the word 'parapsychology' was too revealing!"

The parapsychologist showed some irritation and objected. But G— had lost interest in the dispute. He felt, for the first time, that he understood something of the need or drive which forced so many intelligent persons to maintain a belief, however tenuous, in the occult phenomena. These phenomena promised some glimmer of independence for the mind, of independence from the rigid conditions of nature. If telepathy was a reality, minds could be thought of as in direct communication with each other without the need for the cumbersome media of language and other physical signs and symbols.

Remembering many of his encounters with this tenacious addiction to the supernatural, G— is intrigued to find that what had captured his interest and curiosity a long time before he had dreamed of becoming a therapist has again appeared in the center of his attention in a new and much broader context.

He feels a bit overwhelmed by the vast variety of the instances in which fundamental human desire seems to express itself. Although one could say that in all these different endeavors the common goal is to create a semblance of fusion, the means which are used show such a difference in flavor and in quality that they can hardly be put in any kind of order. There is the thrill of the military parade, the stern demand of tradition, the lofty image of unity with God, the abstract idea of extrasensory perception, the most intimate feeling of "being one" between lovers, the impersonal concept of humanity and the brotherhood of men.

Brooding somewhat unhappily over this confusing multitude of creations of the human mind which seem to reach from wishful phantasies to outright delusions, G— suddenly sees that it is easier to recognize their interrelatedness, if one does not look so much for what condition of the mind they try to picture as real, but rather what inner experience they try to deny.

Within a second, it becomes clear to him that there is something frightening in the thought of what "being an individual" entails—a complete, a fundamental, an eternal and insurmountable isolation. But he is not able to keep the thought, or rather the experience, on the same level of lucidity for more than just this one second. Almost without knowing it, he repeats the words he had formed, "complete, fundamental, eternal and insurmountable." But they do not carry the same penetrating momentum.

He makes an effort to think but his mind's vision is blurred and what appears instead of abstract thought is a recollection: When G—started his second year of studies at the university he lived next door to a friend, Walter, two years his senior and a student of medicine. This tall blond boy, the oldest son of very cultured parents of small means, appeared to G— as the model dedicated student. While G—'s interests were always divided and subjected to sudden changes, Walter, in his quiet way, lived completely in his studies, and though his pitifully small allowance forced him to the strictest frugality he seemed very content and was a very likable companion of imperturbable good humor. To G—, who envied Walter's steadiness, he appeared much older than he really was and when, occasionally, he observed in Walter an attitude of skepticism or even mild resignation, he took it as a natural attribute of maturity.

One day G— received an invitation to attend a show put on by a small group of students who were interested in dramatics and he asked Walter to come along. He was delighted that Walter agreed with unusual eagerness and more so when his friend seemed almost enraptured by the performance. When G— hesitatingly suggested that they meet some of the actors after the play, Walter, in spite of the late hour and his habit of careful time economy, was all for it. There followed a very lively session with spirited discussions, in the course of which the leader of the dramatics group asked G— as well as Walter to join. To G—'s surprise, Walter accepted immediately while he postponed his decision.

Some months later, G— was in the audience watching his friend in the leading part of a modern play that another student had written and was amazed at the display of talent and temperament which he never would have suspected Walter possessed.

G— was by no means the only one to be astonished and impressed by his friend's acting. From this day on Walter was like a different person. He did not slacken his pace in studying but it seemed as if his life had been filled with a new intensity and sparkle. A few weeks later he confessed to G—, during a long and passionate talk, that he thought seriously of quitting medicine and of devoting his life to the stage. His decision was not yet made and, indeed, this decision was not at all easy. Not only did his financial situation make it very risky to delay the moment when he could earn a substantial income but the idea of abandoning the medical profession forever seemed almost as inconceivable as the thought of not throwing everything into the career of an actor. For almost six months, G— witnessed an incessant struggle which seemed not far from endangering his friend's life.

It all boiled down to the fateful question: How great was Walter's talent? At the beginning of the struggle, Walter, as well as G—, assumed that to answer this question decisively nothing more was necessary than to invoke the judgment of an expert.

But, as soon as the expert, an actor-director of the highest rank, after conscientious testing, pronounced his verdict, both friends realized how naive had been their expectation. Now the issue was decided unequivocally.

The famous man was impressed with Walter's endowment, with his good taste, his sensitivity and a certain noblesse and distinction in his bearing. But he was not without reservation.

"I would have welcomed you as a student in my acting class," said the famous man, "and would have considered you a very promising beginner, if you simply had come to me with the risk to be accepted. But you came to me with the question, how talented are you, and this changes the whole picture. I fully appreciate your reasonableness and your decision not to aim at becoming a fairly good actor, but only an excellent one, or no actor at all. But I cannot help holding the fact that you need my judgment for your decision somewhat against you. But don't think that I take this hesitation of yours for an infallible criterion of mediocrity."

When Walter repeated to G—, in good spirit, what the expert had said to him, G— felt sad and could hardly hide his disappointment from his friend. And while Walter mentioned calmly that he thought of consulting another expert it dawned on G— that Walter was expecting the impossible. He was not looking for an opinion. He wanted somebody else to make the decision for him. But this thought was not clear enough in G—'s mind to express it to Walter. In the time that followed, G— could observe how Walter slowly, step by step, discovered that no judgment, no advice from any other person could contribute anything to the decision he had to make. Feeling com-

passionate towards Walter's struggle, he was always willing to
discuss with his friend all the innumerable pros and cons which
could possibly have a bearing on the step considered. Yet, when
they had gone through all the possible consequences, had esti-
mated chances, weighed indications, sifted information and
only the ultimate conclusion was missing, they regularly fell
into a deep, painful silence. G— then sensed Walter's unspoken
question, "Now, what do you think?"

G— had no answer, and knew that he could not have one.
Here was the point where he had to leave his friend, and
Walter seemed to know it too because he never asked G— in
so many words. Sometimes, when he sensed how much Walter
was suffering, G— frantically tried to think of some helpful
remark which could diminish the heaviness of the impending
resolution. To no avail! G— thought that he could hardly feel
different if he had to watch his friend die and leave him to the
infinite loneliness of extinction.

G— wonders whether the recollection of this experience
with Walter had been in his mind all the time and had secretly
prompted the whole line of thoughts along which he was moving. Or was it the other way round? He knows that this question cannot be answered and that, perhaps, it doesn't even make
much sense. However, he feels "in his bones" that being fully
aware of one's being an individual is frightening. He hesitates
at the word "frightening." Is it not an exaggerated expression?
It does not seem so when he thinks of the time of Walter's
struggle. And yet, how far back had he had to think to redis-
cover such an experience? And, even then, there had been only
single moments when he had felt the full impact of the individual's basic isolation.

G— thinks of the travel journal he had read recently in
which the author had vividly described the torments he had
gone through when he had spent five miserable days without
water.

"I know, of course, that it is devilish torture to die of thirst.
But if I had not read this description, and others before, I
would hardly know it. Even now, I cannot quite honestly say
that it is a frightening experience. I never came anywhere
close to it. For, long before thirst became a real hardship I

found an opportunity to drink and I did drink. In the same way we might experience only rarely the full awareness of our individuality and suffer from it, because long before the experience becomes sharp enough to cause pain, we find a protective device which softens its impact—a delusionary device, as I have to say now!

"If all this is so, mankind is suffering from an inborn weakness, a congenital Achilles' heel; or rather we would be suffering from it, if we would not cover it up by some magician's trick. We are marching in step, we are staying in line, and this allows us to feel that one and the same mind controls our bodies. Only when we find a stone in our way and have to decide, individually, whether to pass it to the right or to the left does the delusion break down and we recognize with dismay that the decision is ours. It is not that the delusion is so attractive in itself; the primary fact is our intolerance for what we recognize as the truth when we are forced to think of it— our basic isolation. That explains the large variety of delusional devices. Whatever we can use to obscure our isolation serves the purpose and is welcome.

G—, at this point, thinks of those patients who show neither a submissive nor a tyrannical attitude and realizes that they too have their ways to minimize recognition of their status as being individuals—other ways, but not less delusional ones.

With hesitation and only tentatively, for he now feels reluctant to start another attempt at classification, he sketches a number of types, characterized by the ideational means by which they seem to escape from the burden of being individuals, i.e., of being independent and "on their own."

The types are not too sharply divided from each other. There is much overlapping in the sense that some patients might show features of several types, while some others do not seem to fit in any of G—'s type descriptions. And yet, the very fact that at his first glance some methods of delusion formation are discernible, each of which is used by more than one of the patients he can remember, tends to confirm G—'s hunch that the individual's basic isolation and avoidance of becoming aware of it play a significant role in neurotic disturbances.

Admonishing himself not to consider his list of types in any way complete or systematic, he gives in to the temptation to put it down on paper, and it looks likes this:

Types of Ideation in Neurotic Patients

CHILDLIKE. Patients of this type are *not* characterized by what one would usually call "childish behavior." They can be very competent in many fields; they might even show a high degree of common sense and responsible action. But their behavior seems to suggest: "Do not take me seriously. I do not belong to the category of adults and cannot be counted as such." They are playful but not like someone who likes to play, but like someone who does not want (or does not dare?) to appear serious and matter of fact. Distressing, and even tragic, events are mentioned laughingly, or in a hurried, nonchalant way, as if it were not worthwhile to waste time on them. There is also a readiness to talk of their own shortcomings with an inclination to exaggerate. Achievements and successes are put in a ridiculous light, or the report of them is followed by a compensatory enumeration of failures. Their talk frequently might appear chopped up by quick transitionless shifts in topic. By taking unusual liberties like blurting out naive questions, or using baby talk they indicate that they want to be put into the category "non-adult" and should not be counted among the grown-up people.

PASSION-DOMINATED. These patients claim to be driven by passion. They regret ostentatiously that they cannot control themselves. They are not bothered by guilt and not at all despondent because of their wanton behavior. To the contrary, nothing that they are doing is really done by them but by desire, i.e., in their eyes, an irresistible impulse made them do it. They appear in their own words as the unwilling victims of their drives, wishes and infatuations. When they talk about their desires they seem to talk, not about themselves, but about an impersonal force which directs them.

FATE-DOMINATED. Patients of this type are or appear moody, erratic and unsteady. They abstain from well-planned, systematic work, from keeping regular hours and from organizing their time and their activities. They change between long stretches when they are putting things off and bouts of feverish activity when they work night and day. They are gamblers. Careful preparation and arranging of many small chances, the sum total of which might give success a reasonably high probability is repulsive to them. Such behavior would offend fate, which is friendly only when honored by blind confidence. Taking foolhardy risks is the best way to earn fate's favor. Success makes them triumphant and carefree, while every failure throws them into apathy and exaggerated self-criticism. They are quick to accuse the therapist of every fault imaginable but soon get tired of it and apologize. The past is all-powerful in their eyes.

REASON-DOMINATED. These patients maintain the idea that though they might not always act reasonably they could at least strive to do so. This ideology, of course, implies that reason not only determines the means to an otherwise given end but will also determine the ends which have to be aspired. The result is that in their imagination they do not decide anything, do not want anything, have no preference for anything, but reason decides, wants, prefers for them. If they would only apply themselves consistently to thinking, and would make no error in figuring out what reason requires, they would always invariably do the right thing. They seem to know for themselves only one virtue: to act only after having figured out by strict logic what is reasonable to do. To act on an impulse, and to commit errors in thinking, is sinful.

MORAL-DOMINATED. The place which for the reason-dominated patients is occupied by "reason" is taken by "moral" for the patients who are moral-dominated. For the reason-dominated type, life is a permanent examination and its purpose is to accumulate credit points in reasonableness; for the moral-dominated type, life is a permanent test of morality or "goodness" and its purpose is to get through it with as few black marks against them as possible. If one would take their statements literally, there would be no such thing as morally indifferent behavior. What is not duty for them is already forbidden. Just as the reason-dominated hardly experience "choice" because there is only one action prescribed—the most reasonable one—so the moral-dominated type cannot experience choice because every step is determined by duty and taboo.

It is characteristic of their bookkeeping that black marks cannot be compensated by doing one's duty at another time. Perhaps they feel that an action cannot be rewarded; the omission of it must be punished. But they can, to some extent, compensate for their crimes by a display of high moral standards; that is, by harsh self-condemnation. Their interest is centered more in *establishing* a strict and all-encompassing moral code than in *following* it.

As soon as G— has finished this little catalogue of delusional ideologies, he feels disgusted with it and thoroughly disappointed. He calls it crude and misleading. "It has as little to do with what moves my patients as a school grammar with the spoken language, or as the Lutheran catechism with religion," G— thought; "Patients never say anything as explicit as I have made it appear. One cannot put down in black and white what is said only between the lines without distorting it and without removing the unique flavor which is the personal characteristic of every single patient. The whole idea of describing types is absurd. Even where two patients actually convey the same ideologic principle they might otherwise be as different as day and night. And a metaphoric expression, which is perfectly accurate in the climate of one individual hour, written down for eternity, becomes crude and barbaric . . ."

While G— curses his own inclination to schematize, classify and order, one generalizing thought is growing in his mind and seems to triumph over all his derisive self-criticism. It is the thought that, perhaps, really every neurotic disturbance might center around the patient's effort to obviate the inner experience of being an individual, or, in plain English, of being alone.

Three mental activities—very ordinary activities, indeed— seem especially conducive to producing this fateful inner experience: first, and perhaps foremost, in making a decision; second, in reaching a conviction by thinking; and, third, in wanting something. At least it looks as though whenever one of these mental activities is about to appear in sharp focus within the patient's attention; whenever the patient comes close to having it driven home to him that it is *he himself* who is going to make a decision; or that the conviction in his mind is really his, originated by his own thinking; or that it is he, and he alone, who is wanting something, a piece of delusional ideology rolls like a fog over the mental scenery, softening or even obscuring the lines of the picture.

"Perhaps," thinks G—, giving way to a sudden jump of his phantasy in his eagerness and animation, "Descartes' famous statement *'cogito, ergo sum'* takes its real significance from just this fact—that the sharp and vivid experience of reaching a conviction by one's own mental effort carries with it invariably an awareness of one's own identity as an individual. If so, then the English translation of Descartes' Latin would be voiced, 'I think and, therefore, *I* am,' and not as it is usually quoted, 'I think and, therefore, I *am*.'

"Of course, what is necessary to make the inner experience of deciding, thinking or wanting so potent that it needs obscuring is the condition that the decision is not a routine decision expected and approved of by the patient's environment; the conviction reached by the patient's thinking is not supported by authority; or, in the case of 'wanting,' what he wants must be something he is not supposed or not expected to want.

"But this says no more than that the patient's neurotic arrangements, with which he obscures his functioning as an individual person, become apparent only and impress us as pathologic where the situation itself does not provide a 'natural' cover. When the shy seventeen-year-old girl, who loves to recite poetry, has been scheduled among others to provide entertainment at a class meeting and is asked what she would like to contribute, she says without hesitation, 'I would like to recite a poem.' She might tell me this little incident in the hour just as it happened. But when for a similar occasion the teacher, addressing the whole class, asks for volunteers, and she finds courage to raise her hand and offer a recital, she would not tell me about it without the explanation that she really felt obligated because it was now her turn to offer something; or the teacher had looked her in the face and seemed to expect her to come forward with a contribution. In both cases the girl is happy to do what she likes. But in the first case, her being 'scheduled' to perform obscures for her sufficiently her own wanting so that she can tell what happened without trimmings, while in the second case her volunteering enhances her awareness that *she* wanted to recite. So when she tells of the incident it becomes important to her to add that she felt obligated. This discourse on her motivation, in turn, strikes me, the listener, as unnecessary. It appears out of proportion and like a foreign body in the context of her simple story. I feel the dissonance and can recognize it as a manipulative effort to create a delusion. Or, to put it more mildly, to obscure one fact: her desire to recite. In professional language one would call this little addition a pathologic feature, a symptom. Where action is needed to confirm by an objective fact. . . ."

But something intrudes into the rapid, happy flow of G—'s thinking: "Good heavens, where am I? Am I not building castles in the clouds? Do I already take for granted what might be no more than a fleeting image, a wild conjecture, a playfully concocted phantasy? Could it really be that the struggle against seeing oneself as an individual is the core of every neurosis? Now, when I come to think of what it means and entails, it seems fantastic! It seems radical! For all the hundreds and thousands of different forms and symptomatologies, the innumerable peculiarities of neurotic character formation or deformation, there should be one and the same universal conflict?" G—'s thoughts stop short, arrested by his choice of words. Before, he was wandering around in his room; now he stays motionless. In this moment his mind contains nothing but the two sounds, the two verbal expressions: "Universal symptom—universal conflict! How strange that is! What a fool am I! It might be all wrong and pure imagination, but I should have expected something like this. It is exactly what I once thought I should be looking for, what I hoped maybe to find in the far-off future!

"Why was I looking for a universal symptom? Only because I assumed that there was something, some condition of the mind, common to all neurotics. And under this assumption it seemed plausible that this unknown common element would be reflected in some noticeable common behavior feature. And, lo and behold, there it was: the universal symptom of duplicity!

It was a thrill to find it. I had some qualms about its true universality, but finally I am convinced that the phenomenon of duplicity is really what I had anticipated would exist: a universal symptom. Why am I now so incredulous with regard to the inner experience of which it is the reflection and with regard, especially, to its uniqueness—its universality? Does it appear too much at variance with traditional assumptions—or just too simple?" For a while G—'s thoughts roam around at random. He is not able to keep track of them; and he relaxes and submits to an uncontrolled flux of ideas, half-thoughts, half-daydreams, which circle around the concept of the *universal conflict*.

When G— returns from his dream-like state and feels again ready to put his thoughts into orderly sequence he shrugs off with a smile what had bothered him before; namely, his suspicion that his idea was an over-simplification and looked so very different from those which constituted the now most widely accepted theory.

"I was already sold on the simplification when I formed the concept of the universal symptom, and that of the universal conflict is only a necessary consequence. Besides, simplification which reduces the number of basic concepts signifies progress and it becomes over-simplification, and that is faulty only when it eliminates observable facts illegitimately. What a theory gains in simplicity by reducing the basic concepts it needs grows in complexity by finding the richer variety of circumstances which connect the fewer basic ideas with the same large number of observable phenomena.

"Indeed, there is no lack of questions to answer and problems to solve!" And he enumerates rapidly the most urgent of them which rush into his mind:

(1) "How is the universal conflict connected with the universal symptom of duplicity?

(2) "If the universal conflict, as I am thoroughly convinced, is not only common to all neurotics but an innate feature, I could say, of all humanity, what then distinguishes the neurotic from the reasonably healthy person?

(3) "When I make the universal conflict responsible for every neurotic disturbance and, assuming I can account for

its necessary connection with the universal sympton in some way or other, I still must find a conection between the universal conflict and the motley variety of all the other symptoms. Though not all of them are ever present in one neurosis, there is no neurosis which does not show an impressive selection of them.

(4) "Further, I will have to deal with the disquieting implication that if humanity at large is counteracting the discomfort of the universal conflict by delusion formation I have to consider delusion (usually counted among the more serious symptoms of mental disturbance) as something entirely compatible with mental health."

G— pauses. "And this leaves out the biggest problem of all: How will all this thinking and theorizing affect my principles of psychotherapy?"

The first item on his list of problems did not seem hard to solve: "Whenever the universal conflict is activated the patient will have to do something which softens or obscures it. Therefore his behavior and, especially, his talk will be geared to suggesting a state of affairs where his independence, his functioning as an individual, appears diminished. In other words, whatever he is doing or talking about has the secret task of creating a delusion, and this brings about his duplicity. Now, should I assume that the universal conflict is always activated? That living, or, at least, being awake, is identical with being exposed to its impact, or being threatened with such exposure? Oh, I see . . . well, that's interesting! There is, indeed, something *I* do in therapy which provokes this conflict, something I am doing *now* after I changed my views on therapy. The very fact that I am making no demands on the patient and deny that any way of behaving on his part can promote or delay the effect of therapy, is undermining his comforting assumption that his behavior during the treatment hour is submitted to some rule outside of him. This complete lack of outside direction . . . it would be small wonder if this in itself were not provoking the universal conflict, and, in consequence thereof, provoke a more striking display of the universal symptom of duplicity than a situation where the patient is told what to do.

"When I did what I had learned in my training, and presented the patient with the basic rule, I kept his universal symptom at a minimum. Conversely, when I changed my views and felt that there is no point in requiring anything from the patient I, unwittingly, did the only thing which could possibly activate the universal conflict and in consequence enhance the patient's duplicity! This is most probably the reason why patients always react with disappointment when they learn in one way or another that treatment as such makes no demands on their behavior and that many of them simply cannot believe that this is so."

G— feels very content with his discovery of this unexpected interrelation between his newly formed concept of universal conflict and an actual observation on patients which already had become familiar to him; it shows that his decision not to structure in any way the patient's behavior which he had considered as the simple omission of traditional but now superfluous routine, was an important step, the significance of which he could now see himself, while his patients obviously had sensed it all along.

Encouraged, he turns to the next question. What makes the universal conflict so much more aggravating for some persons who have to counteract it by crude means, which we call neurotic symptoms, while the more healthy part of humanity manages to tolerate the same conflict with the help of less disturbing devices?

G— sees immediately that this question is much less precise and, therefore, harder to handle than the first. He starts with a skeptical rumination with regard to the justification of calling the "devices" of the healthier part of humanity "less disturbing" and those of the so-called neurotics "more disturbing." Both types of devices of softening the universal conflict are "delusional." He asks himself whether the belief of a poorly educated backwoods farmer that his passionate prayer caused the recovery of his sick child, is really less delusional than the sophisticated hypochondriac's unwarranted conviction that his bellyache is due to a fatal cancer of the stomach? The pious farmer might be a paragon of mental health and his life of enviable richness and contentment, while the hypochondriac

might strike everybody as a terribly sick person in urgent need
for whatever help psychiatry can provide.

G— feels very confused and for a time entirely unable to
come to any decision. At certain moments he is assailed by the
suspicion that, perhaps, his whole trend of thought has led
him astray and that he will have to start all over again, dis-
carding all his basic concepts and looking for new ones. But
his inner turmoil subsides, and he succeeds in discovering
some fallacious elements in his perturbing question.

"I think I have taken some liberties with the use of the word
'delusional.' This word evokes in us not strictly *one* concept
but rather two different concepts; which one, depends in every
case on the context in which it is used. Concept number one
can be described as 'an error in judgment qualified by the
condition that it is due to a psychological need or desire.'
Concept number two can be described just as concept one was
with the addition of the connotation 'sick.'

"There are, undoubtedly, phenomena which we subsume
under concept number one, but not under concept number two;
that is, *some* delusions do not strike us as 'unhealthy.' When
a person is waiting with great impatience for a telephone call
and misjudges the ringing of the doorbell, and hurries to the
telephone instead of the house door, nobody is likely to call
such an illusion a sign of mental illness.

"It is, in fact, an abbreviation (or indirect expression) to
call any single occurrence of delusion—or for that matter, any
single reaction—unhealthy. This concept refers directly only
to persons, and where we apply it to any single reaction we
usually mean only that this single reaction is such that we
conclude the person to whom it belongs must be mentally
unhealthy.

"Things would be simple now; that is, if the delusions (in
the sense of concept number one) which we find in healthy
people would occur only sporadically, in exceptional situations.
But this is not so. To the contrary, many of the delusions of
healthy people may last for a lifetime as, for instance, the so-
called superstitions, religious beliefs or faith in the necessary
progress of the human race.

"Perhaps, I have no reason to assume that such lasting

delusions are as necessary to a healthy human existence as breathing. But it is disquieting to think that they are at least compatible with it. It seems such a plausible hypothesis that every lasting dysfunction of our critical capabilities is impairing our mental health, or better, that there is some positive correlation between correctness of our perception of reality and degree of mental health. But that is a prejudice. In fact, it is as arbitrary as to postulate that mental health should correlate positively to IQ or to talent for writing poetry. I must admit that there is something alluring in the idea that by improving a person's mental health one could improve in him every desirable human quality. Yet, I can see that this is nonsense. It is delusional.

"Still the question remains: What persistent and pervasive delusional thinking impresses us as a sign of sickness, and what distinguishes this type of delusion from the type which appears compatible with mental health? I don't know. I can't tell. But this question might wait. It is undoubtedly important but not crucial for the moment.

"I could say the same about the third question: the connection between the universal conflict and the universal symptom on one side, and the multitude of well-known neurotic symptoms on the other side; those symptoms from which the name of specific afflictions is usually derived. Sometimes, I can now see that the one or the other of these symptoms helps to assuage or obscure the universal conflict. I can understand, for instance, that every symptom which limits the freedom of action, like an agoraphobia, may tend to diminish opportunities in which the universal conflict would be provoked or intensified. But I cannot show such an effect for every neurotic symptom, nor are my basic assumptions suited to elucidate what determines the choice of symptoms.

"Interesting as these questions might be from many viewpoints, I doubt that the answers to them would have an immediate bearing on the practical problems of therapy."

This thought reminds G— painfully of the most urgent and unavoidable task he has to face: namely, to determine where he stands now with view to the general problem of psychotherapy. After having lost, or, should he rather say abandoned, the one really normative principle of his original theory—the one which could serve as a directive for his work with patients—he had entrusted himself to the temporary leadership of intuition, until further study, observation, thinking and, last but not least, a stroke of luck would replace the deficient part of his original idea with a new, sound and workable principle.

During the time the concept of the universal conflict had developed in his thoughts, beginning with his miscarried attempt at patient classification, the question had always been present in the back of his mind as to whether the new vision he was acquiring would finally confirm or contradict his intuition. And, although right now he has not even a hunch which it would be, he is almost certain that the decision is just around the corner.

Bravely fighting his trepidation, G— tries to focus on the question of whether any directive for therapeutic action could be derived from what he has understood recently about the universal conflict. But, against his expectation he draws a blank. Beyond a certain confirmation of the importance of the universal symptom (satisfactory as far as it goes), he cannot extract any indication for therapeutic action from the concept.

THE ROLE OF COMMUNICATION

It was, as usual, a chance observation which set G—'s mind in motion again and led him to a view on the whole of psychotherapy, more coherent and more in keeping with what he was actually doing with his patients than any of his former formulations and hypotheses.

During three weeks of vacation in a mountain summer resort, G— found himself thrown together with a married couple, both much older than he. The man, a law school professor around sixty, was an erudite scholar of many interests, quick-witted and of a dry humor, whom G— found very likable. His wife, perhaps ten years his junior, was of distinguished appearance with a very intelligent face though her eyes always had a tired expression.

On the first evening of G—'s arrival, he met the professor in the salon of the little guest house and soon was so involved in a vivid and interesting conversation with the older man that he regretted it when his partner, after half an hour, excused himself in order to look after his wife who had retired early. "Not feeling too well," he said.

The next morning at breakfast, G— met the lady who thanked him with a charming smile for his inquiry about her health and expressed her pleasure that he had been such good company to her husband. During a very leisurely breakfast, G— found himself very well entertained by the woman. An old customer of the place, she informed him, the newcomer, in an amusing and unobtrusive way about its history and development.

G— considered himself lucky to have found such nice and interesting companions. However, his pleasant anticipation met with grave disappointment.

It was at lunch. The few guests, perhaps nine, were sitting around the same table. G—, on the professor's invitation, had taken the chair at his side. Some of the other guests were talking about chess and the marvelous talent a youngster of fifteen had displayed recently in a public tournament. Lydia, the professor's wife, remarked that a cousin of hers had come out best at a local tournament in New London at the age of eight.

"Excuse me," inserted the professor dryly, "he was *nine* at this time."

"The other players," continued Lydia, "were grown-ups who felt all the more taken aback, as the youngster had never before played in the club where the tournament was arranged. Of course, it makes no difference," she added with a sharpened voice, "but I happen to know Teddy was eight years old when he won his victory."

"I am sorry, dear," intruded the professor, laying down his knife and fork, "I think I can prove he was nine." And he mentioned rapidly a number of circumstances—names, age differences, and birthdays from which he quickly and succinctly deduced the correctness of his statement. Lydia smiled. But G— noticed that her nose and lips had lost their color and looked white. "You are quite right, Hugh," she said in a hoarse voice, "but you made one error: Cecily's birthday was not her thirty-second as you assumed but her thirty-third."

With bewilderment G— observed that the professor's face, usually somewhat pale, had reddened. He still managed to smile but his voice sounded harsh when he went into a fluent argument which, if one could follow it, seemed to prove that the birthday in question was the thirty-second of Cecily's— whoever Cecily might be. Lydia's eyes had lost every trace of tiredness when she, very erect on her chair, somewhat short of breath but every word carefully pronounced, countered with, "No honey, you *are* in error. Forgive me, but . . ." and on and on it went.

G—, like most of the other guests, sat for awhile in a be-wildered silence; then tried to make the embarrassing dispute less conspicuous by busily passing dishes around, filling glasses, closing a door, opening a window and readjusting the lid of the salt shaker.

Finally, the professor, obviously exhausted, and looking straight ahead towards the window said, "Well, I might be mistaken. Excuse me, Lydia dear!" But it was clear to everybody that these words meant, "Of course, I am right, but I give up."

Unfortunately, it soon became manifest that arguments like the one at lunch were not the exception but the rule between the otherwise engaging couple. It made no difference what the theme of the conversation was, who started it or how many people participated. At one point or another, when either the professor or his wife had made a contribution to it, the other party raised an objection and off they went on their pathetic argument, polite in words but bitter in tone, each one visibly distressed but compelled to continue relentlessly, oblivious of the squirming audience, until some inner voice told one or the other that it was enough and the battle ended with a non-committal phrase of withdrawal.

The other guests, following the lead of the experienced landlady, soon acquired the technique of ignoring these point-less, unpleasant arguments by continuing their conversation with slightly raised voices. Outside of meal time, everybody avoided the company of the quarreling couple and that was easy enough as the professor and his wife were always the first to leave the dining room, taking a walk or retiring into their little cottage.

G—'s interest in them was not diminished by the disappointing experiences during meals. He tried, however, to meet them separately which was not easy as each of them was slightly disquieted when the other was not present and seemed constantly on the lookout for the spouse. He found that the professor usually spent an hour of the evening alone reading in the little salon where he had met him the first day. When G— entered, the professor put down his book or magazine and invited him to sit down; they would then start talking. These discourses were always pleasant and G— looked forward to them. During the second week of his stay, G—'s talks with the professor touched frequently on personal matters. He learned quite a bit of the older man's life history, his present work and his interest in didactic methods; G— felt that they were becoming friends. Occasionally, their conversation turned to topics in which juristic, as well as psychological viewpoints had to be taken, and, there, their opinions were frequently in sharp opposition. Yet, somewhat to his surprise, G— found in the professor a very considerate, open-minded partner who argued with vigor and skill but without any irritability or obstinacy.

Less frequently, G— chatted with Lydia in the absence of her husband. This happened only at breakfast where she sometimes appeared a few minutes before the professor. She seemed to appreciate G—'s interest in her and in her husband but the conversation with her remained only on the level of social small talk, very friendly, casual, yet definitely impersonal. When the professor had joined them, G— stayed at the table only a short while before he excused himself and left. Although never, during this morning hour, did any of the painful arguments occur, G— could not bring himself to "tempt" fate and remain at the table at leisure.

In the middle of G—'s third week at the guest house, and only two days before his departure was scheduled, an incident occurred which distressed G— considerably and caused intense uneasiness whenever he remembered it. Yet, notwithstanding its unpleasant nature, it triggered off in G—'s mind a chain of thoughts which proved fruitful for his views on therapy.

As on every evening, G— was sitting in the little salon chatting with the professor over a cup of tea. G—'s imminent departure was mentioned, and the professor, who seemed even more outgoing and friendly than ever before, expressed with some warmth his regret at losing a companion whose acquaintance he had enjoyed so greatly. Continuing this friendly expression, he asked G— a few personal questions about his parents, his home country and his childhood, which he had never done before. G— answered readily, describing the peculiar character of the little university town in which he was raised and mentioning casually the melodic, Latinized name by which the university was known. The professor took the cigar from his mouth and throwing a critical glance at the ash which had formed at its burning end, said without looking at G—, "You mean, I suppose . . ." and he repeated the Latin name but with a different ending.

G—, immersed in his memories, paid little attention. "No, no, it is as I said. You know, this is not classical Latin," and continued his narrative. The professor waited until G— had finished his sentence, then waved his hand and said, "Excuse me, but . . ." He followed this with a lengthy discourse about the intimacies of Latin grammar and its treatment of proper nouns, from all of which he deduced, with a scowl on his forehead, and pressing his right forefinger so firmly onto the table top that finger and table vibrated, the incorrectness of the ending which G— had used.

G— could not follow the explanation, because his recollection of the grammatical rules of Latin was very scanty. He suddenly realized, with a jolt, that the man in front of him, the bright erudite scholar, the warm-hearted friendly fellow, was no longer talking to him with the intent to explain, to prove or to teach but was fighting for fight's sake in blind determination. G— felt disgusted, and on the verge of rudely interrupting the argument which, he knew, was nonsensical. But a sense of hopelessness stifled his action. "Either I offend this old man who doesn't really want to hurt me, or, if I say what could be said within the limits of politeness, I will pro-

voke a new stream of arguments, which might even be worse."
So, he raised his hands and with a grim smile said, as if
ashamed of himself: "I can't trust my memory! I never could,
as far as names are concerned. You might be right after all!"
It sounded awfully false to him and for a second he expected
that the other man would burst into laughter. Instead, the professor finished his sentence, then relaxed, looked G— in the
face with a kind of bewildered expression as if awakening
from a bad dream, and said graciously with a little smile,
"Oh, never mind!" G—, after taking a long sip from his tea,
intended to continue the conversation as if nothing had happened but found that he couldn't. So he resigned and a few
minutes later left the room with some pretext or other.

At an early hour the next morning, G— was riding in the
guest house station wagon on his way to the airport, when the
only other passenger, a girl with an expressive and intelligent
face, addressed him suddenly: "We all admired your courage,
Doc. And, I would love to know—did you succeed?"

"You guessed right," answered G— without any hesitation,
"I finally failed."

"So did all of us. Some sooner, some later. It's a pity!"

G— would have liked to continue the conversation but the
station wagon swerved into the last curve in front of the
airport and there was no time left.

"It is the old story," thought G—, when he was sitting
comfortably in his plane and the three vacation weeks had
already faded into a little memory package, not without color
and form but almost without extension. "What makes them so
intolerable to others is probably the very thing which makes
them indispensable to each other. The famous dove-tailing of
neuroses!"

G— remembered a stenographer who had worked as his
secretary at the time he was an employee of the industrial
firm. She was an excellent worker in many ways, conscientious, untiring and reliable. He treated her with respect,
expressed his appreciation of her work and advocated energeti-
cally and successfully a raise of her pitifully low salary. It
looked as if they would get along splendidly with each other.
But it did not last. She, who knew the office routine much

better than G—, never could keep herself from asking about all the little details which she had at her finger tips while G— had to think about them or even consult a colleague. At one point he told her he was confident she would do it right and that there was no point in asking *him*. She did not object but seemed disgruntled and continued asking as before.

One day he corrected, in his own handwriting, a small typographical error in a lengthy memorandum which he had dictated to her. When she discovered this, she reproached him for not having told her about it and wanted to retype the whole page immediately. He said that this was unnecessary, a waste of time. Obviously disappointed, she told him, in contrast to her usual reserved manner, how her former boss would have "raised hell" over such a mistake and would have torn up the whole page. Though, on the surface, her remark appeared as if she appreciated G—'s leniency, it was clear that she felt ill at ease. From that time, G— noticed that she had an obstinate expression on her face whenever he talked to her and had lost all her spirit. While her work remained satisfactory, G— became irritated, for there was an increasing awkwardness in her behavior and her "moping around." He felt relieved when one day she gave notice and announced that she was going to get married. Through the grapevine, he learned that this good-looking girl, who would have had no difficulty in finding a respectable husband, had married a former storekeeper of the same firm, an alcoholic who had been fired because of his irregular working habits and his inclination to get into fist fights with coworkers.

A year later, the secretary was back at work though not in G—'s office. Her husband, whose drinking excesses had increased, was unable to support the family and the little he earned was spent in taverns. For some time, G— did not see her but heard enough through the department gossip about the brutal treatment she received from her husband and the general misery in which she was living.

One day he met her at the lunch counter of the firm. She looked thin and overworked but G— was surprised when she greeted him without any embarrassment and without her usual obsequiousness. She even seemed glad to talk to him. When he asked politely, in a formal manner, how she was, she answered calmly and with a wistful smile, "Oh, Doctor, you know, of course, how bad things are," and sketched, in a few words her daily fight for survival, the humiliations to which she was exposed and her futile efforts to combat the husband's addiction. The picture was sad enough and she did not minimize her plight, yet she did not seem to complain nor to ask for sympathy. Her lunch finished, she got up, said how much she had enjoyed talking to him and hurried back to her work.

G— now remembered vividly what he had thought after this meeting. "She is certainly not happy, nor content, nor even resigned. Yet, she seems in a state of inner equilibrium which she had never reached before."

The two examples of "dove-tailing neuroses," the first one with the secretary and her alcoholic husband, and the recent one with the sophisticated, distinguished couple from the guest house, amalgamated in G—'s mind; and in a kind of mild hypnoid state induced by the vibrations of the airplane and the monotonous droning of its engines, he found himself working on the elusive task of bringing into coincidence two visual images which in a mysterious way represented the two couples. The images appeared somewhat like two very irregular pieces which might belong to a jigsaw puzzle. Each one seemed to possess an elongated protrusion which extended from the more compact main body.

G— found, after some trials, that the best start was to make these two protrusions coincide. They seemed to fit perfectly. Only then, he had trouble doing the same with the remaining parts of the two pieces, without disturbing the perfect congruence of the protrusions. This difficulty appeared all the more disappointing and vexing as G— felt that he was close to a solution. Then something disturbing happened. The two images paled and started to disappear and, with what seemed a gigantic effort, G— realized that the plane's hostess was offering him a cup of tea or coffee, while he, by whatever trick of splitting his attention, retained a faint glimmer of the two vanishing pieces and managed to ask for a cup of coffee. Holding the hot cup in his hands and mechanically taking little sips from its content he tried to return to his "puzzle." Yet, he found that he was now again thinking of the two couples and especially about what he recognized as the "equivalent" of the protruding parts. Both the secretary and the professor of law were not content with rigidly structured relationships with their respective spouses. Though they seemed to need fighting relationships to maintain some sort of equilibrium, they also reached out for a natural, normal and healthier contact with other human beings. This common human desire was not simply absent in their souls, nor completely dead and dormant; it was still alive and prompted them again and again to take some steps towards its fulfillment. Yet these steps did not lead them very far. After some distance had been covered, something like a silent alarm signal seemed to be set in motion, and obstacles arose which barred further progress. Communicative behavior was replaced by some rigid, monotonous and repetitive pattern. The secretary increased her obsequiousness, insisted on being bossed and refused to use her common sense; the professor became over-critical, argumentative and authoritarian.

What caused this alarm? Asking himself this question, G— felt in a strange position. On the one hand, the secretary's as well as the professor's reactions, so annoying when they occurred, appeared to him now understandable in the sense that he could sympathize with them. They struck him as somehow familiar. These people, it was clear to him, lived their lives along a rigid pattern which allowed them to feel embedded in some kind of structure which protected them against the dread awareness of their single selves. They *had* to be disturbed when anybody addressed them simply as fellow men. Being recognized—not as boss or employee, as student or teacher, as members of a class or social stratum—foremost or even exclusively as human beings, it was plausible that this experience tended to shake their protective structure.

Yet, on the other hand, it was equally obvious that, if anything could mitigate the grim aspect of the individual's basic isolation, it was closeness to the other, the sharing of inner experience by communication, a free and unrestricted exchange of thoughts and feelings.

How could it be that the very thing which bridged the gap between one self and another self—this unique possibility provided by language—could be perceived also as a danger?

G— knew that he had once encountered a similar paradox, but it was hard to remember what it was, where it had occurred and when. Slowly, the vague image gained more concrete features. Water was around—the choppy water of the Mediterranean on a sunny but windy day. He had swum out from a beach for what seemed not more than a quarter of an hour and then, looking back, had discovered that the beach with the little village behind it was almost out of sight. Turning right back he soon found his suspicion confirmed that a current must have taken him out for he could make very little headway, if any. At a great distance he could see a rowboat. The boat was to the lee of him and it seemed possible that a call for help could be heard by the fishermen. He thought clearly that to call for help was the most sensible thing to do. But, without quite knowing why, he did not call but changed his direction and swam for a while almost parallel to the coastline and found that he had been lucky enough to escape from the current. Only later, when he was resting in the hot sand of the beach, did he realize that calling for help would have increased his worry into panic.

G— felt certain that his memory of this little introspective observation which had flashed into his mind when, fairly exhausted, he had rested in the sun and of which he had never thought again, in some way contained the solution for his present paradox. But it seemed very difficult to trace the parallel. Again and again he went over the few moments when the thought of calling for help had appeared in his mind and had been rejected. As soon as he had discovered that swimming towards the shore for at least ten minutes had not brought him closer to it he knew that he was in danger. He remembered thinking something like: "Now, this is serious. Under such circumstances people have been carried out into the sea and have drowned. I must make a real effort! There is no point in fighting the current head-on. But I have a chance to get out of it when I swim across it. I have no idea what its width could possibly be, but it cannot be infinite." At this moment it had occurred to him that hailing the boat was another possibility which needed very little effort, would not waste any time and was almost sure to bring help quickly. But he had dismissed the thought without hesitation! Well, it was one thing to know that one's situation is serious and might lead to death and another to send a message about it, even if it is no more than an inarticulate yell. Doing this changes the inner situation immediately. The knowledge of danger turns into fear.

In a very similar sense, "talking seriously and intimately to another person" is first of all an acknowledgment of one's separation. G— remembered a woman he had had in treatment for a long time and who had been silent for long periods in the sessions. "I would like to tell you what has happened to me during the day," she said more than once, "but I think you must know it already. I know, of course, that this is not so. But I cannot overcome my feeling which tells me that it is." G— felt that he now understood more fully what his patient had experienced. She knew that G— could not know, and did not know. Yet, this knowledge would have taken on a new and uncomfortable realness if she had acted upon it and had told him of the little events of the day.

"Maybe," thought G—, "the decision to talk implied the realization that before she talked her thoughts were hers only and not mine, and would have carried for her such a sharp sense of isolation that to avoid its pain she waived the possible but, uncertain, future comfort of communication, and preferred to maintain whatever delusional *feeling* she could preserve in the face of her realistic *thinking*." It seemed that for people like the secretary and the professor, or the woman G— had just thought of, communication appeared just as *dangerous as helpful,* or rather, more dangerous. And, their shrinking from it had the justification that the more intimate, the more free and straightforward the communication, the more we experience the other's "otherness." However, in spite of this being so, not for all people do the "dangers" of communication outweigh its desirable gifts. What, then, is it that causes the difference?

A low voice at G—'s side interrupted his thinking with the distinctly pronounced words, "Fasten your seat belt, please!"

G— complied. The plane descended rapidly. The lights of the city became visible. And soon, G— was on solid ground again and walked slowly with the group of other passengers toward the gate.

THE VICIOUS CIRCLE

At home and in more familiar surroundings G— tried as methodically as he could to put the somewhat disconnected thoughts which had come to him during his return flight into better order.

The idea that every neurosis centered around the universal conflict seemed sound, and he wanted to maintain it; but, as the universal conflict, by definition, was common to all mankind, it was necessary to determine under what circumstances this common condition forced a person to develop the restrictive-protective patterns characteristic of neurotics which became apparent during treatment, especially through the phenomenon of the universal symptom.

He also had great confidence in the thought that it was the ability to communicate freely that prevented the universal conflict from forcing a person into the restrictive delusionary pattern of neurosis.

The third idea concerned the double nature of communication. Communication was able to activate the universal conflict and was, at the same time, the potent antidote against its pathogenic effect. But, obviously, these two functions of communication did not simply cancel out each other. Their effect on the neurotic person was not synchronic. When a neurotic person came together with a healthy one with a communicative attitude, the first effect which was noticeable was the lessening of the neurotic's universal conflict. How long this favorable effect lasted, while communication continued, depended on many circumstances, essentially on the individuality of the neurotic. But, invariably when the communicative contact between the two people was maintained, it increased by its very nature in intensity, depth and intimacy. And, also invariably, while this took place—after hours, days or weeks— a point was reached where the beneficent effect of communication on the neurotic was overtaken by the accumulating activation of his universal conflict. At this point his delusionary protective patterns came to the fore, with the result that communication was interrupted. From there on the relationship between the neurotic and the comparably healthy person was doomed. The latter withdrew in disappointment. He either withdrew physically, i.e., he avoided meeting the neurotic person, or withdrew psychologically, and kept his relationship to the neurotic on a formal, superficial, essentially manipulative level, turning for communication to other, healthier people.

It followed that the longer the neurotic condition existed, the more the social surroundings close to the neurotic were emptied of healthy people; the less of real communication was available to him, and the more he suffered from actual isolation, which again made him turn to more and more radical delusionary and restrictive patterns of behavior. The people with whom he could maintain a steady contact were neurotics themselves, who could tolerate only a minimum of communication and were content with an essentially manipulative relationship.

All this meant that a neurosis was self-perpetuating by the strength of a vicious circle. "The question of the origin of the neurotic condition," thought G—, "is therefore equivalent to the question what starts off the vicious circle? Theoretically, one could think of two possible answers. Either the person who was to become a neurotic was constitutionally less capable of communication than those who developed in a healthier direction, or he was excluded from communication for a long stretch of time by external conditions in his formative years. If the first assumption obtained, successful treatment seemed hardly possible. But the latter assumption allowed for hope. If the vicious circle was started by external conditions one could imagine that breaking the circle would mean—cure! But, how could the circle be broken?"

While G— was going through this chain of thoughts, a vague and nebulous idea had been stirring somewhere in the background. When he thought of the question "How to break the vicious circle?" his breathing stopped suddenly. The answer seemed so obvious but also so primitive and naive that it appeared almost ridiculous. G—'s mind refused to spell it out and for a while turned blank. "Naive, bizarre, ridiculous or not, there can be no harm in thinking it through!"

If it is really true that a neurotic condition is maintained by the vicious circle which feeds the delusion of fusion by starving communication, and starves communication by feeding delusion, then, there is, at least, a theoretical possibility of breaking the vicious circle and thereby arresting, reducing or even abolishing the neurosis. This theoretical possibility, obviously, depends on the fact that one link in the feed-back system which constitutes the vicious circle is lying outside of the neurotic's mind, and consists of the habitual, natural reaction of withdrawal of the healthier elements of his human environment. These healthier people, after a while, give up, withdraw from the neurotic personality physically or psychologically, and leave him to his fellow neurotics. "Just as the people of the guest house shunned the company of the professor and of his wife," G— thought, "as I did, finally, in disgust and annoyance."

But, it is clear that under certain conditions healthy people can be motivated to act differently. And that, it seems, is the essence of psychotherapy! For one thing, we therapists do not withdraw physically. To the contrary! We are seeing our patients again and again for an hour at a time over months and years. Interest in the patient, interest in doing this fascinating job, interest in the satisfaction we derive from successes and, last, but not least, our interest in making a living, lend the motive for persevering.

"Not to withdraw physically" from the patient is necessary for treating his condition; however, this condition is easy to fulfill and creates no problem at all. The crucial condition which makes all the difference between psychotherapy which helps, and alleged psychotherapy which doesn't, is *that the therapist does not withdraw psychologically.* This second condition is indeed of a peculiar and very tricky nature. It is not enough that the therapist recognizes it as a necessary condition of effective psychotherapy; frequently, the one who fails to fulfill it does not notice that he fails. And even the one who notices that he does not fulfill this condition, and knows that it *is* a necessary one finds himself very often unable to fulfill it in spite of all his efforts.

At this point G— felt the need to take his bearings. He had ventured far out on a promising trail which, in any case, would be worth his while to study carefully from every possible angle. But he also felt that he had some menace at his back which he had better face immediately. And, for this purpose he had to know his present position better and the course he had taken.

When he had started out with what he once called "his project," he was in possession of a theory of therapy. A very, very meager theory, certainly, but at least one which provided him with a prescription for therapeutic action: "Make the patient aware of his duplicity!" He had learned something was wrong with this prescription, under pain and scruples, with embarrassment and perturbation. But, when he had followed his intuition and "played it by ear," as it were, he found this state of affairs halfway tolerable, and even felt more confident and closer to his patients, only as long as he expected that, sooner or later, he would be able to replace the deficient prescription with a better one.

Now, he had made some headway in his thinking. He had learned something and could understand more. His skeleton of a theory (a one-bone skeleton, as he called it), had put on, if not flesh, at least some skin and color and looked promising to him. But his new prescription, the replacement for his discarded principle of therapeutic action, appeared very different from what he had expected. Instead of being more precise, more structured and more detailed, it had shrunk to a mere ghost of a principle. It consisted, to all appearances, of nothing but a negative command, a prohibition: "Don't withdraw, neither physically nor psychologically!"

"But, no! It is not as bad as that! The negative form of this principle is only a quirk of semantics; it still means something positive, just as the admonition, 'don't loaf!' means as much as 'work!' So, it must be possible to express the same meaning in a positive formulation!"

G— thought and thought. One version after the other emerged in his mind and was rejected. Whatever sentence he composed sounded stilted, or vague, or simply ridiculous. The *vague* type seemed the less offensive. "Small wonder," thought G— with some bitterness, "the less one says the less chance there is to blunder!" But he could not prevent the vague formulations that prevailed more and more: "Be aware of the patient's duplicity! Let's see, suppose you were, what good would that do, if you would not *act* upon this awareness in one way or another. Try again! *Act* upon your awareness of the patient's duplicity! Fine, but does that in any way describe what you should say or do? And, by the way, if you are *not* aware of the patient's duplicity, or *not* sensitive to it, can you make yourself the one or the other?

"Another attempt: Offer communication to the patient! The word 'offer' sounds idiotic! Perhaps I can find a less pomp- ous expression later, but what in the world should be communi- cated? So, it really says nothing!

"There must be something completely wrong in my effort. What am I trying to do? Doesn't it sound as if I wanted to answer the question: 'How do I become efficient and success- ful? Or, how to be entertaining and popular? Or, how does one become the life of every party? My whole attempt to define what to do in therapy is nonsense. To help a patient you have to keep him company frequently enough for a sufficiently long time, and whether he gets well or not depends on who you are, what kind of person you are, what interests you, and what you are sensitive to. The therapist's task does not consist of doing anything definite; the task is—to be therapeutic! What a formidable paradox."

G— felt alternately dismayed and elated when he looked from different angles at this bewildering formulation. But after he had lived with it for a while it lost much of its paradoxical appearance. Conditions for doing a good job in a certain field could not be expressed in the form of a code of behavior. Personal qualities were not at all a unique feature of the field of psychotherapy. It was equally true for education, for every form of creative art, for any kind of leadership. Even the sim- plest technical skills could be described in step-by-step rules only up to a certain point. Then the workman had to use his own discretion. This did not mean that the personal qualities of a good therapist, technician, artist, leader or educator were all inborn. Although they could not be acquired simply by reading and memorizing a manual, they could, to some extent at least, be acquired by training.

G— could see that the image of psychotherapy which he had finally reached excluded the usefulness of any manual and of any learning by rote; nevertheless, there was a wide range within which personal qualities, necessary for the therapist, could be developed by training. With the recognition of this state of affairs he could feel satisfied. At the same time, he shuddered, thinking how strange it would seem to others. Everyone seemed so accustomed to estimating therapeutic efficiency in terms of applying a certain method, performing a certain activity, that the term "just *being* with the patient" was practically unthinkable. One thought of "advising, encouraging, enlightening the patient, increasing his self-understanding or self-awareness, of making his unconscious conscious, reconstructing his childhood experiences, dissolving his resistances, interpreting his phantasies or dreams or, perhaps, making him feel unconditionally accepted." Not too long ago, G— himself had formulated the rule of "making the patient aware of his duplicity!" He had now abandoned not only every single one of these rules but the usefulness of any rule whatsoever!

He could easily anticipate the objections which would be raised against this "extreme" idea. He could vividly remember how he himself had once argued with passion against colleagues who had ridiculed the whole idea of establishing rules for the technique of psychotherapy. Perhaps their reasoning had been faulty but, it seemed to him now, that they had sensed some truth which he had been able to see only after painfully passing through many stages. He felt certain that he could base his newly gained conviction on better reasons than those his former opponents had brought forward against him. Yet, he still had an almost nostalgic sympathy for his former conviction which he had once defended with the feeling that it was not only correct but "better," "nobler" in some vague, moral sense.

Wasn't the statement that the therapist had to follow no rule whatsoever except *to be with the patient* asking the therapist to abandon reason, intelligent thinking and scientific method; making him rely on mere intuition, the moment's mood and the whims of chance? Wasn't it?

G— sighed. In his mind's eye, he saw himself getting up from his chair before a large group of his colleagues, taking a long look at the questioning faces, with their raised eyebrows and wrinkled foreheads, delivering the following lecture:

"I know that it sounded strange when I advocated that you demand nothing from your patients as a condition for successful treatment—except their presence in your office. It seemed unbelievable! However, you were willing to discuss my suggestion and though we never reached agreement on this issue, it still seemed worthwhile to take up the matter occasionally and pursue the subject somewhat further.

"The thesis which I tried to expound today; namely, that there should be no rules for the therapist either, has struck you as even more bizarre or revolting, like the 'idée fixe' of a monomaniac. Treatment, you believe, is goal-directed activity. Patient and therapist meet, not for a social visit, a picnic, a friendly chat, but for a serious purpose. The purpose is to improve the patient's mental condition, an endeavor of vital interest to the patient and, considering the aggregate of patients, also of vital interest to the therapist. Is it not a matter of simple logic that purposeful behavior is controlled by certain rules, deducible from the purpose on the one hand, and from all the pertinent factual circumstances on the other? Even if there were no rules for the patient's behavior, there *must* be some for that of the therapist!

"I maintain, however, that the purpose of therapy, on which we agree, demands no more nor less than that the patient spends sufficient time with a person of *certain personality characteristics*, who is motivated to give his attention exclusively to the patient at the times they meet. I can imagine your incredulous question: 'Just *being with* the therapist should help the patient, no matter what happens between the two of them?'

"When you ask me this question, with an expression of utter disbelief written all over your faces, my answer is 'Yes, no matter what happens!' But, I must remind you that what happens between them will, of course, depend upon the two persons involved, and that I required certain personality characteristics from the person who is to function as therapist.

" 'What personality characteristics?' you want to know! Fine, I see you will give me a chance! I think you will find that the required characteristics are quite specific though it might not appear so at first glance.

"*The first requirement* concerns an interest of the therapist (or you could call it an inclination or predilection), namely, an interest in people, and more specifically, in establishing straightforward communication with people whose attitude is uncommunicative because of their neurosis. This interest of the therapist has to be genuine in the sense that establishing such communication in the face of neurotic obstacles is for him an end in itself, not only a means to an end.

"*The second requirement* (like the third) is to make sure that the therapist is free and able to have his interaction with the patient determined by the interest which I just mentioned. This second requirement is concerned with the therapist's theoretical convictions. It demands that his views on psychotherapy do not compel him to interfere with the free play of his aforementioned interest in communication for the sake of the patient.

"*The third requirement* demands that this essential genuine interest in establishing communication not be curbed by neurotic protective patterns of his own. This does not mean that he must be a paragon of mental health, but just that whatever his neurotic difficulties might be, they should not be such that they interfere with living up to his crucial interest.

"*The fourth requirement* is not quite as trivial as the second and third. It concerns a mental condition, or disposition, of the therapist which one could call his receptiveness. He must be sensitive towards the noncommunicative elements in the patient's behavior, or to the patient's duplicity.

"I see that some of you have jotted down the four requirements. I appreciate your attention, but I warn you that there is a certain arbitrariness in these formulations. It might be just as well to arrange the description of attitudes desirable in a therapist in three paragraphs as in four, or even in five. My main point is that the conditions for effective psycho-

therapy can be expressed only in terms of personality characteristics of the therapist, and *not* in rules of what he should do.

"If this thesis—no rules for the therapist!—seems bewildering to you, it is, at least partially, due to the fact that usually
books on technique of psychotherapy describe the conditions
of effective therapy in terms of what the therapist should *do*
in the sessions, and only incidentally do they mention, in a
special little paragraph, what personal qualities make for a
good therapist.

"I reverse this emphasis. I do not say what should happen
in the sessions, or what the therapist should do in order to help
the patient. I leave this whole area fluid and, instead, concen-
trate exclusively on what kind of person the therapist should
be. I hope you will recognize that this somewhat unusual way
of defining 'effective treatment' is, *so far*, really not more than
a change of *expression*. It might, in itself, mean just a change
of semantics as if I were to replace the statement 'drivers
should stop at red lights' by the statement 'drivers should be
persons who stop at red lights.' Therefore, your bewilderment,
your raised eyebrows and shrugged shoulders should rightfully
clamor for an explanation *why* do I make this switch in
semantics?

"Ladies and gentlemen, if my change in semantics did not
allow me to indicate something which I could not express without this change, I certainly would not have suggested it! I am
now undertaking to show you that, unlike the 'red light' example, where both modes of expression boil down to one and the
same statement, my definition of the essence of effective treatment can only be given in terms of the therapist's personality,
and *not* in terms of what he does in the treatment sessions.

"If the driver stops at the red light, he does the right thing
with reference to what is desirable for traffic safety no matter
whether he stops just because he sees other drivers stop and
feels an urge to conform, or because he is afraid of getting
a ticket, or because he wants to protect himself and others
against accidents. In short, his motivation does not matter
when our concern is purely with traffic safety—as long as he
acts according to the law. It is decisively different with the
value of a therapist's behavior in treatment as a measure of

helpfulness to the patient. This value is *not* independent of the therapist's inner motivation.

"One could say that whatever influences the patient during the treatment hour must come to him through his own perception, subliminal perception included. Therefore, any aspect of the therapist's inner attitude that influences the patient, in one way or another, must have found some physical expression in the therapist's talk or non-verbal behavior. It must have appeared in the therapist's words, intonation, pitch or rhythm of voice, gesture or posture, raising of an eyebrow, or curving of the mouth. So, in order to define what influences the patient favorably or therapeutically, we theoretically could skip whatever goes on in the therapist's mind; we theoretically can neglect his inner attitude and stick solely to its audible and visible manifestations. This reasoning, so far, is undoubtedly correct, but I think you can already see where the snag is! No expressive behavior can be described with any completeness and reliability, except by naming or describing *what* is expressed. And, this is, of course, always an inner attitude or condition of the therapist. We could never describe or formulate one single sentence as the therapeutically desirable response of the therapist to a given behavior of a given patient because no formulation can guarantee that when the therapist would make this response under the given circumstances to the given patient that it would be a therapeutically spontaneous and genuine expression of the therapist's mind."

G—, exhausted from his imagined speech, fell silent and cast a long searching glance at his imaginary audience. The upturned faces looked as bewildered and questioning as before as if they expected that he would now give the solution to the vexing riddle and show that his shocking formulations, properly understood, meant actually the same as what already could be read in their text books.

"I can't blame them," G— thought with reference to the audience of his imagination. "If I had not already experienced for a year or two, what I know now to be in accordance with my present formulations, a speech like the one I delivered in phantasy would not have convinced me a bit! It is so very difficult to form a concrete picture of what it looks like 'not to withdraw psychologically,' unless one has experienced his own involuntary withdrawal, has become aware of it, has struggled with it, and has become desperate about it. When, at some time or other, for God knows what reasons, one has managed not to withdraw but to stick *with* the patient, and has in this way experienced how it feels to talk 'straight' with him, without being haunted by the obsession that one has to do the 'right' thing—well, one might stumble again later, but, at least, one has an image of what therapeutic communication could be."

FROM WHERE DOES THERAPY DERIVE ITS "MAGIC POWER"?

Several months had passed since G— had delivered his imaginary lecture to his phantasy audience, months in which his daily work with patients had absorbed most of his energies. During this time he was content to take in whatever experience offered and, when his office hours were over, turned happily to other occupations.

He did not deliver any actual speeches nor did he look for an audience. When, occasionally, he looked back at his "airborne" thoughts, he felt as if the tunnel through which he was wandering for years had been shattered by an explosion and light was filtering irregularly through the cracks and openings. He was certain that he would slowly emerge from the semi-darkness, gain a full view of the landscape and find his direction. Yet, the debris of the smashed rocks was still obstructing his vision and much ordering and clearing up would be necessary to bring the isolated landmarks which were already visible into one coherent picture.

Then, one Sunday when he was lying in a small sailing boat on one of the beautiful lakes surrounding his city, his thoughts returned ruefully to the general questions of therapy which now had taken on a more peaceful appearance.

Especially one aspect of his present concept of psychotherapy which made it appear so different from his former concepts came vividly to his mind—the apparent disparity between the means applied and the result one hoped to achieve.

Here was a neurotic patient whose whole life, for years and years past, had been over-shadowed by the all-pervasive effect of numberless subtle misconceptions, strange and destructive rules, peculiar unreasonable fears and expectations; his desperate efforts and good endowments had been thwarted by inhibitions and mysterious mistakes or by inexplicable physical ailments, as if his mind had been invaded by a group of evil spirits. Was it not mere common sense to expect that to exorcise them one had to apply the strongest incantation, the most cunningly devised ritual, as elaborate and foreign to the everyday life of man as the demons it was meant to attack?

In modern language, could anything resembling common human intercourse be an adequate weapon to combat the hydra of neurosis? If no machines or complicated surgical instruments and techniques should be applied; if no other tool but language should be sufficient for the task, the least one had to assume was that the language used would have to deal with new and complex concepts of a deeply hidden, laboriously unearthed anatomy of the soul. One would have to talk about subjects never thought of, let alone mentioned in ordinary interlocution. Yet, what G—was considering now as the effective and sufficient agent for therapy seemed ordinary, non-specific and simple. It contrasted sharply with the elaborate arsenal of psychoanalytic therapy.

In psychoanalysis, the curative agent, the psychological antibiotic, so to speak, which killed the poisonous neurotic germs, was insight into the pathogenesis of the individual neurosis in all its complexities. Everything else, the regular meetings with the analyst, the basic rule of "free association," the analyst's dispassionate, infinitely patient attitude, his measured interpretations, his imperturbably scientific approach, his impartiality and noninvolvement, was only the vehicle which carried the germ-killing agent to the place in the patient's mind where it would be most effective.

This was, roughly, the view transmitted to G— in his training and still prevalent in analytic literature. Freud saw himself in the first place as an explorer who had charted the hidden workings of the human mind, had uncovered the *unconscious,* had found the lawfulness of the dream and had created a psychogenetic and psychodynamic theory of human behavior, especially in its pathologic aspects. Only in the second place did Freud see himself as a therapist. Small wonder that under the sway of Freud's own evaluation, his followers put their emphasis on Freud's theoretical innovations and achievements of "insight" for which he was striving and which he had created in abundance. Comparatively little emphasis was put on the tremendous change he introduced into the therapist's approach to the patient. The new attitude he found in his own therapeutic work and instilled into his students was considered, on the one hand, as a necessary condition for exploration of the patient's mind, and, on the other hand, as a necessary condition for the successful transmission of the therapist's insight to the patient. That this change in attitude on the part of the therapist, which entailed a significant change in the relationship between the two personalities involved, could be a powerful curative agent, if not *the* curative agent in the therapy, was never put at the center of attention. It was never given full priority in comparison with the curative power attributed to insight, though traces of such a view could be found in many places in psychoanalytic literature.

As exploration of the patient's mind was the only way to get at the raw material which had to be subsumed under the concepts of Freud's theory, Freud had to spend many hours, extended over weeks, months and years in daily contact with his patients. The patient's words, complaints, recollections, phantasies and whatever else he volunteered to say, were not considered as mere samples or indicators of the destruction wrought by illness in his suffering mind, nor were they registered as so many symptoms contributing to the forming of a diagnosis.

Freud surmised, and proved, that they had a meaning— like the utterances of any healthy person—and though they appeared weird and sometimes cryptic he did not rest before he had discovered that, in some surprising way, they made sense and expressed something that was understandable and could be empathized with by the sensitive therapist.

So it occurred that in psychological reality, Freud's patients ceased to be to him mere objects of scientific curiosity, or wretched victims of mental illness who aroused compassion and the wish to help; they turned into human beings with whom he exchanged thoughts and observations. He frequently felt impressed with their intelligence, and the nobility of their character, and he found that he not only worked *on* them but rather *with* them. The very concept of Freudian therapy altered—to some extent—the time-honored hierarchical order according to which the medical care extended by the doctor to his patient created a difference in status between them. The spirit of his approach tended to diminish this status difference and almost established a relationship based on a recognition of equality.

In other words, the theoretically prescribed goal of the psychoanalytic precedure (thought of more or less as "making the unconscious conscious") required, as a technical means, that therapist and patient meet regularly over a long period of time under conditions which favored, to a certain extent, real communication between them. To what extent? Well, there were positive and negative factors. In the first place there was the fact that in view of the serious therapeutic purpose therapist and patient could discard many of the rules of conventional social behavior, which in ordinary social contact stifle free interaction. The therapist believed that what he did would be, or at least could be, of decisive help to the patient and so he felt no qualms in expressing thoughts which might upset or displease the patient; and he also would tolerate behavior on the part of the patient that the therapist would not have been able to tolerate in a social setting. Furthermore, the continuity of the meetings gave the therapist a chance of acquiring a comparatively complete vision of the patient's personality which, in many cases, enhanced a very personal and immediate interest in the patient as a person. However, the rules of psychoanalytic technique also put some limitations to the freedom and immediacy of the interchange; there was the analyst's obligation to remind the patient of the basic rule, and his concern with getting information from the patient. There was the therapist's task to use the acquired information for describing the patient's past and present behavior in analytic concepts (though not necessarily in analytic terms) and to transmit the insights he had gained to the patient.

G— knew very well that the rules of psychoanalytic therapy left a very large margin for the manner in which they were applied. Even when two analysts agreed completely with each other in the theoretical and technical principles to which they adhered and which they were teaching to their students, their actual behavior in therapy might be very different according to the differences in their personalities. And their results might be equally different. To the small extent to which it was possible for G— to compare the course and climate of analytic treatments at the one side with the results on the other, it seemed that the patient's improvement depended much more on the personality of his psychoanalyst than on the amount and so-called depth of the insight acquired.

Here, G— remembered a kind of modest criticism which he had heard again and again when he, in former times, had expressed his enthusiasm for psychoanalytic therapy. "Oh well," was the response, "if one can afford to have another person to talk with about all one's problems for hours and hours during several years, no wonder that people get better!" This type of response annoyed G— more than others which were far more derisive. He scorned the naive disrespect it expressed for the tremendous amount of careful observation and thought on which analytic therapy was based. Now, he was amazed to see that just this "silly and obstinate" reaction contained in all its naivete a kernel of truth which he had failed to recognize. The people who raised this artless objection had grasped, instinctively, just that element in psychoanalytic therapy which had appeared to G— for a long time as nothing more than a technical condition for the application of the highly sophisticated really curative agent, namely, insight. The objection now could be regarded as naive only because it did not do justice to the very strict and incisive conditions which a psychotherapist's personality had to fulfill in order for the extended interaction with his patient to become increasingly communicative—which is equivalent to cure

"So, what I now see as the helpful agent in psychotherapy," G— thought, "powerful enough to cope with the hardened structure of neurosis, is essentially the same that was helpful in other brands of therapy—wherever these other therapeutic methods have been helpful, that is, *the therapist's communicative attitude*. And, if anything is new in what I am doing, it is due to my recognition that the communicative attitude is *the* helpful agent, while other therapeutical schools see it, at best, as just one among others and not even as the most important one. And so they dilute and counteract this attitude (even if they have a natural inclination towards it) by burdening the therapy with tasks which are not compatible with it, by striving to support, encourage, direct, and counsel the patient and, above all else, to create insight.

"The apparent disparity between the impressive task of therapy, and the modest, inconspicuous means I am suggesting for fulfilling it is really *only apparent*. The postulated condition that the therapist, by dint of his personality, maintains a communicative attitude towards the patient is much more radical than the words seem to convey. If the interaction with the therapist is new and unique for the patient, it is not less new and unique for the therapist; and the more so the more he fulfills the postulated condition.

"The office looks more or less like any ordinary room with some furniture, as practicality and the taste of the therapist require. And yet, what strange and extravagant undertaking is the therapist going to execute in this commonplace setting! He is going to meet another person, without even a tacit understanding as to what will happen. He has nothing to sell and nothing to buy; he has nothing to teach and nothing to learn; he does not intend to entertain nor to be entertained. He is not geared toward creating a certain reaction in the other person; he is not playing a game with the intention to win or to lose, nor is he acting a role in order to appear in a certain way or to make a certain impression. He has no handrail, no mapped track or charted course to follow. The more of a therapist he is, the more he moves out from any of the hundreds and thousands of patterns which shape the different types of interaction between people and which form our social life in the word's broadest meaning. Such patterns are noticeable in even the most intimate relationships between close friends, lovers, spouses, relatives. As nothing in this world is absolute, the therapist's emancipation from structure in his interaction with the patient is far from absolute or complete. It seems, however, that satisfactory results of treatment can be achieved in spite of such deficiencies. Yet, the difference with regard to freedom of response between the therapist who is trained for a communicative attitude, and the one who is not, can be tremendous.

"I cannot tell what the experience of the patient is but I know what one experiences, as therapist, when one feels a bit freer to leave the rules behind and venture in—well, what could I call it?—that no-man's-land of undiluted humanity! It seemed such an adventure when I had learned in my training to discuss unconventional topics in a matter-of-fact way. But how much more adventurous it is to rely on expressiveness without aiming at an impression, whatever the topic may be!

"The powerful ingredients which convert a conversation, a discourse, an explanation, even a struggle into a therapeutic experience—and which one never can inject just when and because one wants to—is so hard to describe in the abstract without sounding banal or bombastic or both. It has the same elusiveness as the proverbial virtue of the good hostess: It is unnoticeable when it is there and becomes conspicuous only when it is absent. (Heavens, how often I have to confess to myself its absence!) I could identify it by saying, 'One has to *respect* the patient!' I can say that to myself and find it accurate because I know beforehand what I want to express. Yet, if I would say it to another therapist I do not have to wait for his response in order to know that my words had not conveyed what I wanted to convey. 'Of course,' he would say, 'I do respect my patients! What must you think of me? To respect one's patients is the most obvious requirement of common human decency. I try hard never to hurt their feelings unnecessarily. I never show contempt for their weaknesses and failures. I don't judge them nor do I scold them when they behave obstreperously. I am neither sarcastic nor ironical. I try my best always to be understanding, and when I point out their errors, their self-deceptive rationalizations and their childish, irrational behavior, I do so with tact and delicacy.' That is what *the one* type of colleague would answer.

"And, *the other* would say: 'You are a damned hypocrite. Respect my patients! Do not talk humanitarian nonsense! Well, there are patients you might be able to respect, maybe there are. But, how can you respect those wretched creatures who are afraid of everything, lick the boots of every boastful bully, are always complying, appeasing and placating no matter how much the other guy might trample on their rights, their dignity, their honor? Compassion? Yes, I wish to help all right, But, don't tell me I should respect the lazy playboy who has nothing in his mind but the number of girls he was able to lay, or the amount of vodka he could drink and still drive his car at seventy miles an hour. Or the overdressed society woman who goes to the theater and plays bridge, not because she is interested in shows or likes bridge, but only because that is what one does if one wants to belong to the right group and hopes to be invited by the right people! Be realistic and admit that the bulk of our practice consists of freaks and phonies you would not want to associate with, if it were not your job to help them become a little less freakish or a little bit less phony, or to enjoy a bit more their miserable wasteful lives!'

"So, what would I say to them? To number one, the man of *common human decency*, I would say: 'Look, you certainly are harboring the most noble intentions, you *try* hard not to sit in judgment and to be understanding. And you never hurt your patients' feelings unnecessarily. Maybe you do understand what I mean by respecting one's patients. Maybe you do respect them. Frankly, I doubt it. The word *respect* like all other words referring to inner experiences is somewhat ambiguous, and when it matters that we convey a precise meaning we have to talk about it for a while and even around it, as it were. You try to say unpleasant things *tactfully* to them. I have a high regard for tactful people. It is a wonderful gift to be tactful, and to encounter a lack of it is distressing. But listen: I remember a lecture about the technique of therapy. We all raved about this lecture. The teacher talked so freely and relaxedly, so undogmatically and with such a good sense of humor! It was a pleasure to listen to him. Well, after he had stressed the point that the therapist should not mince words; that he should not try to sugar-coat the bitter pills he had to administer, he said with a smile, that this did not mean that the therapist should not use tact and delicacy. *For instance,* he said, *when the patient is just in the process of revealing a painful secret you would not light your cigar!*

" 'When I heard this I found it very plausible and felt sure I would never light a cigar when the patient was about to reveal a painful secret! Yet, when I remember after so many years, this simple humane advice I am not as convinced as I was with regard to its validity. If you are paying attention to the patient, if you are *with* him, as I would like to say, you might not even notice whether you are lighting your cigar or not—and it does not matter! Whenever you feel the need to do something, or to refrain from doing something for the purpose of showing him your concern, you can be certain that your concern is lacking.'

"And, as to number two, the *rugged realist,* who rejects as hopelessly Utopian the idea of respecting the patient, I would say to him that he fails to distinguish between respect and appreciation.

" 'You may feel,' I would tell him, 'that the way your playboy passes his time is utterly worthless and a caricature of human existence. But as long as you recognize him as a human being and, therefore, his potentiality for breaking out of the vicious circle in which he is lost, you will respect him. Look, this playboy, or whatever scoundrel you might find in front of you in your office, may act as if he were entirely at ease with his misdeeds, his shallowness and inane undertakings. But you will notice, sooner or later, that his personality is not the monolithic block of inhumanity which he tries to make it appear. Even if he comes to you under the threat of the probation officer who has left him only the choice between treatment or jail, you will discover a human response when you approach him as a human being—even if it were only the response that he now prefers the jail.' "

G— noticed that a breeze had sprung up as he got hold of sheet and tiller. When he finally had the boat on course he remembered with a smile his imaginary speeches. "I would probably convince neither the one nor the other. Some things are so simple that one cannot express them in just a few sentences. Even a whole book might not be enough. One has to live in order to know what life looks like." He did not feel dismayed by this prospect.

Emergency*

SEVEN DIALOGUES REFLECTING THE ESSENCE OF PSYCHOTHERAPY IN AN EXTREME ADVENTURE

Prologue

Just as the normal function of an organ or an organism is frequently illuminated by pathologic events, so the views of a therapist on the essential nature of his daily work may become unusually lucid when they are applied to an extreme and unusual case which is theoretically possible but has never occurred in real life.

The following seven dialogues sketch such an unusual case. The views of the therapist in the story are my views. They are not easy to present or to transmit, not because they imply a complicated theory, but because they are simple where one expects the elaborate. When they are expressed in abstract terms, as a textbook would do, the reader is likely to miss their meaning, as if he had to decipher a melody from the grooves of a gramophone disk.

The sequence of scenes contains, in condensation, interaction between the therapist and his patient. However, I do not intend to prove, but only to show.

Scene 1

Dr. Terwin's office. Dr. Terwin is in the process of clearing his desk, as he usually does before leaving for the day. He picks up a letter and gets caught up in reading it through.

* Copyright © 1962 by the William Alanson White Psychiatric Foundation, Inc. Reprinted from *Psychiatry*, 25, 1962, 97–118.

SECRETARY: Dr. Terwin—Dr. Terwin!

DR. TERWIN [*his eyes still on the letter*]: Yes, Linda?

SECRETARY: You didn't forget that you still have to see a patient?

DR. TERWIN: A patient?

SECRETARY: You know—the lady who phoned this afternoon, Mrs. Estella Porfiri.

DR. TERWIN [*hardly remembering*]: Oh yes, something urgent, didn't you say?

SECRETARY: Right, Doctor, she made it sound very urgent indeed!

DR. TERWIN [*good-naturedly*]: You never know; it might be a real emergency.

SECRETARY: Anyway, she seemed dead set on seeing you today, no matter what. But I can tell you now: When she complains about lack of will power, general apathy, and no interest in life—don't believe a word of it!

DR. TERWIN: Who knows?

SECRETARY: I know! May I leave? Or—

DR. TERWIN: By all means! Enjoy yourself!

SECRETARY: Thank you. Good-bye, Dr. Terwin!

DR. TERWIN [*after another look at the letter*]: O.K. [*He opens the door to the waiting room.*] Mrs. Porfiri, I assume?

MRS. PORFIRI [*entering*]: How do you do, Dr. Terwin!

DR. TERWIN: How do you do! Will you sit down here, Mrs. Porfiri?

[*Mrs. Porfiri sits down and looks attentively at Dr. Terwin, who takes a chair facing her. She seems surprised by his appearance.*]

MRS. PORFIRI: You look so different from what I had expected!

DR. TERWIN [*with a little smile*]: Maybe you came to the wrong person. I am *Simon F.* Terwin.

MRS. PORFIRI: No, no! Dr. Simon F. Terwin. There is no other Dr. Terwin in the whole city. You know Dr. Redstone, do you?

DR. TERWIN: Dr. Oliver Redstone? He was one of my teachers.

MRS. PORFIRI: I know! [*She lapses into a thoughtful silence.*]

DR. TERWIN: I understood you were in a kind of emergency?

MRS. PORFIRI: Because I insisted on seeing you as soon as possible? I have been in fear for a long time—especially in the last four months. And I did not know what to do. And then, suddenly, I learned that you were in the city—that you have been in this very city for something like a quarter of a year. [*With a faint smile*] So I felt I should not lose any more time!

DR. TERWIN: I am not sure that I understand you fully. Do you mean to say that Dr. Redstone referred you to me?

MRS. PORFIRI: He did, but I should rather say he confirmed my opinion. I'll explain in a minute! [*Tensely*] May I ask you a question first?

[*Dr. Terwin looks somewhat astonished and waits.*]

MRS. PORFIRI: It is very important to me. All depends—

DR. TERWIN: Of course! What do you want to know?

MRS. PORFIRI: About half a year ago I read an article of yours —I forget the title—was it "Talking to People" in the *Clinical Psychologist?*

DR. TERWIN: That's right.

MRS. PORFIRI [*quickly*]: There you said something like, "In order to treat a person, nothing more is required than that the therapist meets this person regularly for a sufficient time in his office. There are no rules for the patient. He need not talk about any specific topics or talk at all." I want to know whether you mean this literally. [*She looks at Dr. Terwin in great suspense.*]

DR. TERWIN [*smiling*]: The answer is yes.

MRS. PORFIRI [*repeating his word*]: Yes. Good—that's very important. [*She seems to rest from the effort of settling this question and to ponder about the next step.*] You—you don't think that it matters where the doctor sees the patient?

DR. TERWIN: I don't know what you have in mind. I would not want to see a patient in—let's say, a restaurant.

MRS. PORFIRI: Of course, of course! That's not what I meant. There is really no point in trying—

DR. TERWIN: Trying what?

MRS. PORFIRI [*impatiently*]: Oh, my God, to trap you! Can't you see? To get you to commit yourself by answering my general questions, so that you cannot back out when I beg your help in my special case! But it won't work! If you are a coward, you will back out anyway!

DR. TERWIN: That might be. But I can neither back out nor accede to your request as long as I am completely in the dark as to what it is you are asking for.

MRS. PORFIRI [*proudly*]: I am not going to ask for a favor. I'll tell you what my fears are and you will either help or refuse to do so! You know who I am?

DR. TERWIN: I understood, Mrs. Estella Porfiri!

MRS. PORFIRI [*waving her hand impatiently*]: I mean, do you know my husband?

DR. TERWIN: You expect me to know him? Don't forget that it's been only three months since I moved to this city!

MRS. PORFIRI: Good, very good! I thought you might have heard the name: Dr. Emilio Porfiri, psychiatrist.

DR. TERWIN: I am sorry. The name sounds only vaguely familiar to me. I would not have known that he is a psychiatrist and lives in this city, if you had not said so.

MRS. PORFIRI: He is not very well known. He is 36, in private practice, and he hasn't published anything—oh, in the last five or six years. We have been married almost eight years. It may sound strange to you when I say that it has only been during the last two or, perhaps, three years that I have come to understand how unhappy Emilio really is. Or maybe it is not my better understanding—it might also be that in the beginning of our marriage he was not so unhappy or disturbed as he became later. I know that during the last four months a change for the worse has taken place.

DR. TERWIN: You would say that your husband is severely depressed?

MRS. PORFIRI: Oh, God yes! Severely depressed! I don't mean that he goes around groaning and moaning; but there is no sparkle in his eye any more. He doesn't complain—or only very rarely. Seeing him from afar you wouldn't notice much. He is well controlled, has always been. He goes to his office, sees his patients, goes to meetings, and even gives speeches occasionally. But it is as if he were far away in his mind, only going through the motions of life.

DR. TERWIN: And you say all this has become more pronounced in the last—I think, four months you said?

MRS. PORFIRI: Yes—as far as I can tell; it began gradually, yet—

DR. TERWIN: Yet?

MRS. PORFIRI: I wanted to say that in the last four months he has become very restless, which he had not been before at all. You know, he used to design furniture; he was quite good at it. When we needed something he did the design. He liked to work it out carefully, and it always took him a long time to do it exactly the way he wanted to. Yet he always finished what he had started. Now he seems unable to stick with anything which is not absolutely necessary.

DR. TERWIN: When you say that there was a deterioration in the last four months, are you only making an estimate of the time, or can you think of an event which occurred four months ago?

MRS. PORFIRI: The latter, Dr. Terwin. There was an event which caused Emilio great concern and distress. And I don't doubt that it contributed in some way to the deterioration. Only, as you will see, it cannot be the clue to everything!

DR. TERWIN: You seem hesitant to describe this event.

MRS. PORFIRI [*thoughtfully*]: I *am* hesitant. It's silly, I know! I feel that this incident will bias you against Emilio, but, as you will see, there was really nothing he could have done to prevent it. It was simply hard luck. This is what happened: Emilio had a patient, a Mr. Dorand, whom he had seen for approximately two years. An addict! Four months ago, the patient, who had improved and seemed decidedly on the way up, had to interrupt treatment for two weeks. Some family problem. When he came back, a few days later than anticipated, he called my husband, as we learned from the answering service which had picked up the call. We got the message late on a Sunday afternoon. My husband called the patient's number several times, but there was no answer. He tried again in the evening; again no answer. The same happened Monday morning. But as soon as Emilio had left for the office, Mr. Dorand called. I told him that Dr. Porfiri had tried to reach him, and that Mr. Dorand should call him at his office in fifteen minutes. The patient remained silent a few seconds, but I could hear him clear his throat. Then the line went dead. I called his apartment, but there was no answer. Apparently he had called from somewhere else, and he never got back home. Somebody found his dead body Monday night in a little motel. Suicide! I have told all the details to show that, as far as I can see, Emilio had done all that could be done under the circumstances. It seemed natural that Emilio was terribly upset when he learned about the suicide. He canceled some of his hours; he went to the police, to the coroner, and to the morgue. He got in touch with the relatives. And for a week or so this unhappy event kept him occupied. I have asked myself, of course, and have asked Emilio more than once, whether his worrying on Sunday evening was completely accidental or whether he had any reason to suspect that something had gone wrong with the patient. "No reason," he said, "not the slightest bit of a reason. But, look, in spite of the lack of any reason I *was* worried, and you know I was. I must have made a mistake and must have known it without knowing when or how."

DR. TERWIN: What followed?

MRS. PORFIRI: Well, to the best of my recollection, Emilio recovered from the shock, I would say, within a week or two. But then—I cannot tell how it started. There must have been a slow transition or—well, I don't know. But he must have slid into his present behavior, this—what should I call it: aloofness, restlessness, silent despair—oh, it is uncanny!

DR. TERWIN: It frightens you?

MRS. PORFIRI: It does! Oh, my God, it does!

DR. TERWIN: I understand your husband is working as before the—the accident?

MRS. PORFIRI: I think so. He keeps his hours, sees his patients. However, during these four months or so he has lost some other patients—not in the same way, of course, but two or three quit prematurely, as I understood. Emilio has mentioned that occasionally, but not as he would have done before—in former times, I mean. It used to concern him a good deal if a patient left without too good a reason, but now he doesn't seem to care. No, that's not right! He does care, but something has changed in him. I think sometimes that he takes the other side, Mr. Dorand's side—he used this expression once, in a different context, but it sticks in my mind.

DR. TERWIN: I see—

MRS. PORFIRI: Dr. Terwin, can you say anything? Can you help?

DR. TERWIN: Possibly! I would certainly be glad to talk to your husband. Isn't that what you have in mind?

MRS. PORFIRI: [*after sighing and then remaining silent for a few seconds*]: I had it in mind. Of course, I had it in mind. I had it in mind a year ago, and during these last four months I've had little else in my mind. But, you know, he does not want to. Calmly and firmly, he refuses to see anybody.

DR. TERWIN: His reasons?

MRS. PORFIRI: I'm not sure that I can answer this question. He says it won't help him—something like that—but this can't be the real reason. How could he know without trying? I have asked, begged, implored him to try. But he seems unassailable.

DR. TERWIN: You know, your husband might simply need more time to make his decision. A psychiatrist has, perhaps, more serious obstacles to overcome than many who are not of the faculty.

MRS. PORFIRI [*intently*]: You tell me to wait?

DR. TERWIN: Let me ask: What is it you are so afraid of?

MRS. PORFIRI [*in a low voice*]: Suicide!

DR. TERWIN: I assume your husband moves in a circle of

psychiatrists. It would be strange if not one of his friends had noticed the change in him which you have observed?

MRS. PORFIRI: I can't tell whether anybody has noticed. Nobody has said anything to me about it—with the exception of our maid. She asked me, oh, some weeks ago: "Is Dr. Porfiri ill? He doesn't seem to feel well." Dr. Terwin—believe me—oh, *do* believe me, it *is* urgent!

DR. TERWIN: Mrs. Porfiri, you will understand that I am in no position to confirm or deny the urgency of the case. [*As he notices a look of despair on her face, he goes on.*] Do not misunderstand me! I am ready to act on the assumption that there *might* be urgency. But I have to get some idea that my action would at least not make things worse! I refuse to act simply for the sake of giving you, or myself, the feeling that action has been taken! Let me ask: What do you think would happen if you told your husband that you had asked me to come and see him? Presenting him with a *fait accompli,* as it were? [*As she makes a gesture to interrupt and even starts to say something, he raises his hands to make her listen.*] Please, don't feel you have to decide in a hurry. Such a *fait accompli* method has an advantage and also a disadvantage, and which prevails depends essentially on the patient's personality. I want you to consider as calmly as you can these two sides. Look, when you want psychiatric help for your husband, you imply that his refusal to go to see somebody is unreasonable and its motivation irrational. You follow me?

MRS. PORFIRI: Yes, but—

DR. TERWIN: All right, listen: We may then assume that what prevents him from consulting a colleague is something like shame or pride. More generally, he might consider it as wrong in some sense or other for him to admit to a colleague his worry, depression, or whatever it is. This would not exclude the possibility that he would like to have somebody help him, but his countermotivation overrides the desire. If this were so, it might help to present him with a *fait accompli.* He would not feel so keenly that he himself is asking for help, because you had taken all the initiative. He might tell himself that not to talk to me, when I had been summoned by you, would be rude. So it would not be his doing if he talked to me, but rather yours.

MRS. PORFIRI: But, Dr. Terwin—   ·

DR. TERWIN: Allow me a minute more—we are not *that* much in a hurry. I said that there is a disadvantage, too, in the *fait accompli* method. I take it that he has no close friends. You are probably the only person at the present moment he feels close to and has some confidence in. Your calling in a psychiatrist, behind his back, as it were, your putting before him a *fait accompli* and trying to force him into treatment, might impress him most of all not as a sign of your caring for him and loving him, but as a sign that you have lost confidence in him—that you, well, declare him incompetent to look out for himself and are now acting like a guardian who forces onto his helpless ward what *he*, the guardian, thinks is best.

MRS. PORFIRI: That is exactly what I am afraid will happen! That's what I wanted to say all the time. Emilio is terribly sensitive about what he calls "people with the best intentions." He would cancel the appointment or, if it were too late for that, he might even leave the house. No, that *fait accompli* method has no chance and would be very, very dangerous.

DR. TERWIN: Hm! Your estimate as to your husband's reaction might be completely correct. But I am baffled! I thought you would take the opposite view. What, then, is it that *you* suggest? I understood you wanted to make a suggestion, didn't you?

MRS. PORFIRI: I *do* want to make a suggestion. It is not by chance that I came to see *you* and no other psychiatrist. [*There is a short pause. She is highly conscious that this is the moment of decision.*] I called you the minute I learned you were here—or rather, I wired Dr. Redstone and called you as soon as I had heard from him. I have a very definite idea how you could help. You remember my question—the one I asked right at the beginning? Well, the answer you gave me confirmed what I had thought. Listen, Dr. Terwin, I can see that you can't simply take my word that there is danger. But, as you admitted—and I appreciate very much that you did—you also can't say for sure that I am in error. I know that I am going to ask something unusual from you—something, let's say, that is not usually done by a professional man. But, please, listen to me with an open mind! [*A little pause*] Let me say something more: Dr. Oliver Redstone is a friend of mine. I had talked with him earlier, over the phone. We had a long discussion. He is very old, but his mind is as sharp as ever. Well, his verdict was: "Not impossible! But who would dare to do it, and be able to do it?" Your name was mentioned. But you lived far away then. Now you will understand how I felt when I heard that you were here in this very city of ours—just now, when I need help more than ever. [*She pauses to catch her breath.*]

DR. TERWIN [*in a low, almost dreamy voice*]: Oliver Redstone!

How strange! [*Without raising his voice, but very firmly*] And your suggestion, Mrs. Porfiri?

MRS. PORFIRI: It can't matter where you see your patient. Emilio is a therapist. So you could go and see him as his patient! [*Her voice is faltering.*]

DR. TERWIN: See him as his patient, you say?

MRS. PORFIRI [*bravely*]: As his patient. You would call him and make an appointment. He has sufficient time open. You wouldn't have to use another name. I know that psychiatrists occasionally ask colleagues for their professional help. [*She smiles breathlessly.*]

DR. TERWIN [*in a controlled voice*]: But he would ask how I came to consult him, wouldn't he?

MRS. PORFIRI: I thought of that. You could mention Dr. Redstone. He doesn't know Emilio personally very well, but he thinks well of him as a psychiatrist..And anyway he would agree to your using his name. He says so in his letter!

DR. TERWIN: As you have read my article so carefully and talked to my teacher and friend, Dr. Redstone, about me, you certainly must know that it is my conviction that treatment can't accomplish anything substantial as long as the therapist keeps pretending, lying, play-acting.

MRS. PORFIRI: I thought of that! Your objections against lying and pretending in such a case are not based, I understand, on moral principles. Are they?

DR. TERWIN: Correct! They are not!

MRS. PORFIRI: But on the thought that lying and cheating would interfere with treatment?

DR. TERWIN: Indeed, they would.

MRS. PORFIRI: Now, listen, Dr. Terwin, I thought of that too. It is true you will have to tell lies in the initial interview—you will have to say or indicate that you want treatment, and probably also why you want treatment. You will have to pretend, invent, lie, and cheat. But as soon as treatment starts, once you are accepted as a patient, you have the inalienable privilege of the patient to say what you like. And it is up to you to limit yourself to truthful statements and leave unsaid the essentially conventional formalities as to whom *you* consider to be the patient and whom *you* consider to be the therapist. [*She looks at him with the courage of desperation.*]

DR. TERWIN: Mrs. Porfiri, you suggest that I, a psychiatrist, call a colleague of mine, another psychiatrist, and ask him for his professional help, ask him to take me into treatment for some real or invented troubles of mine, while, in reality, I am hired by his wife to treat him. Do you realize what that means?

MRS. PORFIRI [*proudly*]: I know what it means! It means doing the only thing which could probably save him!

DR. TERWIN [*with a faint smile*]: That is your point of view, which I certainly respect. But it is not the only possible one. I listened to you, as you asked me to, with a fairly open mind. Now I would like you to return the favor! [*He looks her straight in the face; she answers in the affirmative with a minimal nod.*]

DR. TERWIN: If everything goes well and we get over the point [*he wants to say, which I shudder to think of, but suppresses this remark and replaces it by taking a deep breath*] when I can tell your husband what it's all about, and we can continue the treatment in a more—usual way—it won't matter so much if the thing becomes known—it can be played down. My colleagues will call me a screwball, no doubt, but nothing succeeds like success. As long as neither you nor Dr. Porfiri complains, nothing much can happen. But it would be childish—or worse, it would be ludicrous, megalomaniac, idiotic, irresponsible—not to consider the possibility of failure. Let's say that after three months or so I come to the conviction that I am getting nowhere. Please realize that something like that may happen under absolutely normal conditions of treatment, while here the conditions would be extremely unfavorable. In a normal case I would not worry. I know that it frequently takes more time to tune in, to hear the patient accurately, to acquire the necessary precision of perception. Yet in this case, which would be as new to me as doing psychotherapy with the pet wife of an Arabian sheik whose prisoner I was, I wouldn't know where to look for a helpful idea. I would never know whether it was only I who was not perceptive enough, or whether it was the damned situation I was in which limited my means of expression. If I got desperate enough, I would back out. It wouldn't be too hard to make my withdrawal plausible—at least as plausible as the quitting of most patients who stop prematurely, where nobody can ever tell for sure just what made them quit. But worse might happen. We cannot exclude the possibility that Dr. Porfiri might become suspicious. And then what?

MRS. PORFIRI: Oh God! You are right. We cannot exclude every danger. But you can be sure that as long as *you* didn't confess about our agreement, and I didn't, Emilio would always respect you as a patient and would rather accuse himself of a paranoid delusion and break off the treatment than accuse you of—of—being an impostor.

I can assure you of one thing: Come hell or high water, neither I nor Dr. Redstone will admit as much as even the thought of our agreement, whoever might ask us about it.

DR. TERWIN [*murmuring*]: Crazy, crazy! So what if—your suggestion—

MRS. PORFIRI: Dr. Terwin, let me ask this: When you, for a moment, disregard the unusualness of my suggestion and the trouble it might cause you with your colleagues or your conscience, do you think it could have a chance of success?

DR. TERWIN [*looking at her thoughtfully*]: A chance of success? Heavens, what do you think I am arguing about? The answer is: Yes, a chance! [*For a whole minute the two stare at each other, sometimes frowning, sometimes smiling, obviously intent on reading the other's mind.*]

MRS. PORFIRI [*starts crying. After 20 seconds she manages to say between sobs*]: Excuse me, Dr. Terwin! I have no words any more.

DR. TERWIN [*confused and embarrassed*]: But—but—I—I did not say anything yet! You, you—don't—have to feel so—desperate.

MRS. PORFIRI [*with a faint smile through her tears*]: I don't cry out of despair. I—I am so—grateful!

DR. TERWIN: Who of us is the therapist? How could you know? Anyway, you are right. So cry if you feel like it!

MRS. PORFIRI [*somewhat recovered*]: I—I have this letter from Dr. Redstone—it might help some.

DR. TERWIN [*taking the letter without looking at it*]: Is there anybody besides Dr. Redstone to whom you have talked about your plan?

MRS. PORFIRI: Nobody!

DR. TERWIN: Good! Don't talk to anybody, no matter what happens. And don't get in touch with me as long as the experiment lasts. No need to complicate matters. Should I find it necessary to back out, I'll let you know. Do you think you can agree to that?

MRS. PORFIRI: I agree. About the fee—will you read the letter first?

DR. TERWIN [*reads mumbling to himself for a while, then aloud*]: "I declare that if Dr. Terwin should decide to undertake it, he has my full approval. I ask him in this case to send his statements for the time he will spend and the money he pays as fee to Dr. Porfiri to me. I'll take full financial responsibility for the whole treatment." So that takes care of that. Do you have any more questions?

Mrs. Porfiri: No, I can't think of any. You know how grateful
I am!

Dr. Terwin: That's all right. Let's see what happens. I'll call
your husband tomorrow. [*Both get up.*] Good luck, Mrs. Porfiri!

Mrs. Porfiri: I feel hopeful!

Scene 2

*Dr. Terwin's office. He is dictating a letter to his secretary,
Linda.*

Dr. Terwin: "Dear Oliver: This is not the usual thank-you-for-
the-referral note with the additional information that I have seen
the patient and treatment has been arranged. You will know very
well, dear Oliver, that things are somewhat different. My feelings
are different, my expectations are different—so this letter will be
different, too. It is more like a letter one writes before boarding a
ship for an adventurous exploration of the unknown—a farewell
letter. Big words! They may seem out of proportion to the unspec-
tacular occasion. What, after all, is the big issue? An attempt at
therapy under unusual circumstances? But every patient is unusual.
There is always the risk, there is always a lot of unknown factors.
Maybe it is the starting with a lie? Yet I shouldn't be too impressed
by this bit of initial play-acting. I guess it is rather the challenge
which goes with your expression of confidence! I have made an
appointment with Porfiri for this afternoon, an hour from now.
I liked his voice. I didn't find it difficult to talk to him—at least
over the phone. But I still cannot imagine how it will go. I have a
few sketchy ideas of what I am going to say. But I know that no
preparation at all would be just as good—or better! Mrs. Porfiri
referred to the inalienable privilege of the patient to say what he
pleases. She is right; for a long time there will be no danger of
arousing suspicion. The danger is rather of behaving too much like
a patient. If for one reason or another the plan has to be abandoned
or changed, I'll let you know! Wish me luck and thanks a lot!
Yours. . . ." I would like to sign this letter before I leave and have
it mailed before I come back.

Linda: O.K.

Dr. Terwin: I don't want to be tempted to add something after
I meet Dr. Porfiri.

Linda: I see. You'll have it in a minute!

Scene 3

Dr. Porfiri's office. Dr. Porfiri is sitting at his desk and talking into the telephone.

DR. PORFIRI: Sorry, I have to stop. I'm just about to see a new patient and I'm already late. 'Bye, Bob! [*He puts the receiver down, slumps somewhat in his chair, and sighs. Then he looks at his desk, begins straightening out the things on its surface, interrupts himself, gets up, and wanders about the room, like someone who is trying to bring about order, but is not attentive to what he is doing. Finally he pulls himself together and goes over to the door of the waiting room and opens it.*] Dr. Terwin?

DR. TERWIN [*entering*]: How do you do, Dr. Porfiri? Very glad to meet you.

DR. PORFIRI: How do you do, Dr. Terwin? It is certainly—well, will you sit down? [*He steers Dr. Terwin to the chair at the side of his desk, then sits down behind the desk and takes up a pen.*]

DR. TERWIN: Thank you very much for arranging a meeting so soon after my call! [*He stops somewhat abruptly and looks toward the window.*] Very nice view!

DR. PORFIRI: Thank you, quite pleasant! Did I understand correctly—you wanted to consult me?

DR. TERWIN: Yes! Yes, I mean I would like to ask for your professional help—for myself!

DR. PORFIRI [*frowning*]: May I ask what made you pick me?

DR. TERWIN: I am new here, as you probably know. I relied on the recommendation of an old teacher of mine. [*Dr. Porfiri looks questioningly at him.*] Dr. Oliver Redstone. He was your teacher, too, I understood, though this must have been some years before my time.

DR. PORFIRI: 1937 to '39.

DR. TERWIN: Well, I met him for the first time in—I think '42. [*Pause*] I have been in treatment once, during my training. I thought then that I did it in the first place for learning purposes. I now see it differently. Anyway, I thought I should be used to it by now, but I find myself quite uncomfortable when it comes to discussing my troubles. Mind if I smoke? [*Before Dr. Porfiri can answer, Dr. Terwin pulls out a package of cigarettes and lights one. Then he offers Dr. Porfiri the package.*]

DR. PORFIRI: No, thanks! When did you start this treatment?

DR. TERWIN: During my residency—I think in '43.

Dr. Porfiri: And how long did it last?

Dr. Terwin: Close to three years, I guess.

Dr. Porfiri: Why was it terminated?

Dr. Terwin: Let's say mutual agreement. There were some improvements.

Dr. Porfiri: Improvements? In what?

Dr. Terwin: In what? A good question, Dr. Porfiri. I suppose in my symptoms. I—I had felt all kinds of anxieties, and after three years I felt them less, or less frequently, or I felt more ashamed to mention them. You see, I was then an advanced patient and a budding psychiatrist and—and felt under a kind of obligation to respond to treatment properly—that is, with improvement.

Dr. Porfiri: I see! And now?

Dr. Terwin [*more seriously*]: Now? Now I feel less obligated, or I have lost my power of imagination, my talent for self-deception. In a word, it doesn't work any more! [*Pause*] You probably are going to ask me what my symptoms are at the present time. You know, I often wonder to what degree the symptoms we hear so much about in our initial interviews are really the things our patients are bothered with most. In a way, I feel tempted to enumerate a whole lot of complaints, just because they have names. It is easy to say: I am suffering from insomnia of medium severity. Or to say: When I have to meet new people, I try to delay it, I feel an aversion to talking to them. I have to force myself into a conversation and usually fall silent after a short while. I don't work as persistently as I would like and frequently I waste time. Or, I am irritable with my wife and my children. And so on and so forth. All that would be true. All these things bother me—occasionally—I could even say frequently. And yet—I wonder whether these and, maybe, a dozen similar complaints have made me come and look for help. [*He pauses and looks at Dr. Porfiri in a kind of impersonal evaluation, and then his glance goes toward the window and his face takes on an expression of absent-mindedness.*]

Dr. Porfiri [*after having waited for a minute or so*]: What, then, made you come?

Dr. Terwin: What made me come? Perhaps the fact that two obsessional thoughts creep into my mind every so often. Sometimes they both appear together. The one runs: ". . . and so it will go on forever and ever! How awful!" And the other goes: "Somewhere, at some moment, it will stop and it will be as if there never was anything, as if nothing ever had happened." And that is just as terrible!

DR. PORFIRI: Would you say that these thoughts are—at least sometimes—concomitant with experiences of depersonalization?

DR. TERWIN: I think you understand what I mean. "Concomitant with experiences of depersonalization," very good! I would venture to say that these thoughts or feelings *are* experiences of depersonalization.

DR. PORFIRI: Hm, I see. Can you say anything as to the time when these obsessive thoughts, to use your expression, first appeared or reappeared—or, maybe I should say, when they became so obnoxious that you started to think of—of consulting somebody?

DR. TERWIN: A year before we moved here we lost a child, my oldest daughter. She was 12 and died of a congenital heart disease. The long-drawn-out alternation of hope and despair which preceded the final event was hard on all of us and left my wife, after all was over, in a state of depression or exhaustion which was very disquieting. So, after four or five months had gone by without any noticeable change, I thought that it might help to change our surroundings. It took some time to make the decision and another six months before we actually moved. Well, as far as I can see, it really helped. From the moment the decision was made and the preparations started, there was a marked change for the better. Well, to answer your question: During the time when the decision to move had been made, but the move itself had not taken place, it occurred to me for the first time that it might be sensible for me to go into therapy again.

DR. PORFIRI: Can you say that at the time you thought of returning into therapy your wife's condition had already improved?

DR. TERWIN: I am not too sure, but it could be.

DR. PORFIRI: The illness and death of your oldest daughter must have been a highly traumatic experience, not only for your wife, but also for yourself. And yet you seem in no way to connect your symptomatology with these tragic events.

DR. TERWIN [*after a short pause*]: I do not feel any connection.

DR. PORFIRI: That's what I assume. But isn't it astonishing that you did not even *think* of a connection?

DR. TERWIN: There aren't so many things left which I can find truly astonishing!

DR. PORFIRI: You told me that your wife felt better after the decision to move, and I take it that she has improved even more since the move, but you—you seem to feel worse here than in the other city, don't you?

DR. TERWIN: I have no way to tell, except that here I am

arranging for treatment while there I managed without. But that doesn't prove anything. [*Pause*] By the way, when could you take me? Once I made this decision— [*He finishes the sentence by a silent gesture.*]

DR. PORFIRI: Well, as a matter of fact—I have hours open; you could start any time.

DR. TERWIN: Very good! If it's O.K. with you I'll come twice a week. As to the hours, the later in the day the better.

DR. PORFIRI: How about Monday and Friday at 7 P.M.?

DR. TERWIN: Friday is fine; could we make it Tuesday instead of Monday?

DR. PORFIRI: I guess that will be possible. I'll find out before our next meeting.

DR. TERWIN: Oh—well—what is your fee?

DR. PORFIRI: Twenty dollars the hour.

DR. TERWIN: All right; so I'll see you—

DR. PORFIRI: There is plenty of time left. I am free until six. If you want to start right now?

DR. TERWIN [*after a short hesitation*]: All right.

DR. PORFIRI: Let's sit over there! [*They move to other chairs.*]

DR. TERWIN: It sounds ridiculous, but I feel as if I had really done something—spectacular!

DR. PORFIRI: Well, you made a decision.

DR. TERWIN: No, my mind was made up before I came that I would give it a try anyway. [*Pause*]

DR. PORFIRI: I know so little about you yet. Won't you tell me something about your background, your upbringing, and so on?

DR. TERWIN [*a bit sadly*]: Come down to business? So that work can start? Is that what you mean?

DR. PORFIRI [*with friendly reproach*]: Of course; you know as well as I that I need a lot of information!

DR. TERWIN: Be it as you wish! I am forty-two now. Of my parents I remember only my father. My mother died when I was two years old. I have a picture of her in my mind, but when I describe it to my sister she says it's all wrong. As she is eight years my senior she must be right, and I must have confused our mother with some other female. . . .

Scene 4

Dr. Terwin's office. Linda is sorting some papers.
DR. TERWIN [*entering from the hall*]: Hello, Linda!

LINDA: Hello, Dr. Terwin! Back already? Cured?

DR. TERWIN: Almost, almost, Linda—of my megalomania. What I let myself in for! Likeable person, Dr. Porfiri, very likeable. But I feel lost. You can't make a plan. I mean, I made a plan; but I couldn't stick to it. At the end I felt very exhausted. Not that it had been difficult to talk, on the contrary! I would never have thought before that it could be that attractive to the patient! This inalienable right to say what one pleases!

LINDA: What, then, was so exhausting? Did you have difficulty in sounding convincing?

DR. TERWIN: As a matter of fact, I was not concerned with sounding convincing. The thought never entered my mind. It rather took an effort to keep alert to the purpose of my visit.

LINDA: You know, you sound quite excited!

DR. TERWIN: It is exciting and—confusing; and very different from what I expected.

LINDA: Did the lying bother you much?

DR. TERWIN: I am ashamed to admit that no, it didn't; certainly not much. Once or twice, when I had to invent a bit in answering a direct question, I felt some pangs. But otherwise—no! I must be more used to it than I thought. But, then, there weren't so many lies required. Since the other guy assumes that you are coming for treatment, every little idea which goes beyond "Hello" and "How are you?" will appear to him as a symptom. When I come to think of it—I was more truthful in this one hour than any member of the faculty ever is in any staff conference, myself included. You know: The patient's inalienable right. It includes—strange as it may sound—the right to say the truth.

LINDA: I knew it! It musn't be bad at all to be a patient! What would you think of extending this right to other people too—let's say, to secretaries?

DR. TERWIN: God forbid! What a subversive idea!

Scene 5

Dr. Porfiri's office. Dr. Porfiri is talking through the half-open door to a patient who is just leaving.

DR. PORFIRI: We'll talk about that day after tomorrow—at 10 A.M. Good-bye!

WOMAN'S VOICE: Tell me only one thing: You really think that I wanted to hurt him?

DR. PORFIRI [*against his will*]: I can't know what you wanted. *I* did not say that you wanted to hurt him—only *you* said so!

WOMAN'S VOICE: But Dr. Porfiri, you know very well that I can't really know. *You* have to tell me!

DR. PORFIRI [*pained and without a smile*]: But not before day after tomorrow at 10 A.M. Good-bye!

WOMAN'S VOICE: You are cruel! [*The door is slammed shut.*]

[*Dr. Porfiri almost falls into his chair, drops his arms lifelessly, and lowers his head until his chin touches his chest. He murmurs:* In a way she is right—she is damned right! *He sits motionless, staring at the floor. There is a knock at the stoor. Startled, he jumps up and for a moment faces the door, uncertain what to do. Another knock makes him unlock the door carefully and open it a bit. He says:* Oh, it's you! Come in, quick! [*Mrs. Porfiri enters.*]

DR. PORFIRI: I am sorry. I have hardly any time. What is it?

MRS. PORFIRI: Hi Emilio! I was just at Cynthia's. Her husband, Phil, came home early and we thought it would be nice if the four of us could eat out together. So I ran over to ask you—I thought you had this hour free—would you like to come?

DR. PORFIRI: Too bad! I can't. The hour has been filled again. You're quite right, it has been free. But now it isn't.

MRS. PORFIRI: Can't you skip it?

DR. PORFIRI: No, the patient must be already here, and besides, he's a new patient and a colleague to boot.

MRS. PORFIRI: What a pity! Maybe you can cut the hour short?

DR. PORFIRI: I tell you, I'd like to! The man is a nightmare!

MRS. PORFIRI: So sick, you mean?

DR. PORFIRI: No, not sick, but he's a queer guy, with a very evasive way of talking. It's hard to understand what he's really talking about.

MRS. PORFIRI: Confused?

DR. PORFIRI: No, not confused. He is very bright and yet—sort of unpredictable, I would say. Why don't you go on with Cynthia and Phil and I'll see you later at home. [*Points toward the waiting room.*] He, too, is a student of Oliver's!

MRS. PORFIRI: Really? No, I'll be at home and have dinner with you. We can dine with the Tenners another time! All right? I'm off! [*She leaves.*]

DR. PORFIRI: O.K. [*He sighs. Then he walks slowly toward the waiting room door, looking around as if he were searching for a way out. Finally he shrugs his shoulders and opens the door.*] Hello, Dr. Terwin!

DR. TERWIN: Hello, Dr. Porfiri! [*They sit down in chairs facing each other. There is a pause, during which Dr. Terwin carefully studies him vis-à-vis.*] You look brave. I like brave people. But I don't like to be the one to provide them with an opportunity to prove their courage. [*He pauses a little, so as to give Dr. Porfiri a chance to answer.*] But, as it is, that can't be helped, can it?

DR. PORFIRI: I am not sure that I understand you. You feel irritated?

DR. TERWIN: Not irritated, Dr. Porfiri! No, not irritated! But I notice that you don't seem especially happy to see me!

DR. PORFIRI [*with a smile*]: You expect people to feel happy whenever you appear?

DR. TERWIN: Of course not! I confess I was somewhat facetious when I said that you did not seem especially happy to see me. I meant only that you had a somewhat strained expression on your face, as if—as if you had to brace yourself—you know, a long working day and now, at 7 P.M., one more patient.

DR. PORFIRI: You might be right!

DR. TERWIN: Of course, I don't expect people to be happy just to see me. But maybe it would be nice if it happened—let's say—occasionally. [*Pause*] I am tired too. It seemed a very long day to me. There were not only the patients. I had to talk at a meeting—a group of social workers—quite interesting, but it's difficult for me to see their problems clearly. So it was strenuous. When I feel tired, I tend to become philosophical. I wonder whether other people react in the same way. As long as I am alert and wide awake I enjoy the details, like to see and to listen, to observe, I might say. But when I feel fatigued, I think in generalities, *of* generalities, and everything takes on a philosophical color. It becomes confused and self-contradictory—which is so characteristic of philosophical thoughts. No, no—I don't want to say anything against philosophy! We cannot skip over confusion. It seems an important ingredient of our thinking and its development. What is clear from the beginning isn't worth much.

DR. PORFIRI: If your theory is correct, you must be very tired indeed, as you are becoming more philosophical by the minute. But I don't think that your philosophical bent is the effect of fatigue. It rather serves a purpose. It helps you evade the real issue.

DR. TERWIN: The real issue? What's that?

DR. PORFIRI [*seriously and somewhat sadly*]: I can hardly believe that you don't know what I mean. I mean, of course, the things you want help for! Your philosophical speculations about the worthlessness of statements which are perfectly clear from the beginning might be very true, but in terms of your therapy—as you know as well as I—to dwell on such thoughts is simply a waste of time.

DR. TERWIN [*after some hesitation*]: A waste of time! As a matter of fact, I *don't* know as well as you. I have my doubts there. But be that as it may! You know, I made a discovery, or should I say rediscovery? I even talked to my secretary about it. Linda is her name. She is a very sensible person—originally a social worker but —one of the exceptions. You know, I would say that it belongs to those features of her which constitute her exceptionality that she had no qualms about becoming a secretary instead of continuing to do social work. Well, my rediscovery! I say *re*discovery because I assume I must have discovered this trivial truth in my first treatment with Ingelman. Yet I can't say that I remember doing so, as this whole treatment has almost completely faded from my memory. Even the name of my therapist has only now come back— Ingelman! I am sure that if you had asked me in the previous hour who my therapist was, I would not have been able to conjure up the name. What I wanted to say is that after our previous hour, I realized what a great thing we offer our patients—*that they may say whatever they want to.* Even if we set aside the question of final results and whether we really help them or not, this opportunity to talk—to talk about what you feel like talking about—is unique. However little our patients may avail themselves of this marvelous chance, it is the most humane feature of therapy. You must think differently; or, at least, when you think of results and achievements, you feel that enjoying this unique opportunity to the fullest is a waste of time, or could possibly be a waste of time. And, as a conscientious therapist myself, somehow I have got the notion that you are a very conscientious therapist—you don't want your patient to waste time. Your brows contract a little, almost to the point of a frown. It is as if you had heard the call of duty, and, your face looking strained and somewhat sad, you dismiss humanity with a shrug and offer the warning: "You are wasting time!" [*Pause*] I admit that I respect this conscientiousness of yours—it has dignity. It certainly has. But, since it makes you look sad, it makes me feel sad too. I don't know how I would feel if you were not saddened by your submission to duty but pronounced your warning with a ringing voice and a sparkle in your eye. Maybe I would feel annoyed! Maybe I would laugh. As it is—and I can almost hear you sigh, figuratively speaking—well, here again the thought is creeping up: This will go on and on forever and ever. How awful!

DR. PORFIRI: This?

DR. TERWIN: What I mean by "this"? I'll tell you. Look how many things we have in common. We are approximately the same age and of a very similar background. We have gotten our training, partially at least, in the same place with the same teacher. We are both psychiatrists in private practice, doing psychotherapy essentially and by choice. As I did not know you before I made our first appointment, I would not have come without Oliver Redstone's mediation. But I would not have arranged for further visits, after our first interview, if I had not felt—well, that I could talk to you. Well, all these conditions making for ready mutual understanding being fulfilled in our case, all comes to naught because of the preoccupation with purpose, with rules and regulations, with wasting time and good use of time, with theory and psychological concepts —in one word, with duty!

DR. PORFIRI [*after a pause of a minute*]: You sound so—well, should I say enthusiastic—almost passionate. And yet, would you ever say such things to a patient of yours?

DR. TERWIN: Do you want me to talk to you as if you were my patient?

DR. PORFIRI: Of course not! But you can't have one truth for your patients and another one for yourself!

DR. TERWIN: True, very true—and I don't!

DR. PORFIRI: You know, it seems that you have an aversion to seeing yourself in the role of a patient.

DR. TERWIN: That's very true. I have an aversion to seeing myself in any kind of role. That is essentially what I said before, though in different words. [*There is a pause of more than a minute, and then he continues in a low voice.*] I even find it unsatisfactory to see others acting a role.

DR. PORFIRI: I am not sure that I understand you.

DR. TERWIN: Perhaps you understand but don't like to think you do?

DR. PORFIRI [*after a moment's hesitation*]: I think that is correct. I, somehow, feel that you are critical of me, but I can't put my finger on it. When I listen to you, there are moments when I feel I understand what you mean and, in a way, could agree. But then, a few seconds later, I have lost you, and I get confused.

DR. TERWIN [*after 30 seconds*]: You see, Dr. Porfiri, I feel much better now. It is, of course, not a law of nature, or of logic or anything like that. There certainly are exceptions, but by and large I think it *is* true that if things are clear from the beginning, the exchange is not worth while. Only the transition from misunderstanding and confusion to—maybe only a faint sense of approaching a vague notion of something which was possibly meant. Well, it is completely empirical, but I have come to distrust a conversation where everything is lucid and transparent and one says, "Yes, indeed," or "No, under no conditions." Well, as I said, there are probably exceptions. I am not impatient. I don't have to have everything at once. And I don't expect others to expect that either. Isn't that what our job consists of most of the time, and especially where it is not in vain? Well, we use up a lot of time—we deal with months and years. We are very generous in this respect. And it would not make sense to be impatient. I often think that time has a different significance or, maybe, a different texture, in our job from that it has in many others. Though we are paid by the hour, our achievements do not consist of just surviving or staying awake for a certain number of minutes, as it is with the night watchman. Nor do we work like the pieceworker, who wants to cram into a given time as many holes drilled or springs soldered or bolts riveted as possible. One could say that we are not fighting time, neither urging it on to pass quicker, nor trying to slow it down and make it hold more. If everything goes well—whatever that means—we are at peace with time.

DR. PORFIRI [*with some irritation in his voice*]: You say "we"!

DR. TERWIN: Well, I assume that others might see it the same way I do.

DR. PORFIRI [*with a wry expression on his face*]: Or *should* see it the same way you do? Isn't that what you want to say?

DR. TERWIN [*calmly*]: Of course, I really meant to say something about the nature of our job that—more or less—everybody must notice.

DR. PORFIRI: And if they don't—

DR. TERWIN: Oh, you disagree?

DR. PORFIRI: I did not say that!

DR. TERWIN: But you mean just that! [*Dr. Porfiri keeps silent, although it takes some effort. After more than a minute Dr. Terwin continues.*] So why shouldn't you disagree? Heavens, it wouldn't be the first time that two therapists disagree in how they view their work! I can't see anything bad about that. Do you?

DR. PORFIRI [*with noticeable irritation, although he tries to keep calm*]: It seems to me you constantly manage to ignore the fact that you come to me for treatment as a patient and not for a social visit as a colleague!

DR. TERWIN: And you feel that that is wrong. Well, there you may be right. And yet—I get confused. I may see things in the wrong perspective. But don't you expect that something must be wrong with a man who comes to see you for treatment? If he were not inclined to see himself or the other guy in a somewhat distorted way, what would be there for you to treat?

DR. PORFIRI: Aren't you playing with words?

DR. TERWIN: Good—that you say that! I guess I am. I know that I am tempted to do that very, very frequently. But when I do it, I don't recognize, or don't *always* recognize, that I am doing it. And sometimes—you see—sometimes I feel—Oh, my God, how can I say it and make myself understood? I feel that I am playing with words and at the same time—or by this very thing—but how could you possibly understand me? Well, perhaps I can say it this way: Sometimes—oh, not always, but sometimes—I can't find any better expression for what I want to say than just to play with words. It is like a curse! You'll probably call it an obsession! It *is* an obsession. It makes me sad or even desperate—I mean, trying to find the right words and not finding them, and playing with words instead. I get my thoughts entangled in sentences—and they are all in knots. It's like having a long wet fishing line which is all muddled up. You can't leave it alone, but the more you try to straighten it out, the more it gets entangled. So I can't leave it alone, can't stop talking and allow things to settle themselves. I have to talk on and add words, and more and more and more words, and it goes on and on and looks like an aimless playing and leads to nothing—most of the time. And there again I have the feeling: This will go on and on forever and ever. How awful!

DR. PORFIRI: Well, I think we better stop here. The time is not quite up—but I am tired, I must say—it would not—

DR. TERWIN: Oh, that is all right! We don't have to be pedantic. I am tired myself. I'll see you—?

DR. PORFIRI: Tuesday—same hour.

DR. TERWIN: Good-bye!

DR. PORFIRI: Good-bye, Dr. Terwin! [*He does not look up when Dr. Terwin leaves. He appears disconcerted, brooding and agitated at the same time.*] Thank goodness! It's over—finally. [*He sits down and looks very dejected. Two minutes pass. The telephone rings.*] Hello! Oh, Estella! Yes, I will. I can do that—easily. No, nothing special—tired perhaps. Yes, indeed. I don't know what

Oliver had in mind. He didn't care to send me a note. So I don't know what he thinks about his protégé—or what he knows of him, for that matter. But I will write him. It is really a kind of imposition. Crazy! Yes, I said crazy and I mean it—very obscure—can't make him out. It is really very inconsiderate of Redstone—maybe it *is* old age! Practically no excuse—no, no—well intentioned, sure —but there is only a limited amount of good intentions one can survive—yes, I'll have to write him anyway! No, I won't forget. I'll leave soon! See you! [*He puts the receiver down with a sigh.*]

Scene 6

Dr. Terwin's office, about two weeks later. Linda is working at her desk. The telephone rings. Linda is visibly reluctant to take off the receiver, but when it rings for the fourth time she can't hold out.
LINDA: Dr. Terwin's office! No, not yet, Madam. . . . I don't know. You called earlier? It's all right, but. . . . No, no. . . . Perhaps you can try later in the afternoon. Do you want to leave a message? Well, as you prefer. . . . [*Puts down the receiver.*] That's she!
[*Dr. Terwin enters. He looks tired and preoccupied.*]
DR. TERWIN: I am late, I know. I should really refuse to take part in these conferences. There's no point in it—formalities— [*Looks at her for the first time.*] Eh—what's the matter, Linda, you look so gloomy? [*As she says nothing but seems to be searching for words, he becomes alarmed.*] Has something gone wrong? What is it? Speak up! Dr. Porfiri—?
LINDA: I am afraid that something *is* wrong! Mrs. Porfiri called —I don't know how many times. She didn't give her name, but I recognized her voice. She may call again any minute.
DR. TERWIN [*frowning*]: Well, hm, that's just too bad; I can't talk to her. But, you know, she has been under stress now for a long time. Besides, I am seeing Dr. Porfiri tonight. Today is Friday, isn't it? [*Linda nods.*] O.K.—so I will see him. What more can I do? [*He sits down. The telephone rings.*]
LINDA [*agitatedly*]: If it's she, I think you should talk to her! Dr. Porfiri wants to stop! [*The telephone rings again.*]
DR. TERWIN: What's that? Answer the phone and tell her that I'm not in yet but will be in in 15 minutes.
LINDA [*desperately*]: You have a message from Dr. Redstone about Dr. Porfiri! [*The telephone rings.*]
DR. TERWIN [*firmly*]: Take it and tell her what I told you to!

LINDA [*into the phone*]: Hello, Dr. Terwin's office! Beg pardon? Whom did you say? No, you've got the wrong number! We are *not* the dry cleaners!

DR. TERWIN: Heaven knows what we are! What was that about Dr. Porfiri's stopping? Did he cancel tonight's hour?

LINDA: I should have told you first! [*She is trying to control her voice.*]

DR. TERWIN [*his hands on his forehead*]: My God, already! It would have been the seventh hour—three weeks! When did he call?

LINDA: He didn't! You got me wrong. There was a message from Dr. Redstone—

DR. TERWIN: From Dr. Redstone? [*He takes the receiver off the telephone and puts it on the table.*] I want to get this straight! Not from Dr. Porfiri but from Dr. Redstone?

LINDA: I am sorry; a night letter came this morning from Dr. Redstone. Here it is!

DR. TERWIN [*reading*]: "Decided to let you know. Disturbed letter from Emilio. Accuses me of not telling him in advance about you. Calls you evasive, unpredictable, conceited, crazy, hostile. Without transition says all his own fault. Apologizes, thanks for my damnable, misplaced confidence. Estella called me, desperate about Emilio's getting worse, talking daily about that 'new patient.' Wants to terminate. I am ready to take next plane if you think advisable. Sorry, Oliver." Hm, that's it?

LINDA [*almost in tears*]: Oh, Dr. Terwin, I knew the odds were all against you. But I had wished so much you would succeed. [*She takes the receiver to put it back on the phone.*]

DR. TERWIN: Wait, leave it on the table; let's have it nice and quiet—for a while at least! We'll do some thinking! The night letter was sent last night. Since mail reaches Oliver's mountain retreat only once a day, at 10 in the morning, Emilio's letter must have gotten there yesterday—Thursday morning. An airmail letter takes three full days to get from here to Oliver's wilderness, so Emilio's disturbed message can't have been mailed any later than Monday morning. That fits nicely with the mood of the letter. This type of confused message one may write late at night after a miserable week end.

LINDA: But what's your point?

DR. TERWIN: Now look! I saw Dr. Porfiri in my Tuesday evening hour! Well, whatever he may have felt or thought—and at times he became quite emotional—he neither looked nor acted like one who is about to withdraw! And this was two days after he wrote

the alarming letter, two days in which he had time to plan appropriate action. So he *gets* irritated and furious and *says* alarming
things to poor Mrs. Porifiri. What, really, could we expect? If what
I am doing with him is therapy at all, it must have the effect of
therapy whether he thinks of it as therapy or as a course in Espe-
ranto! And the effect of therapy is what it always is and should
be: It stirs him up, tempts him to step out of his rut; and when he
does and feels the wind blowing and in his first bewilderment and
panic tries to bury himself even deeper—well, that's what every
patient does when therapy takes. Now, with Dr. Porfiri things have
to go at a sharper pace; they simply have to.

LINDA: At a sharper pace?

DR. TERWIN: If any other patient under the influence of treatment steps out of his rut and then, frightened, runs for shelter
again, he can soften the impact of therapy for a while by blaming
the therapist and fighting him. But Dr. Porfiri can't fight his therapist because, so far as he knows, this man is his patient, with whom
he should not get involved in a fight. Here his professional self-
esteem is at stake.

LINDA [*still shaky*]: I am glad you see it that way, and I can
understand what you meant by a sharper pace. But how can you
know that this extraordinary dilemma he is in will not lead to a
disastrous explosion?

DR. TERWIN: I don't know. Or rather, I know it *must* lead to
an explosion. This situation cannot last long. The question is only:
Will the little breeze of fresh air which made him unbutton his
neurotic strait jacket be sufficient to make him accept normal treatment?

LINDA: I see; but how can one take this risk?

DR. TERWIN: Only if one realizes that one would take an equal
or even worse risk by refusing to risk, if you see what I mean.

LINDA [*thoughtfully*]: I do.

DR. TERWIN: I have to leave for my hour! Put the receiver back
and send a wire to Oliver: "Don't see advisability of visit. Tonight's
appointment still uncanceled. Don't see danger increased. Love,
Simon." I'm off!

LINDA: Good luck! [*Dr. Terwin leaves.*] What a life!

Scene 7

*Dr. Porfiri's office. Dr. Terwin is sitting in the patient's chair,
while Dr. Porfiri is talking over the phone.*

Dr. Porfiri [*into the phone*]: No, I can't. I will call you back at, let's see—eight sharp. [*He puts the receiver down and addresses Dr. Terwin.*] Sorry, I interrupted you!

DR. TERWIN: Did you? I can't remember having said anything. As far as I am concerned, you could have continued on the phone for the whole hour. I wasn't sure for a while whether I would come today or not. Isn't that ridiculous? When I ask myself what makes me reluctant to come here, I find that it's stage fright. Will I know my lines? Or more precisely: How can I make you listen? And I resent the effort.

DR. PORFIRI: You have the feeling that I don't listen to you?

DR. TERWIN: That's the trouble. You don't! You are so busy trying to find something you can do for me that you have no time, or rather no attention, left to listen.

DR. PORFIRI [*fairly unperturbed*]: This impression of yours that I do not listen carefully enough to what you are saying—don't you think that this is just a reflection of your own evasiveness, a projection, to use the proper word?

DR. TERWIN [*after a glance at his opponent*]: My evasiveness?

DR. PORFIRI: You—well, sometimes you talk about yourself; yet most of the time you talk about me or what I am doing with you!

DR. TERWIN: When you are at the dentist's and you say to him, "You are hurting me!," are you talking about the dentist or are you talking about yourself? See what I mean? someone might say: "I am afraid to drive home now in the rush hour!," or "The show last night was superb!," or "It's too bad you don't listen to me!" If you are primarily impressed by the grammar, you may say that the one who confesses fear of driving talks about himself, but the one who praises the show talks about the show, and I—when I complain that frequently you don't listen to me—I am talking about you. But all three of us are saying what it is that concerns us—right now, at the moment.

DR. PORFIRI [*slightly uneasy, but forcing himself to speak in a serious, matter-of-fact tone*]: I think I see what you mean. Your little lecture on the ambiguity of language or grammar might be perfectly correct. Yet the fact remains that you prefer to give a little lecture which has nothing to do with the purpose of our sessions instead of talking about your personal problems. [*With a smile which is meant to be friendly but comes out sarcastic*] I am sure if one of your patients talked to you the way you did just now, you would describe him as an intellectualizer.

DR. TERWIN [*thoughtfully*]: The purpose of our sessions—look,

if I were talking to you, for whatever purpose, and I saw you suddenly turn white and shiver and slump in your chair, would you
expect me to continue talking about, let's say, the nomination of
Dr. X for president of our psychiatric association, or about my
insomnia, or about whatever we had planned to discuss? I would
jump up and ask, "What is the matter with you?" and, perhaps,
take your pulse; and it would be ridiculous to do otherwise—to
pursue my topic in the very moment you are fainting.

DR. PORFIRI [*with some sharpness*]: Look, Dr. Terwin, look at
your parallel! That's what you are fantasying about and wishing
for: namely, that I fall ill right here under your nose and you jump
up and take my pulse and act as the doctor and turn me into the
patient. You are fighting your role as a patient and want to reverse
the positions!

DR. TERWIN: I think you have a point there, Dr. Porfiri—although, perhaps, not exactly the point you want to make. Let me
say first that I don't think that I would feel any satisfaction if you
fainted or suffered any kind of physical accident. It would embar-
rass me terribly. I am not good at physical medicine and never was.
I would call the nearest GP and would be afraid I might have failed
to apply the proper first-aid measure. So I don't think that I wish
you to fall ill. But you perceived something which I too recognize
as true. It is—no, let me say it in this way: I am not sure that I
would notice it if you were only to change color. But I do notice it
when you are not listening to me. And it's more than just noticing
it. It jolts me and absorbs my attention. If it happens it is for me:
the business at hand, the one I want to attend to. Well, you see.
here I think you made a good point. This sensitivity—or call it
hypersensitivity if you want to—I developed in working as a
therapist, or maybe it determined my becoming a therapist.

DR. PORFIRI [*puzzled*]: This sensitivity?

DR. TERWIN: Well, the fact that it pains me if the other person
is not listening to my words but is only registering them, as it were
—that he does not talk to me but only exposes me to information,
if I may say so.

DR. PORFIRI [*incredulously*]: And that, you say, determined your
becoming a therapist?

DR. TERWIN: I feel it is the essence of my being a therapist!
Therefore, although I can't quite go along with your formulation,
I would say you made a good point when you complained that I
don't adhere to my role as a patient. As a matter of fact, I don't
know what the role of the patient is. Are there things which only

the therapist should say and other things reserved for the patient? From my viewpoint, that is not so! You are quite right when you assume that frequently the things I am saying to you I could also have said to a patient of mine, and vice versa. Well, the expression "vice versa" is not clear. What I mean is: Sometimes patients say things to me which I could have said to them or to other patients. For instance, it has happened that a patient has said to me: "You are not listening to me!"

Dr. Porfiri [*spontaneously, and regretting it later*]: And how did you react then?

Dr. Terwin [*with a light smile*]: Of course, not always in the same way, but sometimes I have seen that the patient was right. In one case, I remember, I had noticed the patient's beautiful tie and suddenly thought of a suit of mine which I needed for that very evening but had forgotten to fetch from the cleaners. So—

Dr. Porfiri [*interrupting almost against his will*]: And what do you think is preventing *me* from listening to you?

Dr. Terwin: I might say: Your preoccupation with therapy!

Dr. Porfiri: My what?

Dr. Terwin [*calmly*]: Your preoccupation with therapy. What I mean is: You are obviously under the urge to do something—oh —*therapeutic!*—no matter what you feel or how you feel. You are keeping yourself, should I say, protected, or at a distance from what I am saying, so that you can manage not to take it in, not as you would take in an ordinary telephone message or the question of your neighbor when he asks you whether your electricity has been cut off too, or something like that. I am sure, for instance, that in this very moment you are uneasy about whether you are doing right to be interested in my views on therapy, or rather, to permit yourself to act upon this interest and ask questions about them, instead of looking into the significance of my talking the way I do, interpreting it, using it as sample behavior as a psychologist uses the Rorschach responses of his subject.

Dr. Porfiri [*he jumps up from his chair, paces around his desk and, with an effort, sits down again*]: Excuse me—Why are you talking to me in this way? No, that's not what I wanted to say! Sorry! [*He makes several attempts to say something, but unsuccessfully.*]

Dr. Terwin [*seriously*]: Are you sure? I rather got the impression that that was exactly what you felt like saying, while at the same time you seemed to feel you shouldn't!

Dr. Porfiri [*passionately*]: You know damned well I shouldn't!

DR. TERWIN: Not at all! Look, Dr. Porfiri, I think—and I have no doubt you will agree with me—it is a sad truth that rarely, very, very rarely do people say what they feel like saying. Here we are, the both of us, in this office together, free for an hour to say what we think. We do not have to sell anything to each other, nor do we have to agree on by-laws or resolutions. We don't have to fight each other, beguile each other, persuade each other. We might not always grasp immediately the other's meaning, but we have the potential of doing so. Why waste this unique opportunity?

DR. PORFIRI [*he now has one of his knees drawn up, the elbow of his right arm on the knee, and his forehead resting in his right hand. His searching glance, under drawn brows, is on Dr. Terwin's face, with an expression as if he were in a dream and trying to awake*]: Whatever the merits or demerits of your reasoning, if I may call it that, it certainly has the effect of confusing me—surprisingly. No, that is not even the whole story. If you were only confusing me, it would not be so strange! There are many things so complicated, or complex, or maybe even paradoxical—one is uncertain about them, bewildered, and one needs time to get them organized. Nothing unusual about that. So what? I get confused, so I shut up and give myself time to think! But, look, what am I doing? [*With lowered voice*] I don't shut up, I continue talking—in spite of knowing better. I could say—I feel tempted to say: You are seducing me! And so I say it! But what is the sense of putting the blame on you? You are the patient, or supposed to be the patient, so you have the privilege of talking seductive nonsense. But I, supposedly the therapist, should be able to stand up to it. I should be able to hold my own and not to succumb, no matter what you say. [*More firmly*] There is only one way out of this situation—and you know it!

DR. TERWIN: At least, I know what you mean. However, you seem to me like one who has been brought up in a religious faith, and then one day discovers that he does not believe in God. And he is terrified! "My God," he thinks, "what could be a worse insult to God than not to believe in Him!" It is true! I can see it—you have violated your principles, but—does not what you would call the violation consist of doubting them?

DR. PORFIRI [*again in a low voice*]: My principles—?

DR. TERWIN: Well, the word is questionable. It might be more than mere principles. I think it is no accident that it occurs so rarely that people say what they mean.

DR. PORFIRI [*with an effort, looking Dr. Terwin straight in the face*]: I understand what you say, but I cannot help but feel that I should not, and that I would be better off if I didn't or couldn't! But not even that is completely true! Be that as it may—one thing is for sure! I cannot treat you!

DR. TERWIN: Be that as it may—it seems pretty immaterial in comparison with the fact that we—at least at times—have managed to say to each other what we meant! I—I think that I might do even slightly better the next time! I see there are only a few minutes left, and I would like to discuss this matter more fully. Would it be all right if I kept my next appointment—under whatever heading you wish?

DR. PORFIRI: Of course, Dr. Terwin, of course! I really should not—should not have—

DR. TERWIN: Don't worry! I feel fine! Day after tomorrow at 6 —all right?

DR. PORFIRI [*with a half smile*]: All right!

Afterword

LOUIS B. FIERMAN, M.D.

Hellmuth Kaiser's contribution to psychotherapy theory and practice raises new optimism and hope for a curative therapy for the psychoneuroses and possibly the functional psychoses. He identifies the essential ingredient of effective psychotherapy as being the authentic communicative relationship offered to the patient by the therapist. A model for effective psychotherapy can thus be conceptualized as one in which the sole and exclusive concern and interest of the therapist is to maintain a communicative intimacy. No other conditions are required and therapy thus becomes uniquely a nonmanipulative, nonauthoritarian, nondirective, no-demands therapy, the only condition for its process being the physical presence of the patient and the communicative presence and interest of the therapist.

Kaiser's contribution as presented in this book consists of his only three writings in English on the subject of psychotherapy. They were written during the last six years of his life which was ended abruptly by a coronary thrombosis in 1961 at age 68. During his long career as a psychoanalyst, however, he had written in German several articles on psychoanalytic theory and technique.

His most notable psychoanalytic contribution was a monograph on psychoanalytic technique[1] published in 1934 and reviewed by Fenichel in 1935.[2] Kaiser then advocated greater emphasis on character analysis in psychoanalytic therapy and questioned the clinical usefulness of concern with psycho-

203

genetics and pathogenesis. At that time psychoanalysts held that only therapy explicitly concerned with infantile sexuality could justifiably claim to be psychoanalysis. Fenichel criticized Kaiser for deviating from this and insisted that anyone who held such views could not legitimately claim to be a psychoanalyst.

Nonetheless, Kaiser continued in his belief that his clinical approach was compatible with being a psychoanalyst and regarded himself as pursuing needed reform in psychoanalytic theory and practice. Paradoxically, as his ideas evolved and the conduct of his therapy became more and more a function of new thinking, he eventually found, twenty years after Fenichel's reproach, that he had reached a point where his views were no longer compatible with those of the Freudian psychoanalytic community. In 1954, he therefore resigned from the faculty of the Topeka Psychoanalytic Institute and went into private practice in Hartford, Connecticut. He was by then regarded as a deviationist by most of his orthodox colleagues.

The bases of his heresy can be found in the three writings on psychotherapy published in this book. In "The Problem of Responsibility in Psychotherapy," published in *Psychiatry* in 1955, he presented a basic viewpoint of his new theory and practice, namely, that psychotherapy should not be conceptualized in terms of abstractions about the patient's illness and response to treatment, such as is implied in terms like "insight therapy" or "resistance analysis," but rather in terms of the therapist's orientation, intent and activity, such as would be implicit in the terms "interpretive therapy" or "communication therapy." He declared the therapist to be solely and exclusively responsible for the conduct and outcome of psychotherapy. He rejected the traditional psychoanalytic point of view that the patient must be an active collaborator for therapy to occur.

His next written contribution was the heretofore unpublished monograph, "The Universal Symptom of the Psychoneuroses: A Search for the Conditions of Effective Psychotherapy." As the reader has noted, this is written in the form of a novel. The evolution and development of Kaiser's ideas are presented in third person as the reflections and experiences of a hypothetical (albeit autobiographical) Freudian psychoanalyst, "Dr. G—." Dr. G— gradually becomes disillusioned by his clinical ineffectiveness. He rejects his orientation with its emphasis on abstractions about psychogenetics and psychodynamics and shifts to a new emphasis on empirical and observable communicative behavior of his patients in therapy. In "The Concept of the Universal Symptom," Dr. G— conceives of the proposition that duplicity in communicative behavior is a universal symptom; that it is ubiquitous and manifest in all patients with psychological disorder regardless of diagnosis.

In "Theory and Practice in Interaction," Dr. G— shifts his conduct of therapy from that of interpreting psychoanalytically the free associations of the patient on the couch, to that of responding to the patient's unstructured and nondirected behavior simply by confronting him with his universal symptom, namely, his duplicity in communication.

In the third and last section, "Reorientation," Dr. G— observes that duplicity in communication seems to be related to dependency behavior in his patients. To account in theory for the phenomena of his patients' dependency behavior and their duplicity in communication, Dr. G— conceptualizes a universal intrapsychic fantasy of fusion, and the universal psychopathology of attempting to create in the therapy the illusion of fusion with the therapist. Thus, Dr. G— infers that indirect communication creates for the patient the illusion of being understood without explicitness and minimizes and denies the boundaries and separateness between patient and therapist. Conversely, direct communication concedes the separateness and autonomy of the two communicants.

In the climax of this section, Kaiser presents his final formulation about the essential ingredient of effective psychotherapy. Abandoning his short-lived proposition that effective psychotherapy simply required the confrontation of the patient with his universal symptom, he now identifies the essence of therapy as being the genuineness of communicative behavior of the therapist. The therapist's sole and exclusive concern to establish and maintain a genuine communicative relationship with the patient is identified as being the only necessary and sufficient condition for effective psychotherapy.

Kaiser submitted his monograph in its present form to

publishers for preliminary consideration but found their advisers on psychological publications unreceptive to his work. The monograph was turned down by no less than nineteen publishers before finally being accepted by one on condition that he drastically revise it. In the course of these disappointing negotiations, Kaiser set about to rewrite and expand his work. He outlined plans for a fourth chapter which would elaborate views presented in the first three and which would present, also, his general theory of psychopathology and therapy. Unfortunately, he died before he could complete this plan and his monograph remains in essence an unfinished statement in regard to his views. After his death, the one offer to publish his monograph was withdrawn by the publisher.

The central significance of Kaiser's contribution is that it addresses itself directly to the problem of the ineffectiveness of psychotherapy as traditionally and conventionally practiced and offers an alternative approach. There is at the present time in the field of clinical psychiatry, psychology, social work and counselling increasing disillusionment and discouragement over the ineffectiveness of analytic and insight-oriented therapies. The hope and promise that Freud presented to the clinical world that the psychoanalytic method and related therapies offered the basis of a curative and definitive therapy have not been realized over the past sixty years of trial. The turning of professionals away from definitive, individual, curative psychotherapy to the use of palliative, supportive, noncurative measures such as drugs, group therapy, family therapy, and directive and manipulative counselling techniques for the treatment of psychological illness has resulted in large part from this disillusionment.

Despite its simplicity, the model of therapy proposed by Kaiser in his monograph offers to professionals in the mental health field the exciting promise of a definitive and curative therapy. In regard to literary style and organization, the monograph represents the individuality of its author. Kaiser drew on his autobiography in presenting the development and evolution of his ideas. To circumvent the problem of discretion and censorship, he found it easier to write in third person narrative style. Although to some his writing style is refreshingly unpretentious and free of pompous jargon and pseudo-scientificism frequently found in publications on psychotherapy, it may disappoint those readers who require that new ideas on therapy be presented in traditional ways before they will be considered.

In the year preceding his death, while awaiting an answer from a publisher, he wrote a playlet to demonstrate his point of view about therapy. This article, "Emergency," was published posthumously in *Psychiatry* in May, 1962. It illustrates his view that the essence of psychotherapy is the communicative experience offered to the patient, and, as such is independent of the traditional roles played by therapist and patient.

Thus, this is all that remains in written form of Kaiser's contribution to the field of psychotherapy. Beyond this, however, is the profound impact he made on his patients, students and colleagues, with several of whom he maintained an active correspondence. These as yet unexplored and unpublished resources contain much additional information about Kaiser's views. On the basis of this writer's contact and correspondence with Kaiser and his associates, an attempt is possible to formulate in summary fashion a comprehensive presentation of Kaiser's theory and therapy.

While the totality of his contribution is unique and original, particularly in his concept of the use of nondirective communicative intimacy as the basis of psychotherapy, many aspects of his theory and model for therapy may be found in the writings and contributions of others, notably Freud, Rank, Rogers, Sullivan and writers on psychotherapeutic relationships, existentialism and Zen Buddhism. The Kaiserian point of view can be formulated as a triad of universals. The term "universal" means in this context an observation or concept applicable to all people with psychological disorder, which is to say all people, since no one is entirely free of neurosis. The *universal triad* consists of the *universal psychopathology*, the *universal symptom* and the *universal therapy*.

The universal psychopathology is the attempt to create in real life the illusion of the universal fantasy of fusion. The universal symptom is duplicity in communication. The universal therapy is the communicative intimacy offered by the psychotherapist.

The Universal Psychopathology

Man is subject to a basic need that conceptually transcends and cannot be reduced to libido or aggression, the primary drives of psychoanalytic theory. This need can be inferred from such observations as the clinging reflex of newborns, the apathy and depression of infants deprived of maternal-type contact and the psychological disorders that occur in children and adults when they experience prolonged social and sensory deprivation. It is a need for contact with another person, and the psychic derivative of this need may be conceptualized as a universal wish or fantasy of fusion. In infancy this need requires direct, sensory physical contact. In childhood progressing on to adulthood the need seems gratified by verbal and social as well as physical contact. With developing psychic capacity for ideational and symbolic gratification, the universal fantasy of fusion generalizes from persons as objects to substitute symbols and abstractions. The individual then behaves as if fused or dominated by such concepts as cosmic forces, unconscious forces, moral absolutes; God, Duty, Truth or Country. These become substituted in fantasy for the "other" that was in infancy the mother.

If this primary need for social contact is frustrated, the individual is left with heightened subjective awareness of his own existence, individuality, aloneness, separateness and autonomy, all of which arouse primary existential anxiety. The corollary to the universal need for social contact is the universal aversion to awareness of separateness. The individual is impelled throughout his life by this dual psychological phenomenon: the need for contact and the aversion to awareness of separateness. He is impelled to seek contact-need gratification on two levels: one by means of actual, reality-oriented social relationships; the other by means of fantasied, imaginary or distorted contact with persons or substitute symbols. Both means provide some gratification of contact-need and both are accompanied by the universal fantasy of fusion, but the universal psychopathology is defined as the attempt to create in real life by behavior and communication the illusion of fusion.

The Universal Symptom

Communicative behavior is the major means by which individuals achieve contact-need-gratification and avoid aware-ness-of-separation anxiety. Direct communication concedes the separateness and autonomy of the communicants. To engage in direct communication with another person, the individual must be healthy, mature or conditioned enough to tolerate and endure the anxiety of awareness of separateness resulting from this direct communication. He will then be able to enjoy and be comforted by the contact-need-gratification supplied by the other who responds to and accepts his genuine communicative relationship. To engage in indirect communication, the individual blunts and distorts his own awareness of separateness, creates the illusion of fusion, and is precariously gratified on an imaginary basis in a fusion relationship with the other person, who is either alienated by the duplicity or joins in it to maintain a fusion relationship of his own. Indirect communication is the universal symptom of duplicity manifested by patients in psychotherapy.

In psychotherapy, the therapist experiences the patient's universal symptom as a subjective discomfort following from his appreciating his patient's communicative behavior as being devious, indirect, covert, ungenuine; not wholehearted, not integrated or consistent. He feels the patient has some prefer-ence for nonverbal communication, does not entirely say what he means nor mean what he says. Over time the pattern of the patient's universal symptom takes on a consistent config-uration, a sort of style or trademark, recognizable as part of the patient's general character pathology and reflecting his dis-torted attitudes, values, manipulativeness and dependency. The patient avoids and resists an open, direct, nonauthori-tarian, communicative relationship with the therapist.

The Universal Therapy

When, over a sufficient period of time, the therapist consistently offers a spontaneous, genuine, communicative relationship, the net result is that the patient's rigid patterns of attempting to achieve fusion relationships gradually undergo extinction, and new patterns of relating based on *non*fusion communicative modes are conditioned. This process of change also gives the patient increased tolerance and acceptance of the existential anxiety which accompanies his heightened awareness of separateness, autonomy and individuality. The communicative intimacy offered by the therapist is the universal therapy.

It has been the experience of clinicians who have used Kaiser's approach and method that doing psychotherapy this way becomes more comfortable, more effective and more widely applicable than any of their previous ways. Pedagogues find this approach easier to teach to students of psychotherapy. Even in aspects of clinical work outside the field of psychotherapy this orientation seems superior in clinical usefulness. Hospital and ward administrators have found it easier and more useful to conceptualize the behavior of psychiatric patients in terms of fusion theory. The orientation provides a rationale for milieu therapy and ward programs aimed at intruding into the patient's neurotic and psychotic rigidities by offering to patients, regardless of how bizarre they are, multiple communication-oriented relationships with the clinical staff. The model of a relationship based on communicative intimacy becomes readily applicable to the fields of marital and family counselling, child rearing, general education and institutional administration.

Research into modes and effects of communication have long been in effect, but the psychotherapeutic aspects of communication still remain a largely unexplored research area in clinical psychiatry. Fusion-fantasy theory provides an additional dimension of understanding group social behavior, conformity, nationalism, fads, mass movements and mass values.

Kaiser's innovations were originally meant by him to be a reform rather than a break with the psychoanalytic movement. His thinking was influenced and paralleled by other psychoanalysts: Rank, Reich, Ferenczi, Horney and others. Such phenomena and concepts as contact-need, rigidity, duplicity, dependency, fusion relationships, avoidance of reality, and communicative intimacy had all been characterized to some extent in psychoanalytic theory within such hypothetical constructs as instinctual energy, libido and aggression, narcissism, transference and countertransference, repetition compulsion, regression, repression, resistance and insight. Unfortunately, psychoanalytic constructs about intrapsychic phenomena do not lend themselves readily to an appreciation of interpersonal transactions and relationships. The need for a model for therapy that would both account for and also provide a rationale for the communicative transactional aspects of the psychotherapeutic relationship has not been met satisfactorily by psychoanalytic theory.

Yet, even this difficulty need not alienate members of the psychoanalytic community if it were truly organized in the spirit of scientific inquiry and freedom. Surgeons do not ostracize other surgeons who advocate new theories or techniques. It is a deplorable aspect of the history of the psychoanalytic movement that new ideas and new techniques so frequently have led to the expelling of their proponents from the orthodox professional community, the innovators being regarded as deviationists and heretics, deserving of sanctions, ostracism and excommunication.

Kaiser would have preferred to be regarded as a reformer in the field rather than as a renegade from the orthodox church, heretically determined to establish his own splinter movement. But it was his experience and those of his followers to be regarded as anathema by their orthodox colleagues, and forced to go their own way outside the mainstream of the Freudian orthodox psychoanalytic community. It is ironical that this is the same reaction to which Freud was subjected because of his deviant ideas.

Fortunately, there are many professionals in the mental health field and in the psychoanalytic community who are scientifically oriented, open-minded and receptive to new ideas and periodic reevaluation of old ones. It is hoped that these individuals will receive and consider the offerings of this book with sympathy, and give them fair trial. It is not inconceivable that the ideas of Kaiser and his followers may yet be integrated into a new and more effective psychoanalytic theory and model for therapy.

Notes

1. Kaiser, H., "Probleme der Technik," *International Zeitschrift fur Psychoanalyse*, 1934, 20:490–522.

2. Fenichel, O., "Zur Theorie der Psychoanalytischen Technik," *International Zeitschrift fur Psychoanalyse*, 1935, 21:78–95; tr. in *Collected Papers of Otto Fenichel*, First Series, "Concerning the Theory of Psychoanalytic Technique," pp. 339–348, New York: W. W. Norton & Co., 1953.

Index

Index